The Politics of Fertility Control:
Family Planning and Abortion
Policies in the American States

Deborah R. McFarlane
University of New Mexico

Kenneth J. Meier
Texas A&M University

CHATHAM HOUSE PUBLISHERS
SEVEN BRIDGES PRESS, LLC
NEW YORK · LONDON

10/01

Seven Bridges Press, LLC
135 Fifth Avenue, New York, NY 10010-7101

Copyright © 2001 by Chatham House Publishers
of Seven Bridges Press, LLC

Publisher: Ted Bolen
Managing Editor: Katharine Miller
Production Services: Sarah Evans
Cover Design: Stefan Killen Design
Cover Art: PhotoDisc, Inc.
Printing and Binding: Victor Graphics

Library of Congress Cataloging-in-Publication Data

McFarlane, Deborah R., 1951-
  The politics of fertility control : family planning and
abortion policies in the American states / Deborah R.
McFarlane and Kenneth J. Meier.
      p. cm.
Includes bibliographical references and index.
  ISBN 1-889119-39-3 (pbk.)
  1. Birth control—Government policy—United States. 2.
Abortion—Government policy—United States. I. Meier,
Kenneth J., 1950- II. Title.
  HQ766.5.U5 M436 2000
  363.46'0973—dc21

99-050685

Manufactured in the United States of America
10 9 8 7 6 5 4 3 2 1

To Catherine Azalea Arthur Bastian (1902–1994)
for sharing her truth

Contents

Figures and Tables

Preface

IN HANDING DOWN its *Webster v. Reproductive Health Services* decision in 1989, the U.S. Supreme Court not only permitted the states far more discretion in abortion policy; it also revealed itself as very much divided on the abortion issue. This case brought renewed interest to the study of abortion politics, and the ensuing scholarship has increased our understanding of abortion policy, federalism, and state politics. Both the field of public health and the discipline of political science have benefited from this work, and we are happy to be counted among the many contributors.

This book reflects our view that larger questions loom behind abortion politics. First of all, we consider nearly all induced abortions as sequelae to unwanted pregnancy, most of which can be avoided with effective contraception. Second, we contend that abortion politics are part of a larger political struggle about values, which we have termed *morality politics*.

Our focus here is on fertility control policies and politics, namely, those concerned with family planning and abortion. We also consider abstinence policies. We believe that to a large extent, the same political winds affect each. Our methods are both descriptive and analytic. We describe the disparate evolution of national policies toward contraception and abortion. We also describe how fertility control policies developed in the states and how they have been implemented. In analyzing these policies, we use models of policymaking, intergovernmental transfers, and policy implementation and, in so doing, demonstrate how these models can inform our understanding of fertility control policies. We also show how this substantive area can contribute to our understanding of American public policy.

Chapter 1 introduces the concept of fertility control and presents the overall theoretical framework for the study. Fertility control is viewed as part of a set of policies generally called *morality policies*. We argue that this concept is important because it determines how issues are framed and how policies are developed.

The contentiousness of late twentieth-century American fertility control politics has led many observers to conclude that this is a unique period in history. In fact, nearly all human societies have practiced both contraception and abortion. At intermittent times throughout the ages, there have been organized attempts to restrict fertility control. Chapter 2 highlights the universality of fertility control and describes various historical efforts to curtail birth control and abortion. Although this chapter offers thumbnail sketches of other societies, the emphasis is on Western history, particularly the American experience.

Chapter 3 describes how family planning policies have evolved since the mid-1960s. From that time to the present, federal family planning policy has been multistatutory and has employed several grant types. After describing policy developments up to the present, we use criteria from the well-known Mazmanian and Sabatier model of policy implementation to rate the likely effectiveness of each federal statute that addresses family planning.

Chapter 4 reviews the history of federal abortion policy since the *Roe* v. *Wade* decision in 1973. To a large extent, the U.S. Supreme Court has determined the parameters of abortion policy, and the Court's changing composition has made abortion a particularly volatile policy area. The Mazmanian and Sabatier model is versatile enough to accommodate different types of policies, including those created by judicial decisions, and in this chapter, we use it to rate the likely effectiveness of federal abortion policy over time.

Both chapters 3 and 4 show that over the past two decades, much of the responsibility for implementing fertility control policies has devolved to the states. In turn, the states have chosen different ways to implement these policies. Chapter 5 documents this variation and attempts to explain the reasons for state policy variation.

Given the variation in state fertility control policies, it is not surprising that there are vast differences in the levels of services that the states provide. Within the limits of existing data, chapter 6 examines the immediate effects of fertility control policies in the fifty states. These policy outputs include patients served and money spent.

Chapter 7 considers the long-term effects of fertility control policies. Here, we analyze the health and fertility impacts of fertility control policies. We also assess whether statutory structure, or grant type, affects policy effectiveness. In this chapter, we employ not only the Mazmanian and Sabatier model, but also the Gramlich typology of intergovernmental grant mechanisms from public finance economics. While this typology predicts the magnitude of policy effects, it is applicable only to fiscal transfers. In the case of fertility control, the Gramlich typology is thus useful for analyzing family planning policy but not abortion policy.

Chapter 8 concludes the book with a discussion of the implications of our findings for both family planning and abortion. We note how public policies toward family planning and abortion have been rendered less effective over time and how fertility control policies could be designed to be more effective.

The publication of this book marks the tenth year of a collaboration between a political scientist and a public health researcher. During the course of that collaboration, we have learned a great deal and recognized that we have a great deal in common. Each of us recognizes that politics create policies and influence their implementation. Each of us is committed to improving health outcomes. We agree that family planning and abortion comprise an inextricable policy area.

By testing theoretical constructs as well as making policy recommendations, we hope that this book offers something of value to both scholars and practitioners. We certainly are indebted to individuals in both categories. Daniel Mazmanian and Paul Sabatier have contributed a rich framework with a clear hypothesis. Judith Blake, Kingsley Davis, William Gormley, Edward Gramlich, and others have provided valuable conceptual tools for model building. Patrick J. Sheeran, director of the Office of Adolescent Pregnancy, has been an invaluable source of information and insight. Both he and Deborah Oakley of the University of Michigan read the entire manuscript and provided excellent suggestions. Rachel Gold at the Alan Guttmacher Institute answered questions tirelessly and with good humor, as well as giving us many leads. Very early in the project, Barry Nestor, formerly of the Alan Guttmacher Institute, provided data and patient explanations. Gloria Roberts, librarian at the Katharine Dexter McCormick Library of Planned Parenthood of America, generously located historical materials. Joy Dryfoos, Vivian Lee, Jack C. Smith, and the late Paul Smith each provided explanations, offered encouragement, and furnished documents for this endeavor. We also acknowledge the silent contributions of the family planning providers who have shared their expertise; their desire to remain anonymous speaks volumes about morality politics.

We would also like to thank Alesha Doan, Donald P. Haider-Markel, Rebecca Leggitt, and Anthony Stanislawski for research assistance. Deborah McFarlane would like to acknowledge the University of New Mexico for the 1996–97 sabbatical leave provided for this project.

We thank Robert Gormley, our publisher, for his confidence in and support of this book and Katharine Miller for keeping our work on track. We are especially indebted to Sarah Evans, our copyeditor. Her diligence and dedication contributed greatly to the quality of this book. Any remaining errors are, of course, solely our responsibility.

A project of this length takes time and attention away from our families. We wish to thank Juan Javier Carrizales and Diane Jones Meier and to acknowledge their patience, support, and intellectual contributions.

CHAPTER 1

Fertility Control Policy: A Theoretical Approach

THIS BOOK EXAMINES American public policy toward *fertility control*—the actions of individuals or couples to limit the number of children they biologically produce or to space the timing of their children's births. We therefore focus on public policies that address family planning and abortion. We also analyze the politics that produce those policies. Our primary concern is the effectiveness of fertility control policies in the United States.

If we as a nation wish to reduce the incidence of unintended pregnancy—hence, of induced abortion—our policies evidently fall short of achieving that goal. Unintended pregnancy is prevalent in American society. The National Survey of Family Growth reported that between 1967 and 1970, 44 percent of births to married women were unplanned and 15 percent were unwanted (U.S. Commission on Population Growth and the American Future 1972). Three decades later, the picture has improved, but not to the extent that many anticipated. In 1995, married women reported that nearly a third of their live births were mistimed and 9 percent were unwanted. Approximately 30 percent of pregnancies in the United States are terminated by induced abortion (Abma 1997).

Unintended pregnancy is highest among teenagers and low-income women. More than four out of five pregnancies to women fifteen to nineteen years of age are unintended. Women living below the federal poverty level report that three out of four of their pregnancies and over a third of their births are unintended. Both teens and poor women have high abortion rates; 40 percent of their pregnancies end in abortion (Institute of Medicine 1995).

Overall rates of unintended pregnancy are much higher in the United States than in Western Europe. These differences show up in widely divergent abortion rates. In 1990, for example, the U.S. rate was 27.4 abortions per 1,000 women aged fifteen to forty-four,[1] while the rates in Denmark and the Netherlands were 18.2 and 5.2, respectively (Institute of Medicine 1995). Not surprisingly, European policies toward fertility control differ greatly from American policies.

Fertility control policies in the United States are fragmented. Little overlap exists between "preconception" policies that address family planning and birth control and "postconception" policies that address abortion. Much of the funding for family planning in the United States is the result of federal legislation. States, however, have a great deal of discretion in this policy area. Policies toward abortion, the most controversial aspect of fertility control, are made largely through the judicial system. Within those legal parameters, states determine their own policies on funding abortions for low-income women, on requiring parental involvement in minors' abortions, and on mandating waiting periods with "informed consent."

Research on American fertility control policies mirrors the fragmentation in existing policies. Although both family planning and abortion policies address unintended pregnancy, they are rarely studied as a single policy area in American politics. Instead, they are examined separately, as if there were no relationship between the use of contraception and the demand for abortion. In this study, we depart from that convention and consider fertility control as a single policy area.

We view fertility control policy as part of a set of policies generally called *morality policies*—public policies that are redistributive in nature. Unlike other redistributive policies, these seek to redistribute values rather than income. Values are redistributed when government officially puts its stamp of approval on one set of values and rejects some other set. Even if morality policies are totally symbolic and have no enforcement mechanisms, their value dimensions will ensure that the issues are highly salient and the politics controversial.

The policy issues involved with fertility control are complex and multidimensional. Because fertility control involves relationships between men and women, it involves the role and status of women in society. It also has economic and social implications of great magnitude; family size has a direct effect on one's monetary expenditures and thus on one's standard of living, and it may even affect one's social status. Fertility control certainly has technological dimensions; and fetal research clearly has both scientific and moral dimensions (Maynard-Moody 1995). The multidimensional nature of the issues would normally make it difficult to discuss fertility policy and thus to establish coherent policy. The strategy of activists on all sides of these issues has been to reduce the debate to a few issues or even to a single dimension. This reduction, or *framing*, of an issue is extremely important in determining what issues are discussed and which outcomes emerge from the political process.

In this chapter, we first discuss how public policies are usually classified. We then explain how morality policies fit into this typology and describe their basic characteristics. In the third section, we explain why fertility control policies can be considered morality policies; here, we also discuss ways that fertility control issues can be framed. After describing how some of the basic characteristics of fertility control influence policy adoption, we consider the likelihood of policy success.

PUBLIC POLICY CLASSIFICATIONS

Public policies may be divided into three major types: regulatory, distributive, and redistributive (Lowi 1964). *Regulatory* policies restrict the behavior of individuals and groups (Anderson 1997). *Distributive* policies grant benefits to some portion of the population, paying for them out of general tax revenues rather than with user fees. With *redistributive* policy, the government taxes one group of people to provide benefits to another group (Meier 1987).

Although the definition of regulatory policy is certainly broad enough to include social relationships, regulatory policy usually refers to the regulation of economic relationships. Some scholars have addressed this point by identifying policies dealing with such issues as abortion, gun control, assisted suicide, affirmative action, and school prayer as *social regulatory* policies (Tatalovich and Daynes 1988). Social regulatory policies differ dramatically from more traditional regulatory policies in scope, objectives, and politics. The term *morality policy*, on the other hand, implies a type of policy different from either regulatory policy or other forms of policy.

MORALITY POLICY

Morality policies frequently address social relationships, but their primary concern is the legitimacy of values: which values are accepted by the state and which are considered unacceptable. Specifically, these values are related to the demand for or the desire to consume what some people consider to be utterly wrong or sinful. For example, many people consider abortion or contraception, or both, to be transgressions against moral or religious law.

Morality policies generally have three distinguishing characteristics. First, the demand curve for commodities or behavior that some consider immoral is relatively heterogeneous; that is, it varies more across individuals than does demand for many other goods. Second, public pronouncements and private behavior are frequently at odds. Third, the public bureaucracies that usually implement morality policies have inherent limitations that influence the policy process.

Heterogeneous Demand

Although some scholars have conceptualized immoral behavior as just another consumer preference (Posner 1992; Becker 1996), preferences for so-called immoral behavior do, in fact, have some characteristics that make them different from many other consumer preferences. The demand for a so-called immoral behavior or commodity is more heterogeneous than the demand for many other commodities. In other words, individuals differ widely in terms of what they are willing to pay for what some would label as sin. Paying includes risking government sanctions (e.g., arrests, fines) if the behavior (e.g., underage drinking or smoking) or commodity (e.g., marijuana) is illegal.

For some people, the demand for sin is nearly inelastic. Simply put, some individuals will pay or risk as much as they can in order to partake of the so-called immoral behavior or commodity. An example is a drug addict (including an alcohol or tobacco addict) who will continue to consume the substance no matter how high its price rises.

Using this framework of heterogeneous demand, Meier (1998) has provided mathematical support for several propositions in morality policy. First, while any attempt to restrict demand will initially have some positive results, these policies will simply cull those with weak demand from the marketplace. Second, to obtain additional increments of compliance, subsequent policies have to impose greater and greater costs. Third, there will remain a residual of individuals who are relatively immune to the negative costs of public policy, and these individuals will continue to consume the good in question and/or provide it to others. Meier's mathematical work has been empirically validated by Meier and Licari (1997) in the case of cigarette consumption.

Public Expressions and Private Behavior

Public pronouncements about morality often diverge greatly from private behavior. In other words, what people profess publicly and what they actually do privately may be very different, especially when others (or even they) regard the behavior as immoral. Consequently, politicians have skewed perceptions about the actual demand for immoral behavior or commodities; that is, they see demand as weaker than it actually is. By confusing public expressions with private behavior, politicians often promote public policies that are more extreme than the actual preferences of most of their constituents.

Bureaucratic Implementation

The implementation of most morality policies is assigned to law enforcement bureaucracies, which are characterized by low levels of technology, personnel-intensive processes, and an output, rather than an outcome, orientation. For example, law enforcement bureaucracies expect to be rewarded on the basis of the volume of the arrests they make—their output—rather than on the incidence of immoral behavior.

Law enforcement bureaucracies generally lack policy-analysis capabilities, so their bureaucratic role is not one of active participation in the policy process; instead, they act as cheerleaders. They favor more extreme policies because such policies will create a climate that supports more resources. Because their mission is law enforcement, these bureaucracies portray nearly any problem as one of law enforcement (e.g., the need for more arrests) rather than one of alternative solutions to the problems (e.g., reduction of demand, reduction of transaction costs, or treatment).

Together, these factors create the environment that generates morality politics. Bureaucracies lack relevant policy information, so expertise plays no role in the process. Public support for stronger laws is perceived as overwhelming, and entrepreneurial politicians seek innovation at the expense of deliberation. Policies adopted resemble current policies (conceded not to be effective), except the penalties are greater and enforcement is increased. The actual demand for the immoral good or behavior is seldom considered.

FERTILITY CONTROL AS MORALITY POLICY

Controlling fertility requires intervening in human reproduction, which itself requires three steps: (1) sexual intercourse, (2) conception, and (3) gestation and parturition (Davis and Blake 1956). Most public policies that address fertility control focus on the provision of contraception between steps 1 and 2 (see fig. 1.1) and on the provision of abortion between steps 2 and 3. Some policies explicitly promote public intervention before step 1 (e.g., the abstinence education provisions of the Personal Responsibility and Work Opportunity Reconciliation Act of 1996, the so-called Welfare Reform Act).

Fertility control policies have three basic characteristics. The first two—heterogeneous preferences with some highly inelastic demand, and differences between public pronouncements and private behavior—are common to morality policy (Meier 2000). The third characteristic—reliance on both public bureaucracies and private agencies to implement public policy—is the result of the evolution of fertility control policy in the United States.

Heterogeneous Preferences

As with virtually any product, the demand for contraception and abortion is marked by heterogeneous preferences (see fig. 1.2, p. 6). To the left of the demand curve are those individuals with weak preferences for fertility control. At this end of the curve, such policies as restrictions on contraceptives or moral

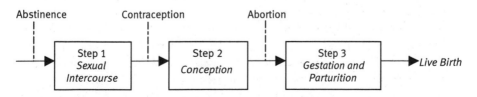

Figure 1.1 The Reproductive Process

Source: Adapted from Davis and Blake 1956.

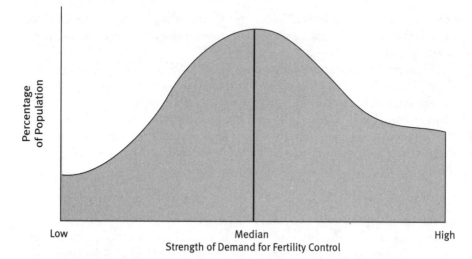

Figure 1.2 Demand Curve for Fertility Control

admonitions concerning abortion will be highly effective. In other words, demand among these people is so elastic that any barrier to fertility control will cause them to avoid it.[2] Some seek large families, some may believe that contraception is immoral, others may believe that their partner should be responsible for fertility control, and still others may have opted for celibacy.

In the middle of the curve are those individuals with moderate demand for fertility control. For many of them, fertility control is a normal economic good with consumption determined by supply and demand.

Finally, to the far right of the curve are those with a high demand for fertility control. For them, the demand for fertility control is highly inelastic. These individuals may be unable to afford children, too immature to undertake the responsibilities of parenting, deliberately delaying childbearing, or simply not interested in procreating. Many of them will ignore laws that restrict fertility control and seek these goods from individuals willing to take the risks to supply them. For such people, conception imposes major costs and is to be avoided as much as possible.

The preference curves for fertility control differ from those for other goods that public policy affects because sexual activity, contraception, and abortion are sequentially related. Without sexual activity, there would be no demand for contraception or abortion. Similarly, the demand for contraception affects the demand for abortion. Because they are sequential, it makes sense to segment the demand for fertility control into three curves: the demand for sexual activity, the demand for contraception, and the demand for abortion.

The demand for sex precedes the demand for fertility control. Unless a woman or a couple is trying to produce a pregnancy, the demand for sex is largely independent of the desire to have children. For most individuals, sex is an

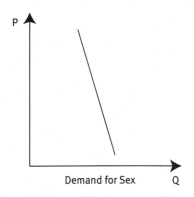

Figure 1.3 Demand Curve for Sex

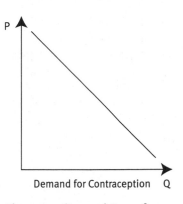

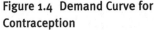

Figure 1.4 Demand Curve for Contraception

enjoyable activity in and of itself. Indeed, most individuals of reproductive age are sexually active. Although some individuals will not initiate or continue sexual activity when faced with certain moral admonitions or public policies (e.g., "Just Say No"), we believe they are a small minority of the reproductive-age population. For the most part, the demand curve for sexual activity is inelastic and probably not amenable to policy intervention.

The demand for sexual activity is depicted in figure 1.3, in which the vertical axis represents *price* (P)—in this case, the price of sexual activity (e.g., the imposition of moral admonitions)—and the horizontal axis represents *quantity* (Q), or levels of sexual activity. The diagonal line, the demand curve, shows the amount of sexual activity in which individuals will engage relative to price. Again, this demand is relatively inelastic, because levels of sexual activity do not change very much relative to price.

Among sexually active individuals, the demand for contraception varies because of different levels of income and knowledge, and also because of different fertility aspirations (some individuals, for example, may have achieved their optimal family size). In many ways, contraceptives can be considered normal economic goods whose consumption is determined by supply and demand (see fig. 1.4). If contraceptive methods are cheap and easy to use, birth control will be practiced. By lowering the price of contraceptives or supporting research on methods that are easier to use, public family planning programs are likely to have an impact. In other words, the lower the price of contraceptives, the more they will be used.

During the course of a lifetime, an individual's demand for contraception may change dramatically. For example, a teenager who is not sexually active would have a low demand for birth control. During her twenties or thirties, before she achieves her optimal family size, she might have an intermittently moderate demand for fertility control. After producing as many biological children as she desires, she might have a high demand for fertility control.

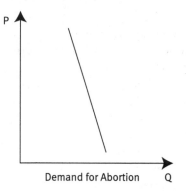

Figure 1.5 Demand Curve for Abortion

The demand for contraception and the demand for abortion are related, of course. If contraceptives are very expensive or otherwise unavailable, but abortion is legal and accessible (as in Japan), then abortion will become a common method of fertility control. If contraceptives are readily available, then the incidence of abortion drops (as in the Netherlands).

Our conclusion from the study of fertility control is that the demand for abortion services is highly inelastic (see fig. 1.5). In other words, the price of induced abortion—even when it includes breaking the law or risking one's health—does not greatly affect the demand for abortions. We base much of our reasoning here on the historical survey in chapter 2. Fertility control, including abortion, has been practiced historically in all cultures linked to the United States. At times, such practices were discouraged, and at times they were illegal, but at no time were contraception and abortion not practiced.

Two additional indicators of the inelastic demand for abortion are available. A variety of scholars have tried to estimate U.S. abortion rates before 1973, when the Supreme Court's *Roe* v. *Wade* decision legalized abortion in this country (Posner 1992). Estimates of the annual number of induced abortions in the 1950s and 1960s range from 200,000 to 1.2 million (Gold 1990, 5); the higher figure is almost 88 percent of the estimated 1.365 million abortions in 1996. Given the high rates of morbidity and mortality associated with illegal abortion, women seeking abortion in the pre-*Roe* era demonstrated a highly inelastic demand for the procedure.

A second indicator of the inelasticity of demand is Haas-Wilson's (1997) study of Medicaid funding for abortions. Haas-Wilson concludes that in states that fund abortions for Medicaid-eligible women, abortion rates are no higher than in states that do not provide such funding. In essence, she argues that the demand for abortion is so inelastic that eliminating all monetary costs will not affect the number of abortions that occur. We disagree with Haas-Wilson that abortion demand is completely inelastic. (If it were, it would be the first case of a completely inelastic good found via applied economics; see Meier and

McFarlane 1994.) However, her findings provide additional support for the notion that the demand for abortion is highly inelastic and that it would thus be difficult to affect that demand using normal public policy instruments.[3]

Inelastic demand for abortion in the United States implies that any attempts by policymakers to change abortion practices in this country will be unlikely to meet with much success. Many individuals will do what they have to do or pay what they have to pay to obtain this service. Changes can possibly be made at the margins, among teenagers, for example, or among individuals with little political clout (e.g., the poor), but massive changes are improbable.

In morality politics, however, such incremental effects are not prized. If fundamental values are at stake, then compromise on policy means compromise on deeply held values. Values such as the sanctity of life, sex within marriage only, or the right to control one's reproductive processes are absolutist in nature. Compromise merely cheapens these values and detracts from the utility an individual gets from possessing such a set of values.

Given this finding, how do we account for the nuances of abortion policy that have occupied policymakers in the United States? Quite simply, we view efforts to ban Medicaid funding and to require parental involvement as searches for alternative frames for the abortion issue. If the abortion issue can be framed along an alternative dimension, elected officials can raise issues to appeal to a highly motivated group of constituents and at the same time not threaten the access of the majority of middle- and upper-income women to abortion. Similarly, restrictions placed on the publicly subsidized family planning program may appeal to certain constituency groups and at the same time not limit access to contraceptive services for voting-age women who can afford them.

Framing Abortion and Family Planning

Any attempt to frame an issue is an attempt to simplify it. To set the agenda and to structure debate, advocates consciously and deliberately frame an issue. Framing occurs when appeals are made to mobilize a broader public. Frames are not neutral. They motivate some individuals and discourage others; they enhance some arguments and reduce others.

Abortion is a complex and multidimensional subject. Framing can remove this complexity and translate abortion into terms that are readily understood. Some common frames for abortion are the sanctity of life, a woman's right to control her own body, the legal-but-discouraged frame, government noninvolvement, welfare, children and families, and health risks/health benefits (see table 1.1, p. 10). Attempts to frame abortion also often frame debates on family planning policy. At times, the salience of abortion policy limits any policy action for family planning.

Sanctity of Life. The traditional pro-life frame for abortion is that human life begins at conception and is sacred. The fetus in this frame is a person, albeit a dependent one, who might need even greater protection than the mother and

Table 1.1 Frames for Fertility Control Policies

FRAME	EXPLANATION	USED IN FAMILY PLANNING POLICIES	USED IN ABORTION POLICIES
Sanctity of life	Human life begins at conception and is sacred.	Sometimes	Yes
Woman's right	A woman has the right to control her own body.	Yes	Yes
Legal but discouraged	Abortion should be legal but discouraged.	No	Yes
Government noninvolvement	Government involvement in fertility control should be eliminated.	Yes	Yes
Welfare	Individuals should be responsible for themselves.	Yes	Yes
Children and families	Parents should make decisions for minors in their families.	Yes	Yes
Health risks/ health benefits	The health risks and benefits of fertility control should be considered.	Yes	Yes

whose claim on life is equal to hers. Under the life-is-sacred frame, no abortions are acceptable. The value of the fetus is not affected by how it was conceived, by its own health or viability, or by economic circumstances; life is a value that trumps all other values. Within this frame, of course, compromise on abortion policy is not possible. Not even exceptions for rape or incest can undercut a frame in which all life is sacred.

The pro-life frame is at times divided on the question of conception. Some would accord potential life the same value as life and oppose the use of contraceptives. Others would permit the use of contraceptives but would still oppose abortion under any circumstance.

A Woman's Right to Control Her Own Body. The dominant frame on the pro-choice side of the abortion issue is a woman's right to control her own body, a fundamental right to be exercised only by the pregnant woman. Here, the policy goal is to have medically safe abortion available for all women who request this procedure. Like the polar position for pro-life, this position is not amenable to compromise. Adding conditions or restrictions on choice essentially denies the fundamental right of all women by limiting it to only some women.

The woman's-right frame easily transfers to family planning policy. If a woman has a fundamental right to control her body, then unlimited access to contraception logically follows. A fundamental right would not recognize economic limitations and thus would require the government to provide for those unable to afford contraception.

Legal but Discouraged. The frame that abortion should be legal but discouraged (or at least not encouraged) is an attempt to impose the equivalent of cost-benefit analysis on abortions. Framed this way, the decision to have an abortion should be undertaken only with a great deal of thought, and abortion should not be used as the primary method of birth control. One might view this as an anti-promiscuity frame or as merely a process frame that encourages individuals to consider all options.

The legal-but-discouraged frame may support some restrictions on abortion; for example, it can accommodate restrictions on length of pregnancy, parental involvement, and waiting periods. At the same time, the legal aspect of the frame suggests that abortions will always be available. At one extreme of this frame, government will restrict choices; at the other extreme, government will provide information and permit individuals to assess the benefits and costs and then decide.

The legal-but-discouraged frame is difficult to apply to family planning policy. Abstinence would clearly fit here, especially as part of an education program. Similarly, a nation could allow access to contraception but place a high tax on it. Because the legal-but-discouraged frame is so difficult to apply to contraceptive policy, it will rarely, if ever, be used.

Government Noninvolvement. The government-noninvolvement frame eliminates the involvement of government in abortion. It is a flexible frame that can be used by both sides of the abortion issue. On the pro-life side, it can be used to oppose abortions in public hospitals, government funds for abortions, and federal aid to domestic or international organizations that perform abortions. On the pro-choice side, this same frame can be used to oppose government restrictions on abortion of any kind, thus leaving the decision in the hands of the woman and her physician as a private-sector transaction.

Despite use by both sides, or perhaps because of use by both sides, the government-noninvolvement frame is inherently contradictory. While adult women with disposable income may have a right to abortion, this frame implies it is more of an economic right than a constitutional right. Because government involvement or government size is a central issue in partisan U.S. politics, the government-noninvolvement frame frequently overwhelms other frames.

For family planning policy, the government-noninvolvement frame implies that government cannot put any restrictions on access to contraception. By the same token, it also suggests that government should not facilitate access. This frame would therefore support a policy of open access for those who can afford to pay.

Welfare. Welfare is a frame with a variety of negative connotations. When applied to abortion policy, it becomes involved with views of individual responsibility; that is, abortions should not be funded for Medicaid-eligible women because that encourages individuals not to take responsibility for their own actions. It is important to understand that this is not a cost frame or a cost-benefit frame, but a frame of individual responsibility. For example, funding abortions for Medicaid-eligible women actually saves far more government money than is expended (Torres et al. 1986); however, individuals using this frame are willing to spend more money in their quest for individual responsibility.

The welfare frame in family planning for the poor takes on a similar tone of individual responsibility. According to this frame, government should not encourage promiscuity by funding contraceptives for low-income women. The massive public benefit-to-cost ratio of such funding becomes irrelevant in the welfare frame.

Children and Families. Children and families are positive social constructs in the United States (Schneider and Ingram 1993). A variety of policies, including those of the criminal justice and Social Security systems and food and nutrition programs, accord children special treatment. In the children-and-families frame, families have responsibility for children, and they should therefore have the authority to make decisions for them.

Requiring parental consent for minors' abortions is a restriction that relies on the children-and-families frame, which presents a minor's pregnancy as a medical or social problem that should be dealt with by the family. This frame is somewhat problematic for pro-life advocates because it is difficult to apply it to other abortion questions (except for attempts at requiring the consent of the father).

Advocates as well as opponents of publicly supported family planning can use the children-and-families frame. It can support both a ban on contraception and the need for contraception to limit family size in order to provide opportunities for children. It can also be applied to contraceptive access by minors. With such a frame, the "squeal rule," requiring notification of parents when their minor children receive contraceptives at Title X–funded clinics, becomes a logical policy in family planning. Parental consent for contraception could be viewed as similar to parental consent for abortions.

Health Risks/Health Benefits. During the early debates on abortion, the pro-life coalition raised the health-risks frame, contending that abortion entailed some major physical and psychological health risks. This frame, however, proved of little value to the pro-life position as medical evidence mounted that legal abortions were relatively safe procedures and in virtually all circumstances entailed less risk than carrying a pregnancy to term (Richard 1989). Risks, however, are based on large numbers; in individual cases, negative outcomes can occur. Because government policy is often based on anecdotal rather than scientific evidence, the health-risks frame is still raised. (For example, during testimony on the federal law that forbids transporting a minor across state lines to obtain an abortion, one mother contended that her daughter died from an abortion performed under such circumstances.)

The health-benefits frame, that there are positive consequences of abortion, is rarely raised. In recent years, perhaps only the fetal research controversy has used this frame, arguing that fetal research can generate effective treatment for some diseases. Only when pro-life advocates have used the frame, however, has it had any impact on fetal research policy (Maynard-Moody 1995).

The health-risks/health-benefits frame works well for contraceptive policy in family planning. In such a frame, the health risks of pregnancy are contrasted with the health risks of using contraception.

Public Pronouncements and Private Behavior

The discrepancy between public pronouncements about sexuality and private behavior concerning it is not uniquely American, but Americans probably take it furthest. Many Americans believe that sexual activity should take place only within heterosexual marriage. At the same time, most Americans initiate sexual activity when they are about seventeen years of age (Upchurch et al. 1998), seven years before their twenty-fourth birthday, which is the average age at marriage (Institute of Medicine 1995). Once married, most Americans believe that sexual contact should be limited to one's spouse;[4] however, a recent study showed that in a twelve-month period, 5 percent of married Americans reported having extramarital sexual intercourse. Only 32 percent of Americans believe that abortion should be legal in all circumstances (O'Connor 1996); however, an estimated 50 percent of American women will experience an abortion during their reproductive years (Gold 1990).

The discrepancy between Americans' beliefs about sexuality and their sexual behavior has serious implications for fertility control practices. The forethought that most contraceptive use requires is difficult to accommodate when one believes that either sexual activity or birth control is inherently wrong, or even when one is just ambivalent about them. Such beliefs and their deterrent effect on contraceptive use contribute to the high rates of fertility and abortion among American teenagers. Adolescents in the United States are not more sexually active than those in Western Europe; they are simply less effective users of contraception (Institute of Medicine 1995).

For the most part, open discussions about actual sexual practices are precluded by strong moral overtones in American society. In fact, the topic has been labeled "taboo communication" (Rogers 1973). When pertinent topics are discussed in the public arena, politicians tend to echo American ideals about sexuality rather than discuss how most people actually behave. Indeed, the public pronouncements of many politicians reflect some of the most extreme beliefs among their constituents. Simply put, few politicians are willing to stand up for sin. As chapter 2 explains, this is not a new phenomenon, especially in American fertility control politics.

Public and Private Implementation

Both public and private organizations implement fertility control policies. In many other policy areas, public bureaucracies alone are responsible for implementation. For example, public schools implement education policies, public law officers enforce statutes on drunk driving, and human services bureaucracies administer welfare policies. Implementation by an organizational hybrid of private and public agencies is not, however, unusual for American health policies.

American fertility control policy permits nearly unlimited access to contraception and abortion for adults who can pay for these services from their own funds or through private insurance.[5] In such cases, contraception and abortion are unaffected by public policy except that the Food and Drug Administration (FDA) must approve of specific contraceptive devices and state agencies must license abortion facilities. Most Americans obtain contraceptive services from their private health care providers. Although the majority of abortions are performed in freestanding clinics, many physicians do perform these procedures for their private patients. These transactions between patient and physician are invisible to government agencies and nearly impossible for them to track. Thus, monitoring compliance with policies when services are provided privately is very difficult.

Public policy is more involved in the provision of services to low-income persons and minors. The implementation of family planning policy, directed toward low-income persons, is assigned to public-sector health agencies and social service bureaucracies, which may contract with private providers. The implementation of abortion policy is assigned to social services bureaucracies, private providers, and the judicial system (e.g., judicial bypasses in lieu of parental consent).

As with other morality policies, the organizational configuration involved in implementing fertility control policy influences policy outcomes. For example, by assigning family planning to a health bureaucracy, fertility control becomes defined as a health problem, not an education problem. The bureaucracy rewards both public and private providers on the basis of their output or production of specific health services rather than for their achievement of a lower level of unintended fertility or even increased contraceptive knowledge.

The social service agencies that administer Medicaid funds for family planning and state funds for abortion function as insurance intermediaries for public and private agencies delivering services to low-income clients.[6] They, too, focus on the production of service outputs. Policy analysis, which might examine the best way to achieve intended fertility in the United States, does not occur in this organizational scheme.

FERTILITY CONTROL AND POLICY ADOPTION

We have argued that fertility control politics are predominantly morality politics. In this arena, policy adoption is a function of the efforts of religious and citizen groups, other political forces, and the demand for the "immoral" good (Meier and Johnson 1990; Morgan and Meier 1980). Governments, particularly at the state level, have a long tradition of enacting policies that are driven by concerns with morality (Gusfield 1963).

Although fertility control policies may be classified as morality policies, they may also involve redistributive or regulatory functions. For example, providing public funding for abortions for low-income women may be considered a redistributive function. Similarly, federal family planning policy is largely redistributive because it funds birth control services for low-income persons.

The combination of a redistributive issue with morality concerns suggests a type of politics that combines aspects of both policy areas. Religious and citizen groups are usually interested in morality issues, while partisan forces and political ideology usually have a large role in redistributive politics.

In addition to being affected by these factors, policy adoption is influenced by the nature of the fertility control issue. Gormley (1986) argues that an issue's salience and complexity determine the actors most likely to have the greatest impact on public policy. A *salient* issue is one that affects a large number of people in a significant way. A *complex* issue requires specialized knowledge and training to address the factual questions (Gormley 1986; Meier 1988).

Abortion is a highly salient public issue; that is, it is characterized by intense conflict of a broad scope. *Roe* v. *Wade* divided the country into "two uncompromising camps"; the pro-choice forces have aimed to protect the policy of legal abortion, while the pro-life forces have been determined to overturn *Roe* v. *Wade*, either by reversal or by constitutional amendment (Sheeran 1987, 1). Abortion policies have been the subject of elections, referenda, protest marches, and even violence.

Although in certain circumstances family planning can generate strong and uncompromising responses, it is generally a less contentious issue than abortion. Much of the time, in most localities, most of the public supports the services offered by publicly funded family planning programs. However, when political opponents are successful at linking family planning services to abortion or are able to focus attention on the provision of birth control to minors, family planning can become a highly salient issue, at least temporarily. Therefore, we would describe family planning as a moderately salient issue.

Neither family planning nor abortion as discussed in policy circles is a technically complex issue, as defined by Gormley. One does not need specialized knowledge to understand that family planning methods prevent conception and abortion terminates pregnancy.[7] Gormley allows that technical complexity can change over time, as may well be the case with emergency contraception (previ-

Table 1.2 Gormley's Typology of Issue Politics

	COMPLEXITY	
SALIENCE	Low	HIGH
HIGH	Hearing room politics	Operating room politics
LOW	Street level politics	Board room politics

ously known as "the morning-after pill"), mifepristone (also called RU 486 or the French abortion pill), and mifepristone-misoprostol.[8] During the time period that we examine, however, the use of both emergency contraception and mifepristone-misoprostol is rare in the United States, so we reassert that family planning and abortion are not technically complex.

Each combination of salience and complexity produces a different policy scenario: hearing room politics, operating room politics, street level politics, and board room politics (see table 1.2). The scenario produced by highly salient issues of low complexity, such as abortion, is known as *hearing room politics* (Gormley 1986). Issues of low salience and low complexity result in *street level politics*. As discussed earlier, family planning is a moderately salient issue of low complexity. We expect that decision making about family planning policies and regulations would be characterized as mostly hearing room politics with some elements of street level politics.

In street level politics, the major players are lower-level bureaucrats and regulated industries. Nobody else is really interested. Family planning, of course, is a redistributive policy, not a regulatory one, so "regulated industries" per se are not really appropriate in this case. Here, the organizations most affected by public policy are the providers of publicly subsidized family planning services. Whether the policy is regulatory or redistributive, however, the major potential pathology in street level politics is bureaucratic inertia (Gormley 1986). Lower-level bureaucrats often lose sight of overriding goals. They tend to be stringent in enforcing regulations that are easily to enforce and lax in enforcing those that are difficult to enforce. Consequently, the distinction between minor and major infractions of policy becomes displaced by the distinction between enforceable and unenforceable regulations. Enforcement or service provision activities are therefore not necessarily supporting the program's goals.

An example of this scenario is the routine monitoring and performance evaluation of Title X–funded family planning programs performed by the Department of Health and Human Services (DHHS). DHHS requires family planning grantees to submit information on the program outputs, but not on the outcomes. Output data or performance data (the number and type of users, income status, contraceptive method used, number and type of visits, type of provider, and revenue generated) can be collected relatively easily. Outcomes, such as the program's success in meeting its primary goal of reducing the incidence of unintended pregnancy, are more difficult to measure and therefore are conveniently overlooked.[9]

In hearing room politics, politicians, citizen groups, and journalists give the issues an open airing. Highly salient issues of low complexity are made to order for politicians. Salience raises the rewards for acting; that is, politicians can generate political support by doing so. If the issue is not complex, it will be much easier to explain to constituents (Meier 1988, 66).

Citizen groups are also influential in areas of high salience and low complexity. Salience aids organizational efforts. Groups can appeal to values held dear by many citizens (see Gamson 1968). Complexity, on the other hand, is a formidable barrier to effective citizen participation. In complex issue areas, only those with access to relevant policy knowledge can participate effectively (Sabatier 1988).

In contrast to other scenarios, in hearing room politics, bureaucrats and specialized interests (e.g., physicians) are not free to do as they please regarding the issues; because the issues are highly salient, journalists, politicians, and citizen groups will be watching their activities. In short, the characteristics of abortion suggest that this issue will be covered by the press and that politicians and citizen groups will have major impacts in determining policy. Bureaucrats who dominate complex issues will have less of an impact here.

Although citizen groups often play a major role in hearing room politics, the policies that emerge from this scenario may not represent the interests of all sectors of society. Most low-income persons do not belong to citizen groups or otherwise participate in politics; therefore, their views may not be aired in the hearing room. Indeed, the major pathology of hearing room politics is that the concomitant democratic politics affect only the more affluent members of the political community (Gormley 1986). Within this framework for public policy, it is noteworthy that the federal government's major abortion restriction—the limitation of funding—affects abortion access only for low-income women. Similarly, the "gag rule" (discussed in chap. 3) restricted mostly poor women from learning about all their legal options in pregnancy.

The salience of the abortion issue has a partisan dimension as well. Although the Democratic Party has consistently endorsed a pro-choice position, many members of its traditional New Deal coalition are pro-life (among them, a number of Catholics). Until recently, Republican politicians often staked out a pro-life position to attract votes from Democratic identifiers. Similarly, Democrats have sometimes stressed their pro-choice position to attract Republican identifiers who support access to abortion. Over time, however, the parties have become more internally consistent, with the Democratic Party's being pro-choice and the Republican Party's being pro-life (Adams 1997; Smith 1994).

In summary, both family planning and abortion are morality issues that may involve other types of policies. For the most part, policy adoption occurs in a hearing room scenario in which politicians, citizen groups, and journalists are prominent. Because family planning is not as salient as abortion, bureaucratic forces probably have more influence on family planning policy than on abortion policies.

THE LIKELIHOOD OF POLICY SUCCESS

The types of policies adopted to address fertility control issues affect policy success. Morality politics often ensure that fertility control policies reflect extreme or uncompromising positions at odds with the behavior of most constituents. These positions may be somewhat mitigated by the presence of advocacy groups in hearing room politics. However, advocacy groups that support birth control and abortion most often succeed at blunting the effect of policy restrictions on middle-class and more affluent women. Low-income women, who are more dependent on redistributive public policy, have faced far more restrictions on fertility control.

Because demand for fertility control is heterogeneous, different policy instruments will work for different groups of people. Abstinence programs will work only for a very few and only for a short period; most people are simply not willing to pay the high price of avoiding sexual activity. Subsidized family planning services essentially lower the price of contraception; thus, more people are likely to consume this birth control commodity. However, every restriction imposed on this commodity will increase its price and thus lower the demand for it. The result will be that a greater number of sexually active persons will not consume it.

The demand for abortion and the demand for family planning are obviously related. Women who use effective contraceptives are seldom in need of an abortion, although contraceptive failure does, of course, occur. However, if the price of contraception is high, fewer people will use it, and the demand for abortion will rise. As discussed earlier, abortion is a particularly inelastic commodity. Many women with unwanted pregnancies will pay a high price for this procedure, either financially or by substituting a cheaper, unsafe procedure for a more expensive, safe one.

Policy success, of course, is a matter of definition. Success in fertility control has been defined in a variety of ways: a reduction of sexual activity, a reduction in unintended pregnancies, a reduction in unwanted births, and an improvement in maternal and child health. If the goal of a public policy is to reduce nonmarital sexual activity, then that policy is doomed to failure because it does not consider actual human behavior.

If policy success is defined as a reduction in unintended pregnancies (and thus of abortions), then public policies that lower the price of contraception (government subsidies for the poor and regulations that require private insurance to cover birth control costs) should be considered successful. What public fertility control policies fail to do now is to expand the demand for contraceptives through marketing. The addition of morality restrictions (such as parental involvement, spousal consent, or ideological patient counseling) will increase the price of obtaining birth control, so that unintended pregnancies may increase. The magnitude of this change will depend, of course, on the shape of the demand curve.

If the goal of public policy is to reduce maternal mortality, then policies that promote access to safe abortion will be effective. Restrictions on abortion that arise from morality politics will not lead to this goal. They are doomed to failure. The demand curve is simply too steep.

CONCLUSION

In this chapter, we defined fertility control as the actions of individuals or couples to limit the number of children they produce or to space the timing of their children's births. Fertility control can be achieved in three ways: by abstinence, with contraception, or through induced abortion. Because fertility control involves human sexuality and reproduction, this policy area is extremely value-laden.

We classify fertility control policies as morality policies—that is, public policies that are primarily concerned with the legitimacy of values. Morality policies address issues that some people consider utterly wrong or sinful, such as contraception or abortion. As with other morality policies, very heterogeneous demand and vast differences between public pronouncements and private behavior characterize fertility control policies. In contrast to the way many other morality policies are implemented, however, both public bureaucracies and private organizations implement fertility control policies.

The adversarial politics surrounding morality issues affect both the adoption and the implementation of fertility control policies. In an effort to garner support, citizen and religious groups often frame fertility control issues as less complex than they really are. In an effort to satisfy these groups, politicians may adopt postures and policies that are more extreme than the preferences of many of their constituents. The resulting policies are not likely to yield optimal outcomes.

By blending constructs from morality politics and other frameworks and applying them to fertility control, this chapter offers an explanation of why policymakers make the decisions they do and how those decisions relate to policy success. The chapters that follow provide a comprehensive view of the policy process from origins to final outcomes.

CHAPTER 2

Contraception and Abortion: A Historical Overview

FERTILITY CONTROL IS a universal phenomenon. In every known culture—literate or preliterate, primitive or modern—people have attempted to regulate their fertility. What has varied is the efficacy and safety of preconception and postconception practices, the dissemination of these methods, and the relationship of the polity to the practice of fertility control.

This chapter provides a brief history of contraception and abortion during ancient, medieval, and modern times. Although many societies have employed a wide range of fertility control practices, such as infanticide, delayed marriage, celibacy, and sexual taboos (Himes 1970, 4), the discussion here is limited largely to birth control and abortion. Our intent is to show the widespread demand for contraception and abortion, both temporally and geographically. We focus on civilizations and countries that have had the most influence on modern fertility control practices in the United States. Throughout much of human history, the state has not tried to regulate fertility control practices. When we are aware of interference by government or other organized interests in the practice of contraception or abortion, we note those efforts.

FERTILITY CONTROL IN ANCIENT TIMES

Ancient Egypt

The oldest known prescriptions for contraceptives come from an ancient Egyptian papyrus. Dating back to 1850 B.C., this document, known as the Kahun papyrus, contained three recipes. The first was for a pessary made of crocodile dung mixed with a pastelike substance.[1] The second instructed a woman to irrigate her vagina with honey and natron (a native sodium carbonate). The third recipe mentioned a gum (Himes 1970, 59–63).

Three hundred years later, the Ebers papyrus described a medicated lint tampon designed to prevent conception. This recipe called for the tips of the shrub acacia, which when compounded produce "the lactic acid anhydride, which is used in modern contraceptive jellies." The papyrus also described abortifacients, listing substances that "stop pregnancy in the first, second, and third [trimesters]" (Riddle, Estes, and Russell 1994, 31; Himes 1970). Ancient Egyptians also used prolonged lactation to reduce fertility. Apparently, ovariectomy (the removal of ovaries) was practiced, too, although it was probably limited to the harems of powerful men, such as pharaohs (Himes 1970, 67).

Ancient Hebrews

Ancient Hebrews practiced what is believed to be the oldest contraceptive method, coitus interruptus, or withdrawal of the penis prior to ejaculation (Tietze 1965). In fact, many rabbis of ancient times recommended coitus interruptus during the two-year lactation period following a birth. In later periods, however, coitus interruptus was widely interpreted as being a mortal sin (Suitters 1968). Ancient Hebrews also placed spongy substances in the vagina to prevent pregnancy. Other contraceptive efforts included magical potions and twisting and performing violent abdominal movements after coitus (Himes 1970).

Like their contemporaries in other parts of the world, ancient Jewish scholars debated the issue of ensoulment. By about A.D. 500, the Talmud had concluded that the question of just when the fetus is endowed with a soul was unanswerable and thus irrelevant to abortion. Moreover, the fetus was considered part of the woman and not fully human until birth. On this point, the Talmud was quite specific, requiring that a fetus be destroyed if it posed a threat to the mother's life during delivery. When the greater part of the body or the head was exposed, however, the fetus was not to be harmed, "for one may not set aside one person's life for the sake of another" (Jakobovits 1967; Sheeran 1987; Rosenblatt 1992, 50–51, 60–61).

According to Jewish tradition, saving a pregnant woman's life was the only justification for abortion. Abortion for other reasons, however, was not considered murder. Traditional Jewish law prescribed penalties for deliberate abortion, but these penalties were not as harsh as those prescribed for homicide, and they were related to gestational age. Up until forty days after conception, the fertilized egg was considered "mere fluid." After forty days of gestation, the formation of the fetus was believed to have occurred. A woman who aborted after the fortieth day following conception was required to make a religious offering, just as she would if she had delivered a live child (Sheeran 1987, 79).

Compared with early Christian writings, Jewish sources have very few references to abortion. Most scholars agree that induced abortion, other than to save the life of the mother, was rare in ancient Jewish society (Jakobovits 1967, 130; Rosenblatt 1992, 63).

Ancient Greece

Egyptian knowledge of birth control may have been available to the ancient Greeks, at least to select physicians and other intellectuals. The Greeks, in turn, made notable contributions. As early as the seventh century B.C., they were importing silphium from a colony in what is now known as Libya. Silphium was a giant fennel known to have contraceptive and abortifacient properties. Attempts to cultivate silphium on the Aegean Peninsula were unsuccessful. Demand for it in Greece and later in the Roman Empire became so great that by the third or fourth century A.D., silphium was extinct. Other plants that did survive—asafoetida, pennyroyal, artemisia, myrrh (myrrhis odorata), and rue[2]—were also used as contraceptives or abortifacients. Modern analyses suggest that many of these are effective methods of fertility control (Riddle, Estes, and Russell 1994, 30–31).

Soranus (A.D. 98–138), the most accomplished physician of ancient Greece, practiced medicine in the first half of the second century. He described about thirty formulas for contraceptive medications having such ingredients as old oil, honey, cedar gum, alum (a metallic astringent), and fruit acids (Himes 1970, 99). These were to be used to medicate wool suppositories. Soranus also recommended four oral contraceptives, which would "not only prevent conception, but also serve as early abortifacients." Like modern physicians, he warned about their side effects (Riddle, Estes, and Russell 1994, 32).

Abortion was viewed in ancient Greek society "with a variety of conflicting attitudes" (Rosenblatt 1992, 58). Both Plato (427?–347 B.C.) and Aristotle (384–322 B.C.) considered it to be a method of population control (Sheeran 1987, 50). Aristotle believed that the state should establish the number of children that any married couple could have. If a woman became pregnant after bearing her allotted number of children, Aristotle thought she should be compelled to terminate her pregnancy before she felt fetal movements (Tribe 1992, 55).

The timing of animation, or ensoulment—that is, when the fetus becomes human—was of great interest to the Greek philosophers. According to their theories, abortion was not murder, at least under certain circumstances (Sheeran 1987, 50). Aristotle hypothesized that the fetus had a succession of souls: vegetable, animal, and rational. The final development, the rational soul, was the most important and constituted the process of animation. Aristotle believed that animation and formation of the fetus occurred at the same time but that they occurred later in female fetuses than in male fetuses. After observing aborted fetuses, Aristotle postulated that animation occurred in male fetuses forty days after conception and in females, after eighty days (Sheeran 1987, 79–80).

Abortion was common in ancient Greek society, though not nearly as widespread as infanticide. Hippocrates (460?–377? B.C.), the most famous Greek physician of ancient times, rejected abortifacients; however, in his book *On the Nature of the Child,* he prescribed a method to procure abortion by jumping so that the feet touched the buttocks (Himes 1970, 89). Greek religion did not profess any strong concern for the unborn, although Greek inscriptions on temples describe birth, miscarriage, and abortion as occasions of ritual impurity. Following these events, a woman was supposed to abstain from worship and follow purification rituals (Rosenblatt 1992, 60).

Ancient Rome

Greek knowledge of birth control was passed on to the Romans, who spread this information throughout their empire (Schnucker 1975, 656). Soranus, the highly accomplished Greek physician, practiced medicine in Rome in the second century A.D. and no doubt dispensed his knowledge of birth control methods among the Romans. As noted earlier, the Romans, like the Greeks, used silphium and other herbal contraceptives.

Views on abortion in Roman society were similar to those of Jewish law (Sheeran 1987, 50). The fetus became a person, an entity with a soul, only at birth when it began to breathe. Before then, it was merely a part of the pregnant woman's body (Rosenblatt 1992, 63). But whereas abortion was rare in ancient Jewish society, it was widely practiced throughout the Roman Empire, and infanticide was even more common than abortion.

Roman law and custom did require the father's consent for an abortion. Indeed, abortion was considered a crime only when it was performed against the father's will (Rosenblatt 1992, 63–64; Tribe 1992, 55). Under Roman law, the fetus had no rights, except the right to inherit (Sheeran 1987, 50).

Christianity

In the early days of Christianity, Christians were relatively few in number and widely scattered geographically. Contraceptive and abortion practices varied considerably, influenced by regional customs and practices (Sheeran 1987, 51, 79).

In A.D. 418, St. Augustine (A.D. 354–430) denounced the practice of contraception. It was unclear, however, whether this written denouncement applied only to persons who did not wish to procreate at all or whether it included those who were or wished to be parents and wanted to limit or space the number of their offspring (Noonan 1986, 135–37). Although St. Augustine's writings were widely read by clergymen, there is no evidence that they significantly influenced the behavior of the clergymen's followers.

Early Christians generally accepted the notion that the fetus was not alive until sometime after conception. The precise time of animation was, however, the subject of considerable debate from about A.D. 1 to 400. Early Christian scholars were certainly aware of Aristotle's theories on the subject.

Between A.D. 300 and 600, the abortion debate among Christian scholars extended to the distinction between a formed and an unformed fetus. St. Augustine contributed a description of fetal development: the first six days in milky form, nine more days for it to turn to blood, twelve days for the mass of blood to solidify, and eighteen more days for the mass to become fully formed with all its members. St. Augustine accepted Aristotle's theory of delayed animation and formation of the female fetus (Sheeran 1987, 52, 80–81).

From A.D. 600 to 1100, the distinction between the formed and the unformed fetus became widely accepted. A woman was considered to have had an abortion only if a formed fetus was extracted. In practice, abortion among early Christians remained a local issue, and penances imposed for procuring abortions varied among localities (Sheeran 1987, 52).

Other Ancient Cultures

In the ancient Islamic world, physicians and scientists recorded valid information on contraception. Although ineffective potions were also prescribed, early Islamic writings on contraceptives were, on the whole, more accurate than early Christian writings. Coitus interruptus was advocated as a method of contraception (Himes 1970).

In ancient India, rock salt was used as a spermicide. Honey and oil were also placed in the vagina for the purpose of preventing pregnancy. Tampons soaked in these substances or in ghee (melted butter) served as contraceptives as well. While these methods have some scientific basis, ineffective methods—such as passiveness or holding one's breath during coitus—were also in common use.

The ancient Japanese used condoms made from tortoise shell or horn. Later, the Japanese would construct condoms from leather. (Rubber sheaths did not come into use until the last half of the nineteenth century.) Prostitutes in ancient Japan used disks made of oiled tissue paper to prevent pregnancy (Himes 1970).

FERTILITY CONTROL IN THE MIDDLE AGES
Contraception

It is estimated that over two hundred contraceptive and abortion methods were in common use during the Middle Ages (Heinsohn and Steiger 1982, 195). Western Europeans were evidently quite successful in controlling their fertility. The average household in medieval Italy had only 2.44 children, and in German territories in the eighth and ninth centuries, there were but 2.36 children per woman. Apparently, much of the knowledge about fertility control in western Europe was transmitted by lay midwives, who served as healers and childbirth assistants (Heinsohn and Steiger 1982, 195–96).

Before the mid-fourteenth century, contraception was openly discussed. The classic medieval textbook *Canons of Healing* included a description of birth control methods. In his *Summa de Creaturis,* Albert the Great (1200–1280), the eminent clerical scholar of the Middle Ages, discussed the contraceptive effects of certain plants and herbs without any indication that he was addressing a delicate or tabooed subject (Heinsohn and Steiger 1982, 201).[3] The subject of birth control even arises in Chaucer's "Priest's Tale" (Himes 1970). Many church records from this period also document that people were practicing birth control (Suitters 1968; Himes 1970).

Although herbal birth control methods were described in the early and late Middle Ages, by the onset of the Renaissance, physicians no longer wrote about these contraceptives. A persistent question for scholars has been why herbal birth control agents faded from common usage at this time. Why was this information lost?

The Witch-Hunts. The witch-hunts that occurred between 1360 and 1700 offer a plausible explanation of the disappearance of many methods of birth control (Heinsohn and Steiger 1982). The witch-hunts began almost immediately after the Black Plague (1347–53), which along with other events had devastated the European population. England was particularly hard hit.[4] The plague produced a massive labor shortage that threatened the position of the landed aristocracy, which depended on having enough people to serve as laborers, soldiers, and civil servants. At the time, the Catholic Church was by far the biggest landowner in Europe.

The notion of a deliberate state-organized system to supply labor was not new; indeed, the Roman Caesars had formulated such a concept, including the prohibition of fertility control. Up until the 1300s, contraception, abortion, and infanticide had been commonly practiced in spite of a nearly thousand-year-old written Christian ethic prohibiting birth control. After the Black Plague, however, midwives, who had been the sources of birth control knowledge, were hunted down and persecuted as witches for the next two and a half centuries.

The witch massacres were massive and widespread, and these executions were sanctioned by the church. Reliable estimates of executions range from a million to multiples of that number, and at least twice as many people were publicly charged. The scale of these massacres can be better appreciated when one considers that in 1600 the entire population of northwestern Europe, the center of witch-hunting, was less than 50 million (Heinsohn and Seiger 1982). That midwives were the major target is confirmed in the *Hammer of Witches* (1487), the first comprehensive apologia for witch-hunts published by the Dominican order. While summing up witch-hunting activities since 1360, the *Hammer of Witches* discussed "midwives who surpass all others in wickedness." Among their listed offenses were contraception and abortion.

Given the scale of the massacres and those who were targeted, one can reasonably assume that when the witch-hunts ended by about 1700, birth control and abortion knowledge had been nearly obliterated in Western Europe. While the practice of reproductive control did not completely cease (Schnucker 1975), contraceptive information was not as widespread or, on the whole, as sophisticated as it had been. Medieval midwives had been replaced by an emerging, largely male medical profession, not as knowledgeable about or as interested in techniques of fertility control.

Although a vital player in the witch massacres, the Catholic Church was not the only organization involved. England made witchcraft a statutory crime in 1541 and in 1562 elevated it to "a crime of the greatest magnitude." In 1563, the Scottish Parliament decreed punishment and death for witches. Indeed, executions, trials, and laws related to witchcraft continued until the beginning of the eighteenth century (Heinsohn and Steiger 1982, 206).

The Puritans. Among other groups that opposed birth control were the Puritans, who arose during the Elizabethan era. The Puritans disapproved of birth control for several reasons. They believed that children were a blessing from God and that by being fruitful and multiplying, they could participate in the Creation. They also feared that birth control could reduce the number of the "Elect," and they worried that birth control might be practiced by the unmarried. Because many Puritans immigrated to the English colonies, these ideas became a part of the American heritage (Schnucker 1975, 661–65).

Abortion

In the thirteenth century, St. Thomas Aquinas (1225–74), a disciple of Albert the Great, expanded upon the ideas of his predecessors. He recognized St. Augustine's description of fetal development and "followed Aristotle in ascribing to male semen the power of creation. . . . In fact, according to Aquinas, since beings tend to produce their own kind, ordinarily the products of conception should be male. Females resulted because of flaws in the semen or some act of God, such as the south wind" (Sheeran 1987, 81).

Aquinas's ideas influenced Pope Innocent IV, who in 1257 declared that abortion before the infusion of the soul was not homicide. He did not, however, specify when animation occurs. In 1588, two years after declaring that abortion constituted "premeditated murder," Pope Sixtus V attached an excommunication to this sin. In addition to being excommunicated, whoever practiced abortion was to be put to death (Noonan 1986; Sheeran 1987, 53, 81).

In 1591, Pope Gregory XIV withdrew these penalties for the sin of abortion. They were believed to be too severe in light of the debate on animation. The declaration of 1591 remained the abortion policy of the Catholic Church until 1869, when Pope Pius IX restored the policy of Pope Sixtus V and "eliminated the distinction between the animated and unanimated fetus" (Sheeran 1987, 53, 81).

FERTILITY CONTROL IN MODERN TIMES
Contraception in Early Modern Europe

The European population explosion began at the end of the fifteenth century. By the late twentieth century, Europe's population had increased tenfold, even though 40 million Europeans had emigrated to the Americas and Australia (Heinsohn and Steiger 1982). By the end of the eighteenth century, Europeans had begun to recognize both population growth and its concomitant poverty as social problems. Nevertheless, there was disagreement about the appropriateness of contraception.

Thomas Malthus. Among those concerned about the population explosion but opposed to contraception was the Reverend Thomas Malthus (1766–1834), who in 1798 published *An Essay on the Principle of Population as It Affects Future Improvement of Society.* This work is important for several reasons, including Malthus's warnings about the likelihood of unchecked population growth. Because of his religious beliefs, Malthus considered birth control immoral, and he did not foresee the widespread use of contraceptives. His concern about the growing masses and subsequent poverty gained a great deal of attention, not only in his time but in the twentieth century as well (Thomlinson 1965, 53–59).

Condoms. While Malthus may have believed that birth control was immoral, at least one contraceptive method came into more widespread use in Europe during the eighteenth century. By about 1700, shops in central London were selling condoms made from animal membranes. These sales were not clandestine operations. Competition in the condom trade spurred advertising jingles and leaflets announcing the availability of prophylactics.

The exact origin of condoms is unknown. The first mention of a condom in the literature appears in a work of 1564 by the great Italian anatomist Gabriel Fallopius. This work, published two years after the author's death, describes an experiment in which he had instructed 1,100 men in the use of a linen condom. Fallopius reported that not one of these men contracted syphilis (Himes 1970; Suitters 1968).

During the eighteenth century, condoms reportedly were used in brothels. The association with sexually transmitted diseases and prostitution has stigmatized this method through current times. In the same century, Casanova (1725–98), the Italian adventurer, reported his personal use of condoms. He used membrane prophylactics not only to prevent infection, but also "to avoid impregnating his women." He even described how he tested them for imperfections by inflating them with air (Himes 1970, 195).

Frances Place and the English Birth Control Movement. Frances Place (1771–1854), a London tailor who strongly disagreed with Malthus about how population growth might be checked, launched the birth control movement in England. In 1822, Place published *The Principle of Population, Including an Examination of the Proposed Remedies of Thomas Malthus.* In this book, he demonstrated the utter futility of deferred marriage or complete abstinence as a means of controlling population growth (Finch and Green 1963, 139).

Even more courageous than his attack on Malthus's ideas was Place's publication of contraceptive brochures in 1823. These were widely distributed in

London and the industrial districts of northern England. The first of them became known as "The Diabolical Handbook." In these leaflets, some of which advocated the use of coitus interruptus and tampons, Place instructed working-class people in practical ways to plan their families. This advice was not an abstract intellectual or theological argument. Place himself was the father of fifteen children, and, as a working man, he knew the difficulty of supporting such a large brood (Finch and Green 1963). Place's activities were groundbreaking for two reasons: his emphasis on the social and economic desirability of birth control, and his organized attempt to educate the masses.

Contraception in Nineteenth-Century America

Although the birth control movement did not take hold in the United States until the twentieth century, the 1800s were an important time for American fertility control. In 1800, a native-born white American woman bore an average of 7.04 children.[5] By 1860, that number was 5.21, and by 1900, it had plummeted to 3.56 (Reed 1978). Clearly, to effect such dramatic change, Americans had to have been practicing fertility control.

At the beginning of the nineteenth century, the major methods of reproductive control were, as they had been in the colonial period, coitus interruptus, abortion, and prolonged lactation. Coitus interruptus, which can be quite effective, had become more widespread among certain communities during the eighteenth century.[6] How knowledge about fertility control was diffused is difficult to ascertain. Both Puritan disapproval of birth control and other social conventions conspired against keeping written records about contraceptive practices and other intimate behavior.

Over the course of the nineteenth century, contraception was discussed in wider circles in America than ever before. Puritan ideas did not disappear from American life, but other ideas gradually surfaced. Two important books in disseminating contraceptive information were Dr. Charles Knowlton's *Fruits of Philosophy* (1831), also titled *The Private Companion of Young Married People*, and Robert Dale Owens's *Moral Physiology* (1831). *Fruits of Philosophy* was the best medical presentation on contraception of its time and also contained an excellent discussion of the reasons for family planning. Proof that in the 1830s the Puritan ethic still held sway is that Knowlton served time in prison for writing and circulating this book.

After the 1830s, however, public lectures on contraception were held frequently. By mid-century, dozens of pamphlets and books on contraception had been published and were widely available. They could be obtained from local newsstands, bookstores, stationers, and peddlers, or by mail order. Indeed, paid agents often passed out contraceptive ads at street corners, railway stations, steamship depots, and other public places (Brodie 1994, 191).

As the nineteenth century progressed, additional contraceptive methods came into more common use. They included douching (with and without spermicide), coitus reservatus,[7] vaginal sponges (with and without spermicide), cervical caps, vaginal diaphragms, and periodic abstinence, or the rhythm method. Periodic abstinence was not very effective because the time of ovulation had not been identified correctly (Brodie 1994).

Indeed, there was a thriving commercial market for birth control methods. In 1872, for example, the Fuller & Fuller Company of Chicago sold seven kinds of troches (small, circular medicinal lozenges) for use in douching. By 1880, a drug company in Boston was selling twenty-five types of such troches. Although contraceptive experts today discourage douching because it is dangerous and ineffective, current knowledge must be placed within the context of the nineteenth century. Even without a spermicidal agent, douching reduces pregnancy rates by 50 percent. With a spermicide, pregnancy rates can be reduced significantly more. Nineteenth-century women were motivated to limit their pregnancies and certainly were not comparing the effectiveness of this method with the hormonal methods of the late twentieth century.

A German physician, Wilhelm Peter Mensinga, is usually credited with inventing the first actual diaphragm in 1882, but American inventions based on the same principle had been patented in the 1840s and were circulating by mid-century (Brodie 1994, 217). Cervical caps, first advertised as "womb veils" in 1864, were probably derived from an obscure 1838 treatise written by a German gynecologist, Friedrich Adolph Wilde. In 1823, Wilde had noticed that the farm families in a particular area numbered only two or three children. Investigating why their fertility was so much lower than average, he eventually traced the secret back to a midwife, who had discovered that placing an object in front of the cervix prevented impregnation. Wilde decided the best way to develop this idea was to take a wax imprint of the cervix and then make a rubber cap of the same size (Suitters 1968, 11). The knowledge of contraceptive pessaries that German immigrants brought with them to the United States may also have contributed to the development of the cervical cap.

Although condoms had been used in Europe as prophylactics against sexually transmitted diseases since at least the seventeenth century, no written records document their use in the United States until the early nineteenth century. At that point, newspapers occasionally carried ads for condoms, usually for protection against syphilis (Brodie 1994, 206). During the first half of the century, most condoms were made of animal skin and were imported from Europe. The use of condoms, however, was limited; they were simply too expensive to be accessible to the middle class.

In the 1850s, after the development of vulcanized rubber, the price of condoms dropped dramatically. Condoms made of this new material became available, and they could be purchased for half the price of skin condoms. But despite their lower price and contraceptive effectiveness, condoms remained tainted by their old association with prostitution and venereal diseases. Moreover, they were most commonly found in shops that also carried pornography and erotica in the seamier areas of American cities (Brodie 1994, 206). Nevertheless, many married couples did use condoms to control their fertility.

Not all groups in American society welcomed the increased interest in contraception. The "social purity" movement, which coalesced after the Civil War, included groups that wished to restrict abortion and contraception.[8] Although birth control was not a focus for most "social purists," the 1873 federal law that they supported—the Act for the Suppression of Trade in, and Circulation of, Obscene Literature and Articles of Immoral Use—prohibited interstate trading in obscene literature and materials, including "any article whatever for the prevention of conception, or for causing unlawful abortion" (Brodie 1994, 255–56). Before the passage of this act—commonly known as the Comstock law—there had been no federal involvement in contraception.

In the original bill, this federal law contained an exemption for physicians from the portion of the legislation that prohibited the possession, sale, or mailing of contraceptive devices. An amendment to the bill struck out the exemption. That amendment set the stage for the separation of contraception from other medical care for many years.

During the next fifteen years, twenty-two states passed similar legislation. Known as the "little Comstock laws," this state legislation sometimes "went considerably further than the federal law." Fourteen states prohibited the verbal transmission of information about contraception or abortion.[9] Eleven states made possession of instructions for the prevention of pregnancy a criminal offense.[10] Four states authorized the search and seizure of contraceptive instructions.[11] Connecticut alone outlawed the act of controlling conception (Brodie 1994, 257).

Support for the ideas embodied in the Comstock laws was broader than the laws' namesake and principal advocate, Anthony Comstock (1844–1915), "the fair flower of Puritanism" (Broun and Leech 1927, 88–89). The Puritan mentality blended contraception, abortion, sterilization, obscenity, and vice and unequivocally condemned them all. Comstock himself believed that law should be used in support of public morality (Dienes 1972, 32–33). He was not an isolated fanatic. Although his fervor was unique, his ideas represented prevailing attitudes toward sexual matters. Behind Comstock stood the influential New York Young Men's Christian Association, particularly its Committee for the Suppression of Vice (Dienes 1972).

While Catholic and Protestant clergy were not the principal proponents of the Comstock laws, they supported their passage, as did feminist groups concerned about the spread of venereal disease. Most feminists believed that the real cause of this public health problem was the double standard of sexual behavior for men and women; that is, extramarital sex was tolerated for men, but not for women. In turn, men contracted sexually transmitted diseases from prostitutes and then infected their wives (Reed 1978).

Birth control was not a central concern for most nineteenth-century physicians. Nevertheless, the moralistic fervor surrounding the Comstock laws probably contributed to the reticent stance that organized medicine adopted after their passage. In 1874, before the "little Comstock laws" started multiplying, the president of the American Medical Association (AMA) recommended the establishment of a national system of regulation for prostitution and control of sexually transmitted diseases, which would have included the cooperation of American physicians with the appropriate international organizations. During the next thirty years, many conscientious medical and public health professionals attempted to regulate prostitution in order to control the spread of sexually transmitted diseases. For the most part, however, their proposals were defeated in local and state legislatures throughout the country, and advocates of these measures were publicly humiliated for their lack of morality.

Eventually, organized medicine abandoned the idea of regulating prostitution as a method of controlling sexually transmitted diseases. Physicians learned that their profession and livelihoods depended on public opinion and accepted one standard of morality for everyone, no matter how unrealistic that standard. Privately, many medical leaders may have recognized that prostitution continued to spread sexually transmitted diseases; they may also have recognized that contraception could be divorced from licentiousness and be used to improve sex in marriage. Publicly, however, they established themselves as guardians of public morality (Reed 1978, 13).

At the federal level, the statutory linkage between contraception and obscenity remained in place for nearly one hundred years. Despite the moderating effect of various court decisions that followed the Comstock laws, these laws had a chilling effect on public and professional attitudes, which was reflected in the policies and practices of health institutions as well as in the media. Not until 1959, for example, did a television program even mention the subject of birth control (Jaffe 1973).

Comstockery's most profound effect was that it created barriers against the dissemination of contraceptive information and services, especially among the poor and uneducated (Littlewood 1977). In addition to being less accessible, most contraceptive literature written in the last decades of the nineteenth century was inferior to that available earlier in the century. Sections on contraception that had been part of larger works were removed (Brodie 1994, 283).

Contraception in Twentieth-Century America
One of the most striking legacies of the campaigns against reproductive control can be found in Margaret Sanger's account of her fruitless six-month search for contraceptive information in "the best libraries in America" (Brodie 1994, 288).

At the time, medical scholars were required to delete sections dealing with birth control methods from their texts because of potential prosecution. In his *Fewer and Better Babies* (1915), William Josephus Robinson introduced two chapters of blank pages with this comment:

> The further discussion of this subject has been completely eliminated by our censorship which . . . is . . . as real and as terrifying as any that ever existed in darkest Russia. . . . Not only are we not permitted to mention the safe and harmless means, we cannot even discuss the unsafe and injurious means. And we call this Freedom of the Press!

Reform was, however, on the way. The country was more urbanized and more affluent, and the participation of women in the labor force was increasing.[12] In the first two decades of the century, members of the Progressive Party were demanding political, economic, and social changes. With an increased recognition of the social problems engendered by urbanization and industrialization, "there was also a deepening recognition that the poor, who had a diminished financial capacity to care for children, tended to produce larger families" (Dienes 1972, 76).

The status of women was also changing, as were relations between the sexes. "The peremptory hold of Puritanism was more clearly on the wane than ever before" (Dienes 1972, 77). Among the upper-middle-class respondents studied by Alfred Kinsey, 36 percent of the women born between 1900 and 1909 reported having premarital intercourse, a major change from the previous generation. Premarital coitus among men of the same generation did not increase, but visits to prostitutes decreased by 50 percent (Reed 1978, 61).

The most influential crusader of the period found her inspiration in the desperate conditions of the poor. Margaret Sanger (1879–1966) "led a successful campaign from 1914 to 1937 to remove the stigma of obscenity from contraception" (Reed 1978, 67). After being jailed for distributing contraceptive literature in 1914, she fled to Europe to avoid a trial. When she returned in 1915, the prosecutor refused to try the case, even though Sanger would have preferred another judicial test of the Comstock laws. She was jailed for thirty days in 1916 after she opened a birth control clinic in Brooklyn, the first of its type in the country. In 1923, she opened the Birth Control Clinical Research Bureau in New York, which dispensed contraceptives under the supervision of a physician and studied contraceptive effectiveness.

On the political front, the persistent efforts of Sanger, the American Birth Control League (of which Sanger was founder),[13] and others resulted in the gradual weakening of the Comstock laws. In 1918, the New York Court of Appeals ruled that legally practicing physicians could prescribe contraceptives for married couples "to cure or prevent disease" (Planned Parenthood Federation of America 1992). By 1937, the birth control movement had orchestrated and won the *U.S. v. One Package* case (86 F. 2d 737), which largely invalidated the 1873 federal Comstock law. In the *One Package* decision, a federal court of appeals ruled that had those who enacted the Comstock law known of the dangers of pregnancy and the usefulness of contraception that was available sixty years later, they might not have outlawed all contraception as obscene. In the court's opinion, the Comstock law was not intended "to prevent the importation, sale, or carriage by mail of things which might intelligently be employed by conscientious and competent physicians for the purpose of life or promoting the well-being of their patients" (Dienes 1972, 112). Although *One Package* opened the mails to contraceptive materials intended for physicians, "the right of individuals to bring such devices into the country was not established until 1971" (Reed 1978, 121).

In 1937, at the time of *One Package*, a national survey showed that 71 percent of Americans were in favor of birth control and 70 percent favored revising the federal Comstock law. In that same year, the American Medical Association recognized birth control as an integral part of medical practice and education (Planned Parenthood 1992). Nevertheless, the birth control movement's experience in both Congress and state legislatures indicated that legislators were not ready to tackle such a controversial subject (Dienes 1972, 95). Indeed, in concurring with the *One Package* decision, Judge Learned Hand commented that legislative action might come "long after a majority would repeal [birth control restrictions], if a poll were taken" (*U.S. v. One Package* [86 F. 2d 737]).[14]

Although *One Package* permitted the use of effective contraceptive methods by married couples, diaphragms and cervical caps were not widely available. A 1941 survey reported that most white Protestant couples used birth control at some point in their lives, but its findings were not specific in terms of particular methods or the duration of their use. Low-income women at this time had limited access to effective methods of birth control and little information about them. In 1942, the U.S. surgeon general addressed this situation by permitting the states to use federal maternal and child health funds for birth control.[15] First Lady Eleanor Roosevelt, a great proponent of family planning, was instrumental in this decision. Another important factor in the decision was that with the outbreak of World War II, women in factories began playing an indispensable role in the war effort, and concern arose that pregnancy would interfere with their vital work.

The baby boom that followed World War II continued throughout the 1950s. Indeed, the 1947 birth rate of 27 per 1,000 population was the highest since 1921. But even with the baby boom in full swing, Americans were using birth control. A 1955 national survey showed that white couples of *all* religious persuasions reported using birth control at some point in their lives. When nonwhites were included in the sample for the first time in 1960, they reported the same pattern.

Diaphragms, the most effective method of birth control in the 1950s, required a medical prescription. Women who had private physicians could be fitted for diaphragms and get prescriptions. Poor women were less likely to have the same access to this method. In 1958, this situation began to change when physicians in New York City's municipal hospitals were permitted to prescribe birth control. This change is viewed as a major turning point in public policy because the New York Board of Hospitals set the standard for the policies of many other municipalities. Shortly thereafter, other cities and states also changed their policies (Jaffe 1973).

In 1959, a presidential committee on foreign aid chaired by General William Draper recommended that assistance for family planning be made available to foreign governments that requested it. Catholic bishops denounced this suggestion, and President Eisenhower opposed it. Nevertheless, the discussion of population control inevitably brought up the issue of funding family planning within the United States, which was to be the focus of considerable legislation in the 1960s (Jaffe 1973; Reed 1978).

More effective birth control methods soon became available. In 1960, the U.S. Food and Drug Administration (FDA) approved the sale of oral steroid pills for contraception. This decision was the culmination of a decade-long effort by birth control advocate Margaret Sanger, philanthropist Katharine Dexter McCormick, and scientists Gregory Goodwin (Goody) Pincus and M.C. Chang (Halberstam 1993). Plastic intrauterine devices (IUDs) also came on the American market in the 1960s (Mishell 1975). Middle-class women accepted these methods rapidly, and the disparity in the percentage of unwanted births between middle-class and poor women increased.

In the 1960s, with the War on Poverty and the Civil Rights movement in full swing, great interest arose in providing poor women the same contraceptive opportunities that middle-class women had. Between 1965 and 1970, Congress mandated no fewer than four federal statutes to fund family planning services (see chap. 3). In less than one hundred years, the Congress of the United States had moved from prohibiting birth control to promoting it.

The last vestiges of the Comstock laws were coming to an end. In 1965, in *Griswold* v. *Connecticut* (381 U.S. 479), the U.S. Supreme Court overturned Connecticut's law prohibiting the use of birth control by anyone, married or single (Brodie 1994, 258). As a result, ten states liberalized their family planning laws and began to fund family planning services (Planned Parenthood 1992). In 1972, in *Eisenstadt* v. *Baird* (404 U.S. 438), the Supreme Court overturned a Massachusetts law that specifically prohibited unmarried persons from obtaining contraceptives (Craig and O'Brien 1993; Brodie 1994).

Abortion in Nineteenth-Century America

In 1800, abortion was not illegal in any state of the Union (Mohr 1978, vii). The minimal regulations that existed were inherited from the tradition in

English common law that abortions undertaken before "quickening" did not constitute homicide and were, at worst, misdemeanors (Luker 1984, 14). Quickening, a notion developed in the thirteenth century, occurs when the pregnant woman feels the first movement of the fetus. An abortion performed before quickening was not punishable by law, and even if quickening had occurred, the patient herself was immune from prosecution (Tribe 1992, 28). Quickening was also the basis for diagnosing a pregnancy. Given the scientific limitations of the time, one could not be absolutely certain that a woman was pregnant until quickening had occurred.

In the early 1800s, abortions were readily available. Many home health manuals prescribed methods and techniques. Single women were most likely to seek an abortion, and the procedure itself was not viewed as a great moral issue. The illicit sexual behavior that led to illegitimate conceptions was, however, considered immoral (Tribe 1992, 29).

Although widely advertised, induced abortion was very risky in the early nineteenth century. For example, it was popular to administer poisons to pregnant women to induce abortion, based on the "dubious theory that a dosage sufficient to kill the fetus might spare the woman." Statistics from the period indicate that mortality from surgical abortion must also have been extremely high. New York at this time had "a *30 percent death rate* from infections after abdominal surgery even when performed in hospitals." During the same period, the mortality rate from childbirth was *under 3 percent* (Tribe 1992, 29). Despite the tremendous risks women took in terminating unwanted pregnancies, demand for abortions was strong. From 1820 to 1830, an estimated one in every twenty-five to thirty pregnancies ended in induced abortion (Sheeran 1987, 55).

The first wave of anti-abortion legislation in the United States occurred between 1821 and 1841. Ten states and one territory enacted legislation that made some abortions illegal (Sheeran 1987, 54). Women's health was the primary motive for these laws. Connecticut passed the first statute in 1821, prohibiting the administration of poisons to produce postquickening abortions. In 1828, New York banned postquickening abortions by all methods (Tribe 1992, 29). However, "there was no popular support for these laws except from politicians and physicians" (Sheeran 1987, 55). Moreover, abortion laws of this period "were little noticed and rarely enforced" (Rosenblatt 1992, 86).

In 1846, Massachusetts launched the second wave of anti-abortion legislation by enacting the most restrictive law in the nation. It is noteworthy that physicians supported this legislation and that the general public did not even testify. This law ignored the notion of quickening and included jail sentences and fines for attempted abortions. New York followed suit in the same year with the passage of an abortion law that disregarded quickening and prescribed punishments for abortionists and abortion patients (Sheeran 1987, 54–55).

The demographics of abortion were changing, but not in the direction those opposed to abortion would have liked. Estimates of the incidence of induced abortion between 1850 and 1860 range from one in four to one in six pregnancies. Moreover, while the majority of women seeking abortions in 1840 were single women attempting to hide sexual activity, the majority in 1880 were rich, married white women (Sheeran 1987, 55).

Beginning in 1860, the American Medical Association became a major advocate of anti-abortion legislation. The leader was Dr. Horatio Robinson Storer, who believed that abortion was professionally and personally wrong. His efforts coincided with trends in Europe to disprove the old theory of delayed animation and replace it with the theory of immediate animation (Sheeran 1987, 56). The AMA's anti-abortion movement also coincided with its efforts to establish monopoly control by physicians over the practice of medicine. Midwives and other alternative practitioners were frequently the source of information on abortion. By repressing abortion, the AMA could restrict the demand for medicine practiced by nonphysicians.

The Catholic Church was not active in the anti-abortion campaigns that occurred before 1850. As noted earlier, the church changed its abortion policy in 1869, when Pope Pius IX decreed that there was no distinction between the animated and unanimated fetus, thus laying the groundwork "within the church for the theological position that all abortion is homicide" (Tribe 1992, 32). Nevertheless, Catholic support for the AMA strategy was tentative. Some conservative Protestant clergy eventually got on the anti-abortion bandwagon, but nineteenth-century clergy were, on the whole, reluctant to deal with sexual matters (Sheeran 1987, 56).

Between 1860 and 1880, forty anti-abortion state laws were passed. The most important common element in these laws was that interruption of gestation at any time during pregnancy constituted a crime. Again, physicians, not clergy, were the driving force. For the most part, this legal situation persisted until the 1960s (Sheeran 1987, 56–57).

Abortion in Twentieth-Century America

By 1910, all but one state (Kentucky) had outlawed induced abortion at any stage and made it a criminal offense (Craig and O'Brien 1993). The only exception was a therapeutic abortion, performed to save the life of the woman (Rosenblatt 1992, 88). Nevertheless, during the first half of the twentieth century, an estimated one in three pregnancies ended in abortion (Luker 1984).

The rationale for therapeutic abortions expanded over time. Poverty was a widely accepted reason for performing therapeutic abortions during the depression of the 1930s. In the 1940s and 1950s, doctors increasingly performed "therapeutic" abortions for psychiatric reasons, especially for women of means. Most abortions, however, were not therapeutic, but illegal and unregulated. Such abortions resulted in especially high morbidity and mortality rates for poor and rural women. However, there were few indictments for performing illegal abortions and even fewer convictions (Tribe 1992, 35).

During the 1950s, therapeutic abortions became increasingly subject to review by hospital boards. Heretofore, physicians had made the decision "to save the life of the mother" privately and independently. In response to the increasing scrutiny of the practices of individual physicians, the American Law Institute (ALI) revised its Model Penal Code to include three defenses against the charge of criminal abortion. The first was that continuation of the pregnancy would gravely impair the physical or mental health of the mother. The second was that the child was likely to be born with grave physical or mental defects. The third defense was that the pregnancy was the result of rape or incest. This widely copied code required certification by two physicians describing the circumstances that justified an abortion (Tribe 1992, 37).

Two events in the 1960s attracted even greater public attention to the abortion issue than the ALI's Model Penal Code had. One was the large number of babies born with missing or undeveloped limbs because their mothers had taken the sedative thalidomide during pregnancy. The best-known case related to thalidomide was that of Sherri Finkbine, an Arizona mother of four and a television personality. In 1962, Finkbine was unable to obtain a legal abortion in the United States despite the fact that she had discovered early in her fifth pregnancy that the tranquilizer she had been taking was thalidomide. The second event was the rubella outbreak of 1962–65. Like thalidomide, rubella causes severe birth defects. This epidemic alone produced some fifteen thousand infants with birth defects (Tribe 1992, 37).

Ironically, the medical profession, which had successfully lobbied for making abortion a crime a century earlier, became a principal advocate for changing the abortion laws. In 1967, the AMA issued a statement favoring liberalization of these laws. By this time, abortion had become a relatively safe procedure. In 1955, 100 of every 100,000 abortions resulted in the woman's death. By 1972, this number was 3 in 100,000 (Tribe 1992, 36, 38).[16]

Between 1967 and 1972, most state legislatures considered changes in their abortion laws. Nineteen states passed new abortion laws, and while more liberal than in the past, most of these were based on the ALI's modest Model Penal Code (Tribe 1992). In 1970, Hawaii became the first state to repeal its criminal abortion law and to legalize abortion performed before the twentieth week of pregnancy. In the same year, New York enacted the most liberal of the new laws, allowing abortion to be performed up until twenty-four weeks of gestation. As a result of these changes, women from more restrictive states flocked to less restrictive states to obtain abortions (Sheeran 1987, 57).

No state repealed any criminal abortion law during 1971 and 1973. On 22 January 1973, however, in a seven-to-two decision, the U.S. Supreme Court struck down every abortion law in the land, whether liberal or restrictive. In handing down *Roe* v. *Wade,* the Court found that a woman's right to decide whether to terminate her pregnancy was a *fundamental right* (Tribe 1992, 10–13, 48–51).

Although *Roe* v. *Wade* legalized abortion throughout the nation, it did not unify public opinion. Activity by interest groups intensified, and abortion became one of the most contentious political issues of late twentieth-century American politics.

CONCLUSION

Fertility control appears to be a universal in human civilization. Within a wide variety of cultures, history shows that people have tried to control their fertility in spite of legal, social, and moral restrictions. While these restrictions have not thwarted demand for fertility control, they have limited access to information and services. Throughout much of history, restrictions on fertility control have ensured that safe and effective methods have been limited to the affluent.

Not until the nineteenth century in England did concern about disparities in access to fertility control arise. In the United States, this issue remained off the agenda until well into the twentieth century. As a result, public policies that promote equitable access to fertility control are a relatively recent phenomenon.

Restrictions on the practice of fertility control remained a part of American jurisprudence until the early 1970s. These legal constraints drove the demand for fertility control, particularly abortion, underground. The reason these restrictive policies were so ineffective is that the demand for fertility control is highly inelastic. Childbearing imposes major economic and social costs on individuals. While many individuals welcome such costs, others seek to avoid them. The consequences of an unwanted pregnancy provide a strong motivation for fertility control either before or after conception.

CHAPTER 3

Family Planning Policies: An Intergovernmental Labyrinth

CLEARLY, FAMILY PLANNING and abortion are related; both address unintended fertility. For the most part, however, different public policies have addressed each. Because abortion is a more controversial subject than contraception, family planning has been easier to get on the agenda for positive action. Since the mid-1960s, both the federal and state governments have funded family planning services for low-income persons. From 1965 to 1994, federal family planning expenditures totaled approximately $7.1 billion, while the states spent an estimated $1.6 billion for family planning (see table 3.1, p. 40). Abortion, in contrast, did not even become legal in all states until 1973, when the Supreme Court issued the *Roe* v. *Wade* decision.[1] Since that time, the courts have determined most of the parameters for the delivery of abortion services.

Because of their different policy histories, we devote separate chapters to family planning and abortion. Nevertheless, the intrinsic relationship between family planning and abortion, as well as a modest overlap in providers, often precludes a complete separation of their politics. We begin with family planning.

The United States does not have a single family planning policy; it has several policies that developed in the context of specific legislation. Since 1965, at least six federal statutes have authorized federal funds to support family planning services. This chapter first presents a decade-by-decade chronology of pertinent legislation and executive branch developments. In the second part of the chapter, we examine the family planning laws more analytically and rate their likely effectiveness, using prescriptive criteria from the Mazmanian and Sabatier framework for policy implementation.

CHRONOLOGY OF FEDERAL FAMILY PLANNING POLICIES
The 1960s
Federal Legislation. In 1965, after the Supreme Court's *Griswold* decision (381 U.S. 479) legalized contraception, the Office of Economic Opportunity (OEO) awarded the first direct federal grant for family planning services—

Table 3.1 Federal and State Expenditures for Family
Planning (in millions of dollars)

YEAR	FEDERAL EXPENDITURES	STATE EXPENDITURES
1965–67	8.1	—
1968	8.1	—
1969	27.0	—
1970	46.0	—
1971	56.0	1.6
1972	101.0	4.3
1973	143.0	5.6
1974	145.8	14.4
1975	157.9	21.8
1976	177.4	22.3
1977	215.9	21.6
1978	239.4	32.1
1979	257.3	48.3
1980	298.5	48.6
1981	324.3	49.8
1982	275.1	53.1
1983	282.9	57.7
1984	308.4	63.9
1985	333.8	63.9
1986	334.3	57.0
1987	334.8	50.0
1988	349.0	94.9
1989	349.0	94.9
1990	363.2	139.8
1991	426.0	147.7
1992	488.7	155.5
1993	521.2	158.7
1994	553.6	161.9
Total	7,125.7	1,569.4

Sources: Doring-Bradley 1977 (1965–76 data); AGI 1979a, 38, 40, 49 (1977
data); AGI 1980a, 49, 50, 57, and AGI 1981a, 26 (1978 data); AGI 1981b,
59, AGI 1981c, 30–31, and AGI 1981d, 34 (1979 data); Nestor 1982
(1980–81 data); AGI 1983a, 147–48, 150–53, 156–57 (1982 data); Gold and
Nestor 1985 (1983 data); Gold and Macias 1986 (1985 data); Gold and
Guardado 1988 (1987 data); Gold and Daley 1991 (1990 data); Daley and
Gold 1993 (1992 data); Sollom, Gold, and Saul 1996 (1994 data).

$8,000 to a project in Corpus Christi, Texas. From 1965 to 1967, OEO spent
an estimated $5.6 million for family planning, although family planning was
not specifically included in the Economic Opportunity Act until 1967.

Title XIX of the Social Security Act, the Medicaid program, was enacted in 1965. The objective of Title XIX was to encourage each state to develop a unified system of financial assistance for persons unable to pay for medical care. Family planning services were not included in the statute, but they were mentioned in the Title XIX regulations published in the *Federal Register* (AGI 1974). In most states, the welfare department was the official Medicaid agency, although some states named health departments or umbrella agencies (i.e., a combination of health and welfare agencies) to perform this function.

In 1967, Congress specifically mandated the provision of family planning services under the auspices of two other federal programs: Titles IV-A and V of the Social Security Act. Title IV-A, the Social Services Program for Mothers and Children, was enacted in 1962 "to help maintain and strengthen family life" through the provision of certain required and optional services.[2] Title V, the Maternal and Child Health and Crippled Children Act, was passed in 1935 to improve the health of mothers and children and to expand and improve services for disabled children. Both programs operated in all fifty states, so each had the potential to be a significant resource for publicly supported family planning services.

Because Title IV-A was tied to public assistance, state welfare departments administered this program. States had the option of including only current recipients of Aid to Families with Dependent Children (AFDC) or of including three additional categories: past AFDC recipients, current applicants, and potential recipients.[3] The federal government covered 75 percent of the costs of Title IV-A services; the states were responsible for the remainder (AGI 1974, 31).

State health departments administered the Title V program. Until 1967, the only explicit Title V directive concerning family planning was a 1942 memo from the surgeon general, permitting state health departments to include family planning as a maternal and child health (MCH) service. The 1967 legislation[4] not only made family planning a required Title V service; it also specifically stated that not less than 6 percent of the funds appropriated for MCH were to be spent for family planning services (AGI 1974, 22). However, this requirement was national and not imposed on individual states.

The States. Changes in explicit federal policy echoed what was already happening in the states: the 1960s were a time of transition for state policies toward family planning services. Although North Carolina established the first state-supported family planning program in 1937 and was followed by six other southern states—Alabama, Florida, Georgia, Mississippi, South Carolina, and Virginia (Eliot et al. 1968)—not until 1961 did any state outside the South adopt an affirmative policy on family planning. In that year, California's state health department began to provide both technical and financial assistance to local communities for the development of family planning services (Lee 1970). By 1963, three more states (Maryland, Colorado, and Kansas) and the District of Columbia had begun to offer family planning services through their public health departments. During 1963, programs were started in eight more states (Arkansas, Indiana, Kentucky, Michigan, North Dakota, Oklahoma, Oregon, and Tennessee). The following year, public health departments in eleven more states (Arizona, Illinois, Maine, Missouri, Nevada, New Jersey, New Mexico, New York, Texas, Washington, and West Virginia) began offering family planning services (Corsa 1966). By the end of 1967, forty-seven states were providing or at least had adopted an affirmative stance toward family planning (AGI 1979a).

The Executive Branch. The executive branch did not neglect the family planning issue. In 1968, President Johnson appointed the Committee on Population and Family Planning to assess the adequacy of the federal family planning program. That committee recommended a drastic increase in funding for domestic voluntary family planning services, as well as substantial changes in their administration (Jaffe 1974).

A year later, President Nixon sent a message about population to Congress, asking for increased federal support for domestic family planning services and requesting the establishment of a population commission. Legislation creating the two-year Commission on Population Growth and the American Future was enacted early in 1970 (Jaffe 1974). Congress, however, preempted the recommendations of this commission by passing Title X of the Public Health Service Act, the Family Planning Services and Population Research Act (PL 572), in December 1970.

The 1970s

Federal Legislation. The overall goal of Title X was "to assist in making comprehensive voluntary family planning services available to all persons desiring such services." The focus of Title X, however, was to provide categorical (i.e., specific) funding for family planning services for low-income women. Title X also provided support for population research.

Title X not only authorized an increase in funding for family planning services; it also mandated the establishment of the Office of Population Affairs (OPA) in the upper echelons of the Department of Health, Education, and Welfare (DHEW).[5] OPA was to serve as a primary focus within the federal government on matters pertaining to population research and family planning and was to be headed by a deputy assistant secretary for population affairs (DASPA) (U.S. DHHS 1978). Statutory framers intended that OPA would coordinate all federal funding for family planning services (PL 572).

Congress authorized Title X at a level at which it would dominate other federal funding sources of family planning, although it would take a couple of years for appropriations to come near the authorization figures (see table 3.2).

Table 3.2 Title X Authorizations and Appropriations for Family Planning (in millions of dollars)

YEAR	AUTHORIZATION AMOUNT	APPROPRIATION AMOUNT
1971	30.0	6.0
1972	60.0	61.8
1973	111.5	100.6
1974	111.5	100.6
1975	111.5	100.6
1976	115.0	100.6
1977	115.0	113.0
1978	136.4	135.0
1979	200.0	135.0
1980	230.0	162.0
1981	264.5	161.7
1982	126.5	124.2
1983	139.2	124.1
1984	150.8	140.0
1985	158.4	142.5
1986	0	136.4
1987	0	142.5
1988	0	139.7
1989	0	138.3
1990	0	139.1
1991	0	144.3
1992	0	149.6
1993	0	173.4
1994	0	180.9
1995	0	193.3
1996	0	193.3
1997	0	198.0
1998	0	203.5

Congressional intent, however, was not for Title X funds to meet the national goals alone. Each year, OPA was required to submit a five-year plan to Congress explaining how the nation's family planning goals would be met and with what resources.

Although family planning was required under Title IV-A and permitted under Title XIX, many states did little to make these services available. Consequently, a substantial proportion of welfare recipients remained at risk of unwanted pregnancy (Rosoff 1972; Fisher and Rosoff 1972). In 1972, Congress addressed this situation by adding family planning incentives to both Titles IV-A and XIX. Federal reimbursement for family planning services provided under the authority of these statutes was increased to 90 percent. In addition, these amendments included a 1 percent penalty on the federal AFDC payment to a state when family planning services were not offered to needy families; however, this penalty was never imposed.

In 1974, two years after significantly strengthening the family planning provisions of Titles IV-A and XIX, Congress repealed the special legislative authority for family planning that it had granted OEO in 1967. The 1974 legislation formalized what was already an administrative fiat. Under the direction of the Nixon administration, the War on Poverty was being scaled down. OEO had begun transferring its family planning projects to DHEW in 1971; this process was completed in 1974.

Title XX of the Social Security Act, Block Grants to the States for Social Services, was passed in January 1975. Federal block grants are lump sums that the national government gives to subnational governments, usually the states. Block grants allow state and local governments to choose how to spend their federal money within broad policy areas. Title XX incorporated and revised many Title IV-A social services provisions, including three that affected family planning: the priority federal matching rate of 90 percent, the requirement that states must provide family planning services under their social services programs, and the 1 percent penalty on the federal share of AFDC when family planning services were not provided under this program. In September 1976, Congress amended Title XX, giving states the option to provide family planning services on a universal basis without regard to income. Family planning and day care were the only programs to receive such preferential treatment (AGI 1976a).

The Executive Branch. Although Title X authorizations and appropriations increased during his tenure, President Nixon, an advocate of revenue sharing, did not endorse the increase in categorical family planning funding. Nixon did appoint a deputy assistant secretary for population affairs, Dr. Louis Hellman, the physician who had written the first contraceptive prescription in New York's municipal hospitals in 1958. Providing earmarked federal funds directly to local communities, however, was antithetical to the New Federalism policies of the Nixon administration. The intent of New Federalism was to shift control of funds from federal to state officials (Dryfoos 1976). Interestingly, a House Republican research task force on population policy, chaired by Congressman George Bush of Texas, "released a dissenting report urging that states not be given control over family planning grants for at least four years." This report recommended that family planning be exempt from the transfer of decision-making power to the states. The Bush committee said it had to be recognized that state health departments lacked adequate systems for "delivering birth control services to the poor" (Littlewood 1977, 63–64).

Nonetheless, the Nixon administration's opposition to categorical family planning legislation, as well as its emphasis on state decision making, was reiterated during the May 1973 Senate hearings on the extension of Title X. While acknowledging that past inadequacies in state Medicaid programs had made categorical family planning grants necessary, the administration pointed out that the 1972 amendments to Titles IV-A and XIX of the Social Security Act made categorical funding superfluous (Weinberg 1974).

Ironically, in 1973, the same year that DHEW encouraged states to make use of the Title XIX mechanism as the principal funding source for publicly supported family planning services, Title XIX also became the primary source of funds for federally subsidized abortions. Nixon had made his abortion position known the previous year when he denigrated the largely noncontroversial final report of the Commission on Population Growth and the American Future because of his opposition to two of its recommendations (Littlewood 1977, 61; U.S. Commission on Population Growth and the American Future 1972). The recommendations opposed by the president were (1) to remove restrictive state laws concerning abortion and to provide public funding for these procedures and (2) to adopt affirmative legislation permitting minors to receive contraceptive information and services. From its inception, Title X specifically forbade the use of its funds for abortion, whereas Title XIX had no such restrictions.

Both the Nixon and Ford administrations struggled with Congress about the New Federalism generally and health programs in particular. This situation clearly affected family planning. For fiscal 1974, Title X was funded by a one-year extension, the Health Programs Extension Act (PL 45), which had been "strenuously opposed" by the Nixon administration (AGI 1973). In October 1974, President Ford vetoed two appropriations bills for fiscal 1975. That year, Title X was funded by no fewer than five continuing resolutions.

Family planning was not a central theme for Jimmy Carter when he assumed office in 1977. Moreover, Carter's own position on fertility control was ambivalent. As governor of Georgia, he had been a well-known supporter of the state family planning program (Donovan 1973). He campaigned, however, on an anti-abortion platform early in the presidential primaries. During his presidency, the controversy about federal funding for abortion continued to rage in Congress.

During the Carter years, the administration of Title X was transferred to the Bureau of Community Health Services (BCHS) within the Health Resources and Services Administration (HRSA), thus shifting administration from the level of assistant secretary mandated by Title X. Individual Title X grants continued to be administered by the ten regional offices of the U.S. Public Health Service (USPHS). The BCHS director pursued a consolidation policy under which Title X funds were increasingly channeled to comprehensive health centers, which had less interest in and less accountability for family planning services than did many specialized family planning agencies.

In addition, the accountability of Title X was threatened by less reliable patient data. The reason for this was that the National Center for Health Statistics converted the National Reporting System for Family Planning Statistics (NRSFPS) from a universal system to a sample system. This sample system was implemented over the protests of the family planning community.

The 1980s

The election of Ronald Reagan in 1980 brought significant changes to the national family planning effort. Public funding for family planning was imperiled for two reasons. First, restructuring federalism was a major priority for President Reagan, who believed that the national government had usurped too many domestic responsibilities. Second, Reagan owed a political debt to the conservative coalition, which opposed public support of family planning (McKeegan 1992, 62).

Reagan envisioned a smaller government with more state authority (Williamson 1990). He believed that the accomplishment of this goal would require a two-stage process. First, the federal grant system required dramatic changes. Initially, the president proposed consolidating ninety of the three hundred federal categorical grants into three block grants with reduced funding. In the health area alone, he wanted to aggregate forty categorical programs into two block grants (Peterson et al. 1986). Block grants would remove categorical restrictions and turn most of the policy discretion over to the states.

The second stage was to occur more slowly. As states became accustomed to making their own policy decisions with more flexible federal dollars, they would eventually assume full fiscal responsibility for their own programs. Reagan argued that states would be more responsive to their own needs than the federal government was (Rosoff 1981).

Not all of Reagan's proposals were enacted, but major changes were implemented. In 1981, Congress consolidated fifty-seven (instead of ninety) categorical grants into nine (not three) block grants. Overall, funds were reduced by 9 percent from the 1981 categorical grant levels. For individual health programs, these reductions ranged from 17 to 45 percent (Peterson 1984). Although these changes were less than what the president had proposed, the 1981 block grant consolidations represented the largest grant conversion in history (Benda and Levine 1988).

Reagan singled out the family planning program for special attack in order to placate the pro-life right wing of the Republican Party. These "right-wing abortion foes saw little difference between abortion and family planning." Ironically, by preventing unwanted pregnancies, the public family planning program was averting an estimated four hundred thousand abortions per year (McKeegan 1992, 64–65).

Federal Legislation. Each of the four federal statutes that funded family planning services in 1980—Titles V, X, XIX, and XX—survived the budgetary politics of 1981, albeit with substantial changes. Table 3.3 (p. 48) summarizes these statutes in terms of their respective grant and administrative mechanisms, specific family planning provisions, and the 1981 changes.

Under Title V, maternal and child health monies are awarded on a formula basis to state health departments. Before 1981, states were required to match the federal dollars one-to-one. This match rate was changed in 1981; since then, for every three dollars contributed by the federal government, the states have had to match with four. Another change in 1981, which became effective the following year, was the removal of the requirement that 6 percent of Title V funds be spent for family planning. In addition, eight existing federal grant programs—including maternal and child health—were consolidated under Title V, with a 17 percent reduction in the fiscal 1981 appropriation. At the state level, these changes meant that Title V family planning services had to compete with more programs for less money than before.

Title X, unlike the other three federal grant programs, is administered not by state health or welfare departments, but by the ten regional offices of the U.S. Public Health Service. Grants are awarded on a competitive basis to projects that either provide or subcontract for services. Title X does not mandate that a state agency be the grantee, although state agencies have never been excluded from seeking these funds. Despite the Reagan administration's effort to block categorical programs, Title X was reauthorized for fiscal 1982.

The salience of family planning contributed to preserving Title X as a categorical program. By 1981, it had been a categorical program for over a decade. Many of the ideological battles (e.g., over parental involvement and abortion referral) had been fought repeatedly on Capitol Hill. Among members of Congress, advocates and opponents had made their positions known. The constituency groups on both sides had been mobilized. While many opponents of the family planning program linked the provision of contraceptive services with the abortion issue, many in Congress viewed family planning as "the only national and logical alternative to abortion." In fact, more than one hundred members of Congress signed a letter to the president expressing their support for family planning, despite their differing views on abortion (AGI 1981g, 1–2).

Another factor that saved Title X from being blocked was that some of the other public health programs did not want family planning included in their block grants. There was, for example, "a conspicuous lack of enthusiasm" among some supporters of maternal and child health programs for family planning to be folded into that block grant. They worried that the entire maternal and child health program "might be adversely affected by the 'controversy' attached to family planning" (AGI 1981f, 2).

Table 3.3 Statutes Authorizing Federal Funding for Family Planning

STATUTE	GRANT AND ADMINISTRATIVE MECHANISMS	SPECIFIC FAMILY PLANNING PROVISIONS	1981 CHANGES
Title V of Social Security Act (Maternal and Child Health and Crippled Children Act)	Formula grants matched by the states; administered by state health departments	FY 1968–81: 6% of Title V funds to be spent on family planning	(1) 6% requirement removed; (2) more programs consolidated under Title V; (3) 17% reduction in funds; (4) less favorable federal match rate
Title X of Public Health Service Act (Family Planning Services and Population Research Act)	Project grants administered by regional offices of U.S. Public Health Service	Categorical legislation	(1) 20% reduction in funds; (2) reassignment of many grants to state health departments
Title XIX of Social Security Act (Medicaid)	Reimbursement of providers for individual services; administered by state health or welfare departments; no federal ceiling on expenditures	FY 1972–present: 90% federal match for family planning services	No changes for family planning: (1) 90% match retained; (2) no federal ceiling
Title XX of Social Security Act (Block Grant to the States for Social Services)	Block grants to state welfare departments	FY 1976–81: 90% federal match for family planning; 1% penalty for failure to provide family planning services to AFDC recipients	(1) Elimination of all state match; (2) reduction in funds

Ironically, the controversial nature of family planning also caused some Reagan supporters within Congress—namely, Senator Jeremiah Denton (R-Ala.) and Senator Orrin Hatch (R-Utah)—to consider breaking ranks with Reagan's federalism and supporting Title X as a categorical program. That way, they would have more control over reworking Title X according to their own ideology, rather than leaving such important matters as teen pregnancy to state discretion (AGI 1981g).

Title X did survive, though its funds were cut sharply—a 20 percent reduction from the fiscal 1981 appropriation. After Senator Hatch informed the president that Congress was against the idea of blocking Title X, Reagan replied, "I regret that we do not have the votes to defeat the family planning program. . . . Perhaps we can remedy some of the problems in the family planning program *administratively* [italics added] in the three years that it will remain a categorical grant" (McKeegan 1992, 66). This program was to be under siege for the next decade.

Title XIX, the Medicaid program, reimburses providers for medical services rendered to eligible persons. Eligibility levels differ widely by state. Except for a 90 percent federal match for family planning services, the federal reimbursement rate to the states varies by state per capita income. After Reagan became president, the rates of federal reimbursement to the states were reduced; Congress, however, retained the 90 percent federal match for family planning. The Reagan administration was also unsuccessful in its attempts to cap or place a ceiling on total Medicaid expenditures. The more the states spend, the more the federal government has to spend for the program. Not surprisingly, the Medicaid program was the only federal source of funding that actually increased its family planning expenditures during the Reagan years.

Title XX allocates block grant funds for social services to the states on the basis of population. State welfare departments administer Title XX funds. Under Reagan, Title XX was reduced overall from $3.0 billion to $2.4 billion. The revised Title XX does not require a state match for any services. Without the 90 percent federal match for family planning services, states no longer have a direct fiscal incentive to spend Title XX funds for contraception.

Related to these conservative developments was the Adolescent Family Life Act of 1981 (PL 35). This legislation replaced the Adolescent Health Service and Pregnancy Prevention Act of 1978 (PL 626), which had funded comprehensive pregnancy-prevention and pregnancy-related services for adolescents, including family life and sex education. The 1981 legislation, which some liberals called the "Chastity Act," took a new tack by focusing on the prevention of adolescent sexual relations. It is noteworthy that while this act provided funding for "necessary services to prevent adolescent sexual relations," it stated that no funds could be used for contraception unless these services were "not otherwise available in the community" (PL 35).

More Executive Branch Developments. The executive branch's efforts to diminish Title X's impact persisted throughout the 1980s. Political appointees were selected because of their anti-abortion, pro-life positions (Craig and O'Brien 1993), which extended to family planning. To quote McKeegan (1992, 62), "Family planning programs offended pro-lifers in myriad ways: by serving teenagers without their parents' consent; informing women with problem pregnancies about the full range of options, including abortion; funding clinics run by the notoriously pro-choice Planned Parenthood; and distributing birth control methods, such as the pill and intrauterine device, which many pro-lifers claimed to be abortifacients."

Once inside the bureaucracy, anti-abortion appointees could tinker with Title X's administrative mechanisms. For example, acting under administrative directives (McKeegan 1992, 67), the regional offices of USPHS consolidated the Title X grants, so that in many states, the state health department became the only grantee (Orr 1983; McFarlane 1992). This move was important because state health departments were more likely to siphon family planning money off to less controversial health programs (McKeegan 1992, 65), less likely to expand family planning services, and much less likely to lobby their state legislatures or Congress than were freestanding, specialized family planning projects.

The first deputy assistant secretary for population affairs under the Reagan administration, Marjory Mecklenberg (former president of the Minnesota Citizens Concerned for Life and a founder of the National Right to Life Committee), recognized the political benefits of consolidation and instructed the regional offices to act quickly (McKeegan 1992, 67; Gorney 1998). They responded; the number of Title X grants for family planning services was reduced from 222 in 1981 to 88 in 1982 (U.S. DHHS 1994). For example, Texas had 37 Title X grantees in 1980; in 1981, the state's sole Title X grantee for family planning services was the Texas Department of Health (Smith 1991).

Other developments in family planning administration in the 1980s included transferring the Office of Population Affairs back to direct administration by the political appointee (DASPA), entirely disbanding the patient data system for family planning, issuing the "squeal rule," and promulgating the "gag rule." The squeal rule required Title X–funded family planning clinics that dispensed contraceptives to minors to notify the minors' parents. The gag rule barred any mention of abortion in Title X–funded clinics or any sharing of staff or space with a clinic that provided abortions, even though only eighty-seven of the forty-five hundred clinics funded by Title X even did abortions and half of these were hospitals (McKeegan 1992, 67–72, 117–21). In short, these administrative maneuvers, along with the funding cuts, "virtually guaranteed that the nation would make little progress in dealing with the problem of unintended pregnancy during the eighties" (McKeegan 1992, 75).

The 1990s

The Bush administration maintained the same policies as the Reagan administration and retained the same DASPA (Craig and O'Brien 1993). The gag rule remained in litigation throughout Bush's tenure; consequently, it was never fully implemented. No Title X authorization was enacted during the Bush years (in fact, there has been no such authorization since 1985). Title X limped along with appropriations from continuing resolutions. On the abortion front, Bush supported the ban on fetal tissue research promulgated by the Reagan administration. In 1991, the FDA banned the import of RU 486 (mifepristone) for personal use (McKeegan 1992,126).

The 1992 election of Bill Clinton signaled a temporary end to the siege of the federal family planning program. Two days after being sworn in, President Clinton began the process of repealing the gag rule (AGI 1993f, 1993l).[6] Clinton's appointments for surgeon general—Joycelyn Elders—and for assistant secretary for health of the Department of Health and Human Services (DHHS)—Philip Lee—were both longtime supporters of family planning (AGI 1993k, 1993p).

Although congressional developments looked promising for Title X in early 1993, the legislation was not reauthorized. Subsumed by Clinton's ill-fated health care reform package, consideration of Title X was also entangled by antiabortion politics (AGI 1993d). Clinton appointed Felicia Stewart, a prominent physician, to the post of DASPA, but she did not fill the position until 1994. During her short tenure, one major policy innovation occurred: emergency contraception was made available to all Title X clinics.

The 104th Congress and Welfare Reform. Any consideration of further expanding the national family planning program came to a screeching halt with the 1994 midterm elections. For the first time in forty years, Republicans gained control of both houses of Congress. Immediately after the 1994 elections, some Republican governors and pivotal House members discussed replacing more than three hundred federal assistance programs worth $125 billion per year with block grants to the states (Congressional Quarterly 1995). Once again, there was serious discussion about collapsing categorical programs like Title X into broader block grants to the states. Overall, these proposals dwarfed even the most sweeping changes that Ronald Reagan had entertained in 1981.

Blocking federal grants, especially for health and social service programs, has been a consistent Republican goal. This time, however, blocking grants had a new twist (Katz 1995). Congress considered not only consolidating federal categorical grants to the states, but also blocking federal entitlement programs. (Entitlement programs, such as unemployment insurance, provide benefits to anyone meeting their qualification criteria.) Turning a federal entitlement program into a block grant was unprecedented (Katz 1996). Both Congress and the

National Governors' Association, however, proposed this change not only for welfare, but for the Medicaid program as well (Pear 1996; MacPherson 1995).

Medicaid was the largest intergovernmental entitlement, accounting for more than 40 percent of all federal outlays to the states (ACIR 1995). With its huge cost increases and "a constituency with relatively little clout," the Medicaid program had been an obvious budget target (Congressional Quarterly 1995). At a mere $17 billion in 1995, federal outlays for welfare (family support) were eclipsed by the $88.4 billion Medicaid program. Nevertheless, welfare was even less popular than Medicaid (Schlesinger and Lee 1993), so Medicaid emerged mostly unscathed while AFDC was altered profoundly.[7] Because most of the growth in the public family planning program was financed by Medicaid funds, this move left family planning funding intact.

The 104th Congress succeeded in changing the national welfare system. Clinton had vetoed similar legislation, but in the 1996 election year, the president signed the Personal Responsibility and Work Opportunity Reconciliation Act (PL 193), the so-called Welfare Reform Act. A block grant, Temporary Assistance for Needy Families (TANF), replaced AFDC, "the nation's main cash welfare program," as well as several related programs (Katz 1996, 2192).

Although those who crafted the legislation were clearly concerned about human reproduction, no funds were earmarked for family planning services. Instead, the Welfare Reform Act deleted the provision that for over a quarter of a century had required states to provide family planning services to welfare recipients. The new act permitted states to spend a portion of their block grant money on "pre-pregnancy family planning services." In a last-minute concession to the White House, Medicaid benefits were made available to those who would have been eligible for AFDC, even if they were not eligible for the "reformed" state welfare programs under TANF.

The framers of TANF focused on the relationship between out-of-wedlock births and welfare dependency. "A particular hallmark of the legislation is language permeating throughout decrying 'illegitimacy,' the clear implication being that out of wedlock births, especially those to teenagers, are both a cause of illegitimacy and a direct result of the 'culture' that it creates" (AGI 1996b). Congress elected to address its concern not by funding family planning services, but through various sanctions. States were permitted to deny welfare benefits to unwed parents under age eighteen. The act also prohibited states from giving benefits to these young parents if they were not living with an adult and not attending school. States could impose "child exclusion policies," whereby no benefit increases would be given if a woman on welfare had another child (AGI 1996b).

Other provisions of the law also concentrated on reproductive behavior. These provisions included (1) a state bonus to reward decreases in illegitimacy, (2) the establishment of national goals to prevent teen pregnancy, (3) the enforcement of statutory rape laws, and (4) an abstinence education program (PL 193, 2118–19, 2349–50, 2353–54).

The state bonus rewarded the five states showing the greatest decrease in out-of-wedlock births with $20 million apiece, provided that these states also had lower induced abortion rates than they did in 1995. Apparently realizing the difficulty of affecting demographic rates, Congress added that if fewer than five states met these criteria, then the bonus would be $25 million to each state that did.

The establishment of national goals to prevent teenage pregnancy required the secretary of DHHS to establish and implement a program for preventing teenage pregnancies by 1 January 1997. At that point, the federal family planning program had been in place for nearly thirty years, and other federal programs, such as the Adolescent Family Life program, funded teen pregnancy prevention. This plan simply repackaged existing federal, state, and local programs in a single document. After all, the new welfare legislation included no funds to support this effort.

Section 906 of this law dealt with "the sense of the Senate regarding enforcement of statutory rape laws" and directed the attorney general to establish and implement a program to study the linkage between teenage pregnancy and statutory rape, "particularly by older men committing repeat offenses" (PL 193, 2349). Also included was the directive to educate state and local law enforcement officials on the prevention and prosecution of statutory rape and "any links to teenage pregnancy" (PL 193, 2350). In fact, only 8 percent of women fifteen to nineteen years old who give birth are unmarried and have partners five years older than they or older (Lindberg et al. 1997). Obviously, this section reflects the ideology of the dominant policymakers rather than illuminating a significant cause of teenage pregnancy, illegitimacy, or welfare dependency.

The new welfare legislation did allot $50 million a year for the purpose of funding abstinence education programs in the states. This section of the law specifically described an educational or motivational program that

a. Has as its exclusive purpose, teaching the social, psychological, and health gains to be gained by abstaining from sexual activity;

b. Teaches abstinence from sexual activity outside marriage as the expected standard for all school age children;

c. Teaches that abstinence from sexual activity is the only way to avoid out-of-wedlock pregnancy, sexually transmitted diseases, and other associated health problems;

d. Teaches that a mutually faithful monogamous relationship in the context of marriage is the expected standard of human sexual activity;

e. Teaches that sexual activity outside of the context of marriage is likely to have harmful psychological and physical effects;

f. Teaches that bearing children out-of-wedlock is likely to have harmful consequences for the child, the child's parents, and society;

g. Teaches young people how to reject sexual advances and how alcohol and drug use increases vulnerability to sexual advances; and

h. Teaches the importance of attaining self-sufficiency before engaging in sexual activity.

Because numerous studies have demonstrated that abstinence cannot be counted on as a major means of reducing rates of unintended pregnancy (Institute of Medicine 1995), this section, too, reflects a particular ideological position rather than likely program efficacy.

In sum, the 1996 welfare reform legislation did not offer support for contraception, nor did it require states to spend money for birth control services. The irony here is that within five years of delivery of their first child (usually unintended), nearly 77 percent of single teenage mothers receive public support (Katz 1996).

Family Planning Funding. Although Title X was not reauthorized during either of Clinton's terms in office, appropriations for the program grew modestly each year. Most of the growth continued to be in the Medicaid program, which increasingly was moving in the direction of managed care. Given the favorable match for family planning, most states devised ways of ensuring that patients could continue going to traditional family planning providers for birth control services.

Summary

In spite of the controversy that has surrounded it, federal legislation concerning family planning has remained remarkably stable. In three decades (1965–95), only six statutes have authorized nearly all of the federal support for family planning: Title IV-A, Title V, OEO, Title X, Title XIX, and Title XX. Four of these, Titles V, X, XIX, and XX, have constituted almost all federal support since 1975. These laws differ in many ways, including their purposes, grant mechanisms, and the roles of the states.

This is an unusual policy configuration. Title X, which provides categorical funding, was also intended to serve as a flagship for family planning within the federal government. The other statutes are not categorical; family planning is just one of the many programs that they fund.

While this combination of statutes may not comprise an ideal policy design, current family planning politics indicate that this amalgam is likely to continue into the near future. In the following section, we use a well-known model from the policy implementation literature to assess the likely effectiveness of each statute.

THE MAZMANIAN AND SABATIER MODEL: ASSESSING FAMILY PLANNING POLICY

The policy implementation literature in political science arose in response to the alleged failures of federal laws enacted from the mid-1960s to the early 1970s. What began as many disparate case studies of different policy areas culminated in the development of general models of the implementation process. Among the most important models were those of Van Meter and Van Horn (1975), Bardach (1977), and Berman (1978). Each contributed to the development of the widely cited and applied Mazmanian and Sabatier implementation framework (1981, 1983, 1989).

Public policies—whether legislative enactments, executive orders, or judicial rulings—are implemented in complex environments. Among the many factors influencing their implementation are socioeconomic conditions, public support, and administrative behavior. This complexity is recognized in the Mazmanian and Sabatier model, which comprises sixteen independent variables from three categories (see fig. 3.1, p. 56). Despite this complex environment, Mazmanian and Sabatier (1989, 25) maintain that "the original policymakers can affect substantially the attainment of legal objectives by utilizing the levers at their disposal to coherently structure the implementation process."

What are these levers at the disposal of the original policymakers? In the Mazmanian and Sabatier framework (1989, 25–30), they consist of the following statutory variables: (1) precise and clearly ranked objectives, (2) the incorporation of adequate causal theory, (3) the provision of adequate funds for the implementing organizations, (4) hierarchical integration within and among implementing organizations, (5) the presence of favorable decision rules for the implementing organizations, (6) the commitment of the implementing agencies and officials, and (7) opportunities for formal participation by supporters of statutory objectives. The statutory coherence hypothesis can be deduced from this model; that is, effective implementation is a function of the extent to which the above conditions are met. In other words, a coherent statute is more likely to work. (McFarlane 1989; Meier and McFarlane 1996).

Given all the problems likely to occur during implementation, a coherent statute improves the odds of successful implementation—that is, of producing the desired results. Precise and clearly ranked goals mean that a policy is not handicapped by vague or conflicting mandates. Incorporation of a causal theory means that policymakers understand why a problem exists and know the way to solve it. The need for adequate funds is self-evident. Hierarchical integration means that the various agencies involved will be coordinating their efforts to manage policy implementation successfully instead of obstructing it. Favorable

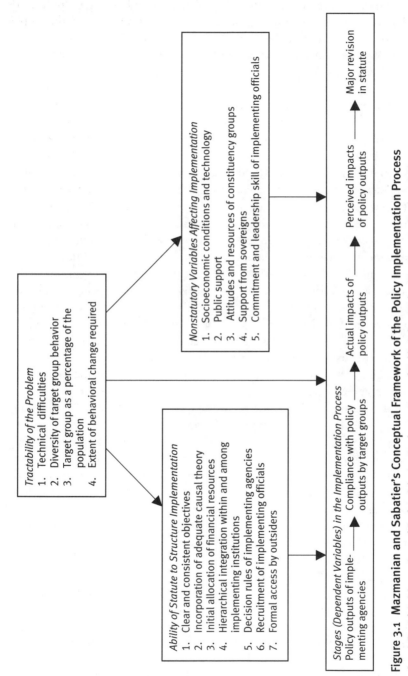

Figure 3.1 Mazmanian and Sabatier's Conceptual Framework of the Policy Implementation Process

Source: Daniel A. Mazmanian and Paul A. Sabatier, *Implementation and Public Policy: With a New Postscript* (Lanham, Md.: University Press of America), 1989. Reproduced with the permission of University Press of America.

Tractability of the Problem
1. Technical difficulties
2. Diversity of target group behavior
3. Target group as a percentage of the population
4. Extent of behavioral change required

Nonstatutory Variables Affecting Implementation
1. Socioeconomic conditions and technology
2. Public support
3. Attitudes and resources of constituency groups
4. Support from sovereigns
5. Commitment and leadership skill of implementing officials

Ability of Statute to Structure Implementation
1. Clear and consistent objectives
2. Incorporation of adequate causal theory
3. Initial allocation of financial resources
4. Hierarchical integration within and among implementing institutions
5. Decision rules of implementing agencies
6. Recruitment of implementing officials
7. Formal access by outsiders

Stages (Dependent Variables) in the Implementation Process

Policy outputs of implementing agencies → Compliance with policy outputs by target groups → Actual impacts of policy outputs → Perceived impacts of policy outputs → Major revision in statute decision rules are consistent with policy objectives and further stipulate the behavior of the implementing organizations. The commitment of the implementing officials will ensure that the day-to-day activities of the program reflect the intent of the original objectives. Opportunities for formal participation provide a means of generating political support for the program.

Measuring the Statutory Coherence of Family Planning Statutes

To assess the likely effectiveness of the family planning laws, we compared the characteristics of each family planning statute with the prescriptive statutory variables of the Mazmanian and Sabatier model. Measures were developed so that the higher score reflects more statutory coherence (McFarlane 1989, 397).

Precise and Clearly Ranked Policy Objectives. The first concept underlying this statutory objective is the precision of policy objectives. Precise objectives "serve as a resource to actors both inside and outside the implementing institutions who perceive discrepancies between agency outputs and those objectives" (Mazmanian and Sabatier 1989, 25). For example, the implementation of a family planning program would be subject to much less interpretation by the implementing agencies if the target population, services to be provided, and eligibility criteria were precisely specified in the legislation. The indicators and concomitant measures for this dimension of the variables are the following:

Precision of Policy Objectives

Target population	Specified (1)	Not specified (0)
Eligibility	Specified (1)	Not specified (0)
Services to be provided	Specified (1)	Not specified (0)

Closely related to the precision of policy objectives is the ranking that the new objectives are given within the totality of the implementing agency's programs. "If this is not done, the new directives are likely to be delayed and accorded low priority as they are incorporated into the agency's programs" (Mazmanian and Sabatier 1989, 25–26). In spite of the conceptual importance of the ranking concept, none of the four statutes specifies a clear ranking for family planning within the totality of an implementing agency's programs. The closest that any of them come to the ranking concept is Title XIX. The Medicaid statute encourages states to purchase family planning services by providing an advantageous 90 percent matching rate for family planning services (AGI 1978, 38).

Adequate Causal Theory. The second statutory variable is the validity of the causal theory incorporated into the policy. "An adequate causal theory requires (a) that the principal causal linkages between government interventions and the attainment of program objectives be clearly understood; and (b) that the officials responsible for implementing the program have jurisdiction over a sufficient number of the critical linkages to actually attain the objectives" (Mazmanian and Sabatier 1989, 26). Whether it is possible to accomplish the statutory objectives was measured as follows:

Causal Linkages
Well understood (1)   Not well understood (0)

The causal linkages between the interventions spelled out in Title X and the attainment of program objectives—to enable all Americans to voluntarily plan and space their children's births—are well understood. By the time Title X was enacted in 1970, contraceptive technology was very effective. Middle- and upper-income women were already using modern contraceptive methods, and there was a great deal of evidence that low-income women would use accessible family planning services (Harkavy, Jaffe, and Wishik 1969; Dryfoos 1973).

The linkage between government intervention and the attainment of program objectives is not as well understood for Titles V and XX as it is for Titles X and XIX. The purpose of Title V was to extend and improve the "services for reducing infant mortality and otherwise promoting the health of infants and mothers" (AGI 1974, 22). The causal linkages for maternal and child health are complex, and what the most effective government interventions should be is not entirely clear. Title XX was enacted to enable the poor or near poor to become or remain self-sufficient. As is the case with many anti-poverty programs, the causality chain here is not well understood (Manhattan Institute 1985). Finally, the purpose of Title XIX (Medicaid) was to pay for medical care for low-income women and children. There is no complex chain of causality here—the state simply pays for specific health services for certain categories of impoverished individuals.

Whether officials have jurisdiction over a sufficient number of the critical linkages to attain the objectives is the second concept in this causal validity variable. Although this is a logical deduction from the first concept, it cannot be measured when the chain of causality is not understood. Because this concept is applicable to only two of the four statutes, no measure was developed.

Adequate Funding. Money is obviously important for any program. In general, a threshold level of funding is necessary to achieve policy objectives. In fact, the adequacy of funding is relatively easy to calculate for family planning services. One would divide the available funding by the average annual cost of serving a family planning patient in order to estimate the number of patients who could be served by this funding. One would then divide the estimated number of patients who could be served by the number of women at risk of unintended pregnancy, the target group for the program (AGI 1997a). However, for three of the federal statutes concerned with family planning, the states themselves determine how much of an intergovernmental transfer will be allocated to family planning services. Because specific family planning funding is determined by statute in only one of the four pertinent laws, it does not make sense to use adequate funding as an independent variable here.

Hierarchical Integration within and among Implementing Organizations. "One of the best documented findings in the implementation literature is the difficulty of obtaining coordinated action within any given agency and among the numerous semi-autonomous organizations involved in implementation efforts. This problem is especially acute in the federal policies that rely on state and local organizations for carrying out the details of program delivery in a very heterogeneous system" (Sabatier and Mazmanian 1981, 11–12). A decentralized approach to the implementation of a national policy means that another layer of bargaining, and hence of contingencies, is introduced (Stein 1984).

Title X awards grants directly to family planning projects, while the other three statutes were mandated to fund state agencies. We would expect more variation in the implementation of programs administered by fifty state agencies than in those that are federally administered. This variable was measured as follows:

State Administration Mandated
No (1)   Yes (0)

Favorable Decision Rules. A statute can further the implementation process by stipulating the formal decision rules of the implementing agencies. The cumbersome registration procedures and eligibility criteria of many health care providers often deter low-income women from obtaining family planning services (Radecki and Bernstein 1989). Title X recognizes these difficulties and mandates that neither grantees nor their subcontractors can deny services to anyone on the basis of age, marital status, or income. While many of Title X's regulations support statutory intent, there was much administrative effort during the 1980s to alter these regulations so that they conflicted with statutory objectives (e.g., the squeal rule and the gag rule). The ensuing confusion on the part of Title X grantees and patients did not promote compliance with statutory objectives. We conclude that, on the whole, none of the four federal family planning statutes had favorable decision rules or regulations during the period of study; this variable is therefore omitted from the analysis.

Assignment to Implementing Agencies Committed to Statutory Objectives. No matter how well a statute structures the formal decision process, the attainment of its objectives is unlikely unless officials in the implementing agency are committed to attaining those objectives. While recognizing that "there are a number of ways in which the framers of statutes can reasonably assure that implementing officials have the requisite commitment to statutory objectives," Sabatier and Mazmanian emphasize assignment to agencies whose organizational goals are consistent with the statute. Such consistency makes it likely that the implementing agency will give the program high priority. When a new agency is created specifically to administer a statute, the likelihood that the agency's goals will be consistent with the statute is maximized (Mazmanian and Sabatier 1989, 28).

Only one of the four statutes, Title X, permitted the assignment of funds to new agencies. Initially, Title X grants were awarded to agencies on a competitive basis. This type of administrative arrangement enhanced the opportunity to implement the program through agencies and officials whose goals were consistent with Title X. Title V had to be administered by state health departments, Title XX mandated administration by state welfare departments, and states had the option of administering Title XIX through either their welfare or health departments. For the most part, neither state health departments nor state welfare departments were strongly supportive of this program. This dimension was scored as follows:

Opportunity for Assignment to New Agency
Opportunity (1)   No opportunity (0)

Formal Access by Outsiders. Not only can a policy specify its implementing organization; it can also affect the participation of two groups of actors external to those institutions: (1) the potential beneficiaries and target groups of the program, and (2) the legislative, executive, and judicial "sovereigns" of the agencies (Mazmanian and Sabatier 1989, 28–30). Of the four statutes, only Title X specifies how its supporters will exercise oversight. At the grantee level, "persons in the community knowledgeable about the community's needs for family planning services" must be allowed to participate "to the maximum extent possible" in the "development, implementation, and evaluation of the project" (U.S. DHHS 1981). At the national level, OPA is required to send a five-year report to Congress each year, thus giving the program visibility and maintaining the oversight of the legislative "sovereigns." This access concept was measured as follows:

Access for External Supporters
Yes (1)   No (0)

Composite Scores

A composite statutory score was developed from the weighted measures of each of the statutory variables. Because the first variable had more than one measure, these measures were adjusted so that each was given equal weight. Table 3.4 shows that Title X had by far the highest statutory coherence score. Therefore,

Table 3.4 Statutory Coherence Scores for Titles V, X, XIX, and XX

STATUTORY VARIABLE	TITLE V	TITLE X	TITLE XIX	TITLE XX
Precise and ranked objectives[a]	0	1	0	0
Adequacy of causal theory	0	1	1	0
Hierarchical integration	0	1	0	0
Officials' commitment	0	1	0	0
Formal access	0	1	0	0
Total	0	5	1	0

a. The individual measures for this variable were weighted and added.

the statutory coherence hypothesis would predict that Title X has been the most effective federal statute in terms of both policy outputs and policy impacts.

CONCLUSION

In 1965, the same year that the *Griswold* decision legalized contraception, the Office of Economic Opportunity awarded the first direct federal grant for family planning. Despite the political controversy surrounding family planning, federal support for it has persisted. Title X has not been folded into a block grant, and the favorable federal Medicaid match rate (90 percent) has been retained for family planning services.

Since 1975, the same four federal statutes, together with state appropriations, have provided public funds for family planning. The link between family planning and other types of policies (e.g., maternal and child health, welfare) has generated a complex policy apparatus with multiple statutes, multiple goals, and multiple implementing agencies. While this structure may be unusual in many policy arenas, it is not atypical in American health policy. An understanding of this complex structure is necessary in order to comprehend the politics, policies, and impacts of family planning programs.

In addition to being multistatutory, national family planning policy is largely redistributive. Statutes that fund family planning subsidize services for those unable to pay. Although the original purpose of Title X was "to assist in making comprehensive voluntary family planning services available to all persons desiring such services," the implementation of this statute, as well as of the three related ones, has focused on low-income and teenage women.

Given the differences in their structure, these four statutes are likely to vary in how effective they are in implementing even redistributive family planning policy. We test the statutory coherence hypothesis from the Mazmanian and Sabatier model of policy implementation in terms of policy outputs in chapter 6 and in terms of outcomes in chapter 7.

CHAPTER 4

Abortion Policy

IN HANDING DOWN *Roe* v. *Wade* (401 U.S. 113) on 22 January 1973, the Supreme Court held that a woman's right to choose abortion was constitutionally protected as a part of her right to privacy; abortion thus became legal throughout the United States. This decision prohibited any level of government from interfering with abortion during the first trimester of pregnancy "except to insist that it be performed by a licensed physician." During the second trimester, the state had only the power to regulate abortion in ways designed to preserve and protect the woman's health. In the third trimester, the protection of fetal life became a compelling reason sufficient under *Roe* to justify interference with the exercise of the right to choose abortion (Tribe 1992, 10–13).

By permitting state discretion, *Roe* v. *Wade* federalized, rather than nationalized, abortion policy. States thus became key players in developing abortion policies (Halva-Neubauer 1990). Although *Roe* did not settle the abortion issue, it has served as the benchmark for American public policy since 1973.

We begin this chapter by reviewing U.S. Supreme Court decisions that have addressed abortion since *Roe* v. *Wade*. In the second section, we look at recent developments in the executive and legislative branches that have affected federal abortion policy. Finally, we assess the likely effectiveness of federal abortion policy by examining how well it has compared over time with Mazmanian and Sabatier's elements of statutory coherence.

SUPREME COURT DECISIONS SINCE *ROE* V. *WADE*

Since *Roe* v. *Wade*, the Supreme Court has been continuously involved in abortion policy (see table 4.1). On the same day it ruled on *Roe*, it ruled on a less well known companion case, *Doe* v. *Bolton* (410 U.S. 179). This decision articulated some of the implications of the *Roe* decision. It struck down state residency requirements for abortion patients, as well as state requirements that all abortions be performed in specifically accredited hospitals. States could no longer mandate that abortions be approved by hospital committees or by other physicians overseeing the performing physician's judgment. (Tribe 1992, 42, 140; AGI 1983b, 3).

Table 4.1 Supreme Court Decisions on Abortion since *Roe* v. *Wade*

YEAR	RULING	CASE	MAJOR POINTS
1973	7 to 2	*Doe* v. *Bolton*	Struck down state residency requirement, as well as requirement that abortions be performed in specially accredited hospitals
1975	7 to 2	*Bigelow* v. *Virginia*	Permitted advertisements for legal abortions
1975	9 to 0	*Connecticut* v. *Menillo*	Permitted states to require that abortions be performed by physicians
1975	0[a]	*Greco* v. *Orange Memorial Hospital Corporation*	Permitted private hospitals financed by public funds to refuse to perform elective abortions
1976	6 to 3	*Planned Parenthood* v. *Danforth*	Disallowed partner veto; struck down prohibition against saline abortions after 12 weeks of gestation; forbade absolute parental veto of a minor's abortion; upheld written informed consent and reporting requirements
1977	6 to 3	*Beal* v. *Doe*	Held that a state's refusal to use Medicaid funds for nontherapeutic abortions did not violate Title XIX of the Social Security Act
1977	6 to 3	*Maher* v. *Roe*	Held that a state's refusal to use Medicaid funds for nontherapeutic abortions was constitutional
1977	6 to 3	*Poelker* v. *Doe*	Held that a city-owned hospital did not have to provide nontherapeutic abortions
1979	8 to 1	*Bellotti* v. *Baird*	Struck down requirement for parental consent unless a confidential alternative was provided
1979	6 to 3	*Colautti* v. *Franklin*	Struck down requirement to save fetal life that might be viable
1980	5 to 4	*Harris* v. *McRae*	Upheld the Hyde amendment, restricting the use of federal Medicaid funds for abortions to medically necessary ones
1980	5 to 4	*Williams* v. *Zbaraz*	Ruled that states do not have to pay for medically necessary abortions for Medicaid-eligible women
1981	6 to 3	*H.L.* v. *Matheson*	Allowed states to require parental notification of abortion for an immature and unemancipated minor

(continued)

Table 4.1 *(continued)*

YEAR	RULING	CASE	MAJOR POINTS
1983	6 to 3	*City of Akron v. Akron Center for Reproductive Health*	Struck down 24-hour waiting period, elaborate informed consent rules, parental or judicial consent for all minors, and hospitalization for all second-trimester abortions
1983	6 to 3	*Planned Parenthood of Kansas City v. Ashcroft*	Struck down a Missouri hospitalization requirement for second-trimester abortions
1983	8 to 1	*Simopoulos v. Virginia*	Upheld Virginia hospitalization requirement because it included outpatient clinics
1986	5 to 4	*Thornburgh v. American College of Obstetrics and Gynecology*	Struck down elaborate informed consent rules and standards of care for postviability abortions
1989	5 to 4	*Webster v. Reproductive Health Services*	Upheld a state's right to prohibit state-employed physicians from performing abortions that are not medically necessary and to ban the performance of such abortions in a state facility; also upheld requirement that physicians determine fetal viability at or after 20 weeks of gestation
1990	5 to 4	*Hodgson v. Minnesota*	Upheld notification of both biological parents of a minor's abortion if judicial bypass is provided, as well as 48-hour waiting period between parental notification and minor's abortion
1990	6 to 3	*Ohio v. Akron Center for Reproductive Health*	Upheld one-parent notification if judicial bypass is provided; ruled that states need not guarantee absolute anonymity to minors seeking bypass; upheld more difficult standard of proof for minors seeking bypass
1991	5 to 4	*Rust v. Sullivan*	Upheld federal "gag rule" prohibiting employees of federally funded family planning clinics from any discussion of abortion with their patients
1992	5 to 4	*Planned Parenthood of Southeastern Pennsylvania v. Casey*	Upheld *Roe* v. *Wade* in principle; replaced *Roe*'s trimester framework with "undue burden" standard; upheld 24-hour waiting period, elaborate informed consent rules, reporting requirements, and consent of one parent or judge for minor's abortion; struck down spousal notification

Table 4.1 *(continued)*

Year	Ruling	Case	Major Points
1993	6 to 3	*Bray* v. *Alexandria Women's Health Clinic*	Ruled that a particular federal civil rights statute could not be used to protect abortion patients from protesters
1994	9 to 0	*National Organization for Women* v. *Scheidler*	Allowed a federal anti-racketeering statute to be used in lawsuits against protesters who engage in violent action intended to put abortion clinics out of business
1994	6 to 3	*Madsen* v. *Women's Health Center*	Ruled that some court-ordered restrictions on abortion clinic demonstrations are constitutional
1995	0[a]	*Cheffer* v. *Reno*	Upheld constitutionality of FACE
1997	8 to 1	*Schenck* v. *Pro-Choice Network of Western New York*	Struck down a floating bubble zone, which would have established a protected zone around patients and vehicles entering and leaving an abortion clinic

a. The Supreme Court let a lower court's decision stand here.

Soon after the *Roe* decision, states, particularly anti-abortion states, passed laws to probe the Supreme Court's policy. These state laws were then challenged by pro-abortion activists. In 1975, the Court handed down *Bigelow* v. *Virginia* (421 U.S. 809), finding that "the First Amendment guarantee of free speech protects advertisements for legal abortions" (AGI 1983b, 1975a). In another 1975 ruling, *Connecticut* v. *Menillo* (423 U.S. 9), the Court held that "states may require abortions to be performed by physicians" (AGI 1983b). In the same year, the Supreme Court dealt access to abortion a blow when it refused to review—and therefore let stand—a decision by a U.S. circuit court (*Greco* v. *Orange Memorial Hospital Corporation*) that permitted a private hospital, financed largely by public funds, to refuse to perform "elective abortions" (AGI 1975b).

In 1976, in *Planned Parenthood* v. *Danforth* (428 U.S. 52), the Court held that the state could not interfere with a woman's right to choose abortion by granting a veto to the man who shared responsibility for her pregnancy. Here, the Court also struck down a prohibition against saline abortions after twelve weeks of pregnancy, reasoning that this restriction was designed to inhibit the vast majority of abortions after the first trimester. In addition, the Court ruled that parents could not have an absolute veto over an abortion for a daughter under the age of majority; it did suggest that something less than a "blanket" parental consent requirement would pose a different constitutional question. Finally, this ruling permitted the state to require a woman's written certification that her consent was informed and not the result of coercion, and it upheld the provision of the Missouri law requiring health facilities and physicians to report all abortions to the health department and to keep all records for seven years (Tribe 1992, 13–14; AGI 1976b).

In 1977, the Supreme Court decided three companion cases: *Beal* v. *Doe* (432 U.S. 438), *Maher* v. *Roe* (432 U.S. 464), and *Poelker* v. *Doe* (432 U.S. 519). In *Beal*, the Court found that a state's refusal to use Medicaid funds for "nontherapeutic" abortions (i.e., abortions not necessary to protect the life or health of the woman) did not violate Title XIX of the Social Security Act (Medicaid). In the *Maher* case, the Court ruled that a state's refusal to use Medicaid funds for nontherapeutic abortions was constitutional. In *Poelker*, the Court held that a city-owned public hospital was not constitutionally compelled to provide nontherapeutic abortions (Tribe 1992, 15; AGI 1977; Goggin 1993).

On 2 July 1979, the Supreme Court issued *Bellotti* v. *Baird* (443 U.S. 622), ruling that a state could not require parental consent for a minor's abortion unless it offered a confidential alternative. Although their reasoning differed, eight justices struck down a Massachusetts law requiring the consent of both parents. The Court insisted that states provide minors a judicial bypass, rejecting the constitutionality of any absolute requirement of parental consent or notification for minors of any age (AGI 1980a, 1979b; Drucker 1990). Also in 1979, in *Colautti* v. *Franklin* (439 U.S. 379), the Court struck down a law requiring that a physician try to save the life of a fetus that *might* be viable (AGI 1983b; Drucker 1990).

Important setbacks for low-income women seeking abortions occurred in 1980 (Henshaw and Wallisch 1984). In *Harris* v. *McRae* (446 U.S. 907), in a five-to-four ruling, the Court upheld the Hyde amendment, which prohibited the use of federal monies to fund abortions "except where the life of the mother would be endangered if the fetus were carried to term."[1] Although the Hyde amendment applied to all federal funding, its major effect was to curtail federal Medicaid funding for abortions for poor women (AGI 1978, 84; 1980b). In *Williams* v. *Zbaraz* (448 U.S. 917), in another five-to-four ruling, the Court found that a state did not have to provide reimbursement for medically necessary abortions for Medicaid-eligible women, even when federal funds were unavailable (AGI 1983b).

In 1981, the Court ruled on *H.L.* v. *Matheson* (445 U.S. 959), a case that addressed a Utah law requiring a physician to notify a minor's parents before performing an abortion. Here, the Court held that a state may require parental notification when an immature and unemancipated minor seeks an abortion. In this context, *emancipation* refers to "the partial or complete extinguishment of parental rights and duties." The most common way that minors become emancipated is through marriage (AGI 1978, 102). Because the *Matheson* decision "did not address the issue of whether a state may require parental notification for mature and emancipated minors" (AGI 1981e), it differed from the *Bellotti* and *Danforth* decisions, which also dealt with parental approval or veto of a minor's decision to have an abortion (Drucker 1990, 77–79).

City of Akron v. *Akron Center for Reproductive Health* (462 U.S. 416) was decided in 1983. In this six-to-three ruling, the Court struck down a variety of state and local restrictions, "including a 24-hour waiting period, elaborate 'informed consent' rules, parental or judicial consent for all minors and hospitalization for all second trimester abortions" (AGI 1983c). In this case, the Court reaffirmed that any statutory requirements for parental consent must provide for an alternative method of approval for a minor who (1) is sufficiently mature to make the decision herself or (2) has good reason for not seeking parental consent and can demonstrate that an abortion would be in her best interest. In addition, the Court ruled that any parental consent rule must be accompanied by procedures ensuring that the judicial bypass would be accomplished quickly and confidentially (Tribe 1992, 14).

The Supreme Court issued two other abortion-related opinions on the same day it ruled on *Akron*. In *Planned Parenthood of Kansas City, Missouri, Inc.* v. *Ashcroft* (462 U.S. 476), the Court struck down a requirement in the Missouri abortion law that second-trimester abortions be performed in hospitals. In *Simopoulos* v. *Virginia* (462 U.S. 506), the Court upheld a similar Virginia requirement because Virginia's hospitalization law included licensed outpatient clinics in the definition of hospital (AGI 1983b; Drucker 1990).

On 11 June 1986, the Court handed down *Thornburgh* v. *American College of Obstetricians and Gynecologists* (476 U.S. 747). This five-to-four ruling struck down informed consent and reporting requirements for abortions, as well as standards of care for postviability abortions (i.e., abortions performed after a fetus has become viable, or able to survive outside the womb). The Court found that the elaborate requirements for informed consent mandated by the commonwealth of Pennsylvania were designed to persuade the woman to withhold consent; moreover, they intruded on the discretion of the physician (AGI 1986). In 1976, in the *Danforth* case, the Court had ruled that recordkeeping and reporting requirements were permissible if they protected a patient's confidentiality and privacy and were intended to preserve maternal health. In *Thornburgh*, however, the Court concluded that the Pennsylvania reporting requirements went well beyond the patient's health-related interests, and it showed no tolerance for extreme reporting requirements that might be made public. The postviability standards of the law were struck down because they failed to make maternal health the physician's "paramount" consideration (AGI 1986; Drucker 1990,128; Tribe 1992, 14–15).

The 1989 case of *Webster* v. *Reproductive Health Services* (492 U.S. 490) revealed a Court that was very divided on the abortion issue. Indeed, no single opinion was endorsed by a majority of justices. At issue was a Missouri abortion law with twenty provisions. Because of the way the case was argued, the Court ruled on only three. The Court upheld the provision that prohibited state-employed physicians from performing abortions that were not necessary to save the life of the woman. Furthermore, a state could forbid such abortions from being performed in state facilities. Finally, a state could require physicians to determine fetal viability at or after twenty weeks of gestation (Annas 1989).

The *Webster* case is regarded as pivotal because after years of turning down state restrictions on abortion, the Court finally upheld three. The plurality also questioned the trimester framework established in *Roe*, and it ignored the "right to privacy," one of the foundations of the *Roe* decision (Tribe 1992, 20–24; Annas 1989, 1202). In his dissent, Justice Harry Blackmun warned that "a plurality of this Court invites every state legislature to enact more and more restrictive abortion regulations in order to provoke more and more test cases" (Drucker 1990, 180; Greenhouse 1989). The section of the *Webster* opinion dealing with fetal viability was especially problematic because it required tests that a physician never uses until the fetus is twenty-eight to thirty weeks old. In fact, the early use of these tests actually poses substantial risks for both the fetus and the pregnant woman (Tribe 1992, 20–21).

In 1990, in *Hodgson* v. *Minnesota* (497 U.S. 417) and *Ohio* v. *Akron Center for Reproductive Health* (497 U.S. 502), the Court allowed further state restrictions. Both cases dealt with parental notification for minors seeking abortions. In *Hodgson*, the Court ruled that although states could not impose a blanket two-parent notification requirement on minors seeking abortions, they could require notification of both biological parents as long as they also provided a judicial bypass for minors who did not want to inform their parents about their plans. The Court also upheld a state requirement that minors wait forty-eight hours between parental notification and the abortion procedure. In the *Ohio* case, the Court upheld the state's policy of requiring notification of one parent and of providing for judicial bypass. Here, the Court explicitly refused to decide whether a state had to provide a bypass with a one-parent notification requirement. The judicial bypass option itself was weakened in *Ohio* on two counts. The Court ruled that states did not need to guarantee absolute anonymity to the minor. States could also require that minors meet a difficult standard of proof— showing either that they were sufficiently mature to consent to abortion on their own or that parental notice was not in their best interest (AGI 1990, 1991a).

On 23 May 1991, the Court ruled five to four on *Rust* v. *Sullivan* (500 U.S. 173). The majority upheld the federal regulation popularly known as the gag rule, which barred employees of federally financed family planning clinics from all discussion of abortion with their patients. The dissenting justices expressed great concern about an abrogation of First Amendment rights (AGI 1991b).

On 29 June 1992, the Supreme Court handed down *Planned Parenthood of Southeastern Pennsylvania* v. *Casey* (510 U.S. 1309), "the most eagerly awaited decision on abortion since 1973." Here, the Court reaffirmed five to four what it termed "the essential holding of *Roe* v. *Wade*": that a woman has a constitutional right to obtain an abortion if the procedure is performed before fetal viability. The four dissenting justices called for an outright reversal of *Roe*. Explaining that *Roe's* trimester framework "undervalues the state's interest in potential life which exists throughout the pregnancy" (AGI 1992a), the majority discarded this framework and replaced it with "undue burden," a more lenient standard for analyzing the constitutionality of abortion restrictions.

Under the undue burden standard, the Court upheld four sections of Pennsylvania's Abortion Control Act and struck down one. The Court found that requiring teenagers to have the consent of one parent or a judge did not constitute an undue burden, nor did the requirement that a twenty-four-hour waiting period follow an "informed consent" presentation intended to persuade the woman not to have an abortion. The Court also upheld the section of the act requiring the doctor or clinic performing the abortion to make statistical reports to the state, as well as a section that specified the medical emergencies under which the other state requirements would be waived. The requirement that a married woman inform her husband of her intent to have an abortion was struck down (AGI 1992a; Greenhouse 1992).

On 13 January 1993, in *Bray* v. *Alexandria Women's Health Clinic* (506 U.S. 263), the Supreme Court ruled that a federal civil rights statute dating from the Reconstruction era could not be invoked to protect abortion patients from protesters who block access to abortion clinics (AGI 1993l). That law, designed to protect blacks, had been enacted "to offer protection against discrimination aimed at a certain group of people." The Court ruled six to three that "women seeking abortions do not qualify for this protection because anti-abortion protesters are not targeting them on the basis of gender." The opinion, written by Justice Antonin Scalia, stated that the right to abortion is not among protected rights. A major consequence of this ruling was that abortion providers became more dependent on state and local law enforcement, which is often less reliable and less effective than federal intervention (Congressional Quarterly 1993b).

On 24 January 1994, the Supreme Court again ruled on anti-abortion protests, this time in *National Organization for Women* v. *Scheidler* (510 U.S. 249), a case brought on behalf of abortion clinics in Delaware and Wisconsin. In this unanimous ruling, the Court allowed the Racketeering Influenced and Corrupt Organizations Act (RICO), a federal anti-racketeering statute, to be invoked in lawsuits brought against protesters who engage in violent activities intended to put abortion clinics out of business (AGI 1994i). The ruling did not determine whether anti-abortion protesters had engaged in activities prohibited by RICO. Rather, the Court determined that RICO was an appropriate vehicle for litigation against certain anti-abortion activities. Those found guilty of violating RICO's civil provisions would be liable for triple monetary damages;

criminal defendants would face up to twenty years in prison for each violation of the law. Additionally, RICO would allow abortion providers to "target the masterminds of anti-abortion activity, rather than just the protesters at the scene" (AGI 1994i).

In July 1994, the Court ruled on another case that addressed anti-abortion protests, *Madsen* v. *Women's Health Center* (512 U.S. 1277). The case dealt with an injunction issued by a Florida judge, which "established buffer zones and noise restrictions around a clinic and employees' private residences that had long been the targets of demonstrations." The Court upheld a thirty-six-foot buffer zone around the clinic's entrances and driveway, as well as noise restrictions on protesters outside the clinic. The Court, however, struck down a three-hundred-foot buffer zone around the residences of the clinic's staff, although the opinion emphasized that "more narrowly targeted noise, time and/or place restrictions would be permissible" (AGI 1994c, 3).

In July 1995, the Supreme Court declined to review a lower court's decision on *Cheffer* v. *Reno*, which upheld the Freedom of Access to Clinic Entrances Act (FACE). The Court stated that FACE was a valid exercise of congressional power under the Constitution's commerce clause because it regulates a commercial activity: the provision of reproductive health services (Bureau of National Affairs 1995). This action effectively ended a challenge brought by a conservative activist group, Concerned Women of America (AGI 1995h).

In February 1997, by a vote of six to three, the Supreme Court upheld a New York law establishing a "15-foot fixed buffer zone around facilities providing abortion services." In the same case, *Schenck* v. *Pro-Choice Network of Western New York* (519 U.S. 357), the Court struck down, by a margin of eight to one, "a so-called floating bubble zone, which would have established a protected zone around patients and vehicles entering and leaving the clinic." The ruling explained that a "floating bubble zone" would not only be an undue burden on protesters' right to free speech; because such a zone would be difficult to designate or measure, it would also be difficult to enforce (AGI 1997b).

RECENT FEDERAL DEVELOPMENTS IN ABORTION POLICY
The Executive Branch

The election of Bill Clinton to the presidency in 1992 signaled a change in the anti-abortion policies that had accumulated during the previous decade. Only two days after being sworn in, Clinton signed five memoranda that (1) began the process of repealing the gag rule, (2) reversed the Mexico City policy, (3) overturned a ban on abortions in military hospitals overseas, (4) lifted a moratorium on fetal tissue research, and (5) ordered the Food and Drug Administration to review the scientific basis for continuing the import ban on mifepristone (AGI 1993e). Moreover, within two years of taking office, Clinton had nominated, and the Senate had confirmed, two pro-choice Supreme Court justices, Ruth Bader Ginsberg in 1993 and Stephen Breyer in 1994. Given the close margins of the *Webster* and *Casey* decisions, these appointments were considered pivotal for American abortion policies.

The Gag Rule. On 22 January 1993, President Clinton signed an order initiating the process to repeal the 1988 regulation known as the gag rule, which, as noted earlier, banned abortion counseling in federally supported family planning clinics (AGI 1993e). The gag rule, however, was already in trouble. On 3 November 1992, the U.S. Court of Appeals for the District of Columbia had ruled that the Bush administration illegally ordered a substantive reinterpretation of this 1988 regulation by not providing an opportunity for public comment. The reinterpreted gag rule, which had not gone through the entire federal rule-making process, allowed physicians but not nurses and other trained counselors to provide abortion-related information in Title X–funded family planning clinics (AGI 1992b; Kerwin 1999).

Mexico City Policy. The Mexico City policy was initiated by the Reagan administration in 1984. This policy disqualified nongovernmental organizations (NGOs) from receiving family planning funds from the U.S. Agency for International Development if the NGOs used their own funds (1) to provide legal abortion services overseas or (2) to lobby for legalizing abortion in foreign countries. A related policy was the Kemp-Kasten amendment to the Foreign Assistance Act. Passed by Congress in 1985, this amendment prohibited giving funds to any organization that supported or participated in the management of a program of coercive abortion or involuntary sterilization. Among the funding casualties were the United Nations Fund for Population Assistance (UNFPA), the International Planned Parenthood Federation (IPPF), and the Human Reproduction Program of the World Health Organization (WHO). Within its first year, the Clinton administration reinstated funding for each of these groups (McKeegan 1992, 86–91; AGI 1993c).

Abortion Ban in Military Hospitals Overseas. This ban was in effect from 1988 until 1993, when President Clinton overturned it. It decreed that no abortion could be performed, even if all costs were fully paid in advance by the patient, in U.S. military treatment facilities outside the continental United States. The only exception for military personnel and their dependents was life endangerment (NARAL 1991; AGI 1988b).

Fetal Tissue Research. An absolute ban on the use of federal funds for research using fetal tissue had been in effect since 1988. By lifting the ban, the Clinton administration allowed the National Institutes of Health (NIH) to perform and fund carefully monitored fetal tissue research, including projects studying in vitro fertilization, Parkinson's disease, cancer, birth defects, and contraceptive development. When issuing that order, President Clinton said, "We must free science and medicine from the grasp of politics and give Americans access to the very latest and best medical treatments . . . we must let medicine and science proceed unencumbered by antiabortion politics" (Donovan 1990; Family Planning Perspectives 1991; AGI 1988a, 1988b, 1994a).

In December 1994, Clinton ordered NIH "not to fund work involving embryos created for research purposes." This action effectively blocked the findings of a special panel of experts convened by NIH to establish guidelines for federally funded research on human embryos in the first fourteen days following fertilization. Most of the work that NIH was considering would have involved only "so-called 'spare' embryos generated in *in vitro* fertilization programs." However, the NIH panel had approved the use of embryos fertilized for research purposes for up to fourteen days after fertilization "but only when important research, such as a careful study of the fertilization process itself, would otherwise be impossible to conduct." Clearly, Clinton's action in December 1994 contradicted his statement in early 1993 (AGI 1994a).

Nonsurgical, or Medical, Abortion. The Clinton approach to mifepristone, also known as RU 486 or the French abortion pill, differed completely from that of the Bush administration. Under Bush, the FDA banned the importation of RU 486 for personal use (AGI 1993a). Under the Clinton administration, FDA commissioner David Kessler, who had held the same post during the Bush administration, met with the French manufacturer of the drug—Roussel-Uclaf—to encourage the company to apply for approval to market mifepristone in the United States (AGI 1993o).

In May 1994, Roussel-Uclaf turned over mifepristone's U.S. patent rights to the Population Council, a nonprofit organization based in New York City. By acquiring the rights to RU 486, the Population Council assumed sole responsibility for shepherding the drug through the FDA approval process and overseeing its introduction to the U.S. market, which included the selection of a manufacturer (AGI 1994e; Smolowe 1993). Part of the FDA approval process required clinical trials, which were underway within eight months of the Population Council's acquisition of the drug.

The approval process has been lengthy. The U.S. clinical trials, which included testing of misoprostol (see chap. 1, n. 8), ended in September 1995, and in March 1996, the Population Council submitted a 164-volume "New Drug Application" to the FDA. The FDA issued an approvable letter in September 1996 saying that mifepristone, in combination with misoprostol, was safe and effective for early medical abortion. An *approvable letter* is an action that the FDA frequently takes to indicate that safety and efficacy data have passed agency review but that additional information must be submitted before final approval for marketing is granted. In this case, the FDA required that the Population Council provide additional information on labeling and manufacturing. The Population Council's licensee, the Danco Group, expected that the drug would be available sometime in 1999 (Population Council 1999).

The Legislative Branch

Abortion Funding. Abortion funding remained a point of contention during the Clinton presidency. In spite of a pro-choice White House, Congress retained the long-standing Hyde amendment, which since 1980 had permitted Medicaid coverage of abortion only in cases of life endangerment. In 1993, Congress expanded the Hyde amendment to include cases in which the pregnancy was the result of rape or incest (AGI 1993q, 1994f). That year, however, the larger issue concerning abortion funding was what seemed at the time to be the possibility of health care reform (AGI 1994a). When comprehensive health care failed to pass, abortion returned to its own policy sphere.

Freedom of Access to Clinic Entrances Act. Harassment of abortion patients and providers escalated into violence during the late 1980s and early 1990s (Henshaw 1995; Hern 1994; National Abortion Federation 1993). During a hearing before the Senate Appropriations Subcommittee on Labor, Health, and Human Services in the spring of 1995, Arlen Specter (R-Pa.), the subcommittee's chairman, observed that there had been five murders and eleven attempted murders in the previous two years alone. He also noted that there had been 211 death threats and 210 stalkings since 1985 (AGI 1995d).

Abortion providers and pro-choice advocates sought protection through a variety of means. On 3 February 1993, less than a month after the Supreme Court's *Bray* ruling that a federal civil rights statute from the Reconstruction era could not be used to protect abortion patients, the Freedom of Access to Clinic Entrances Act was introduced in the House. FACE reached the Senate seven weeks later (Congressional Quarterly 1993a, 1993b; AGI 1993i). This bill proposed to make it illegal, and punishable by criminal and civil penalties, to physically impede access to a medical facility (AGI 1993b). FACE received increased attention and support after the assassination on 10 March 1993 of David Gunn, a Florida physician who performed abortions. Attorney General Janet Reno strongly endorsed the FACE bill, pointing out that no existing federal law could be invoked to protect access to clinics (AGI 1993i; Rubin 1993c).

Because of the maneuvers of anti-abortion members of Congress, most especially Senator Jesse Helms, FACE was not signed into law until May 1994 (AGI 1994c). It became the first freestanding federal legislation designed to protect a woman's access to abortion. This statute established "a new federal offense prohibiting force, the threat of force, physical obstruction or destruction of property intended to interfere with access to reproductive health services" (AGI 1994f, 1).

Freedom of Choice Act. FACE was not the first pro-choice legislation to be introduced in Congress. The Freedom of Choice Act (FOCA), codifying the principles of *Roe* v. *Wade*, had been introduced in 1989 in response to the Supreme Court's *Webster* ruling (Rubin 1993a). FOCA got as far as the authorizing committees in both the House and Senate in 1992 (AGI, 1992c). In 1993, with a new Democratic president and Congress, as well as public revulsion at the murder of David Gunn, FOCA appeared to have some real momentum. That year, the bill was approved by committees in both the House and the Senate, but it never reached the floor of either chamber (Rubin 1993b; AGI 1993j). Both versions of the bill had clauses that gave the states discretion in the areas of parental involvement and funding.

Ironically, in committee, abortion opponents voted to strike parental involvement because its omission would make the bill harder to pass. Even many politicians who were otherwise pro-choice were uncomfortable about not involving parents in a minor's abortion decision (Rubin 1993c). Other pro-choice politicians, including Senators Carol Moseley-Braun (D-Ill.), Dianne Feinstein (D-Calif.), Patty Murray (D-Wash.), and Barbara Boxer (D-Calif.), eventually withdrew support for the bill because it left the issues of parental involvement and funding to the states (AGI 1993j).

Parental consent had been upheld by the Supreme Court in *Casey* (1992), *Akron* (1991), and other decisions; therefore, explicitly deferring to the states the power to legislate on parental involvement was unnecessary. Nonetheless, this clause did point out an important facet of public opinion—that a large majority of the public approves of laws requiring parental involvement in a minor's decision to have an abortion. However, these laws, even with judicial bypass, fail to accomplish what most people think they will, that is, the protection and guidance of minors (Donovan 1992).

Congressional support of the Hyde amendment in 1993 sounded a death knell for pro-choice legislative efforts. FOCA was not introduced in 1994, although the abortion controversy remained—this time in the context of health care reform (AGI 1993d, 1994b). In spite of the Clinton push and active congressional consideration, health care reform was not enacted. Moreover, the mid-term congressional elections in November 1994 virtually assured that health care reform would not be on the agenda in the foreseeable future.

The 104th Congress.   The 104th Congress, which assumed office in January 1995, was further to the right than any in recent memory; indeed, the House of Representatives had not been under Republican control for forty years. Its anti-abortion agenda was obvious and very much related to the plans of the Christian Coalition (1995). Not only did Republicans in Congress act upon the agenda of the Christian Coalition; they extended it.

Among the policies that the new Congress tried to impose were some that President Clinton had taken action against immediately after assuming office in 1993. The 104th Congress proposed a reinstatement of the Mexico City policy, or a kind of Hyde amendment applied overseas; a prohibition on induced abortions, even if paid for privately, in U.S. military hospitals overseas (AGI 1995f); and a ban on the use of federal funds for fetal research. The House also voted to nullify the 1995 requirement of the Accreditation Council for Graduate Medical Education (ACGME) that residency programs in obstetrics and gynecology provide training in abortion services.[2] Although it is not considered within the purview of the federal government "to interfere in the process of setting medical training standards," abortion opponents used the fact that an institution's eligibility for federal funding is contingent on accreditation as justification for federal involvement in the issue (AGI 1995b, 2).

In 1995 and 1996, both houses of Congress passed the Partial Birth Abortion Ban Act (AGI 1995e), a bill that stemmed directly from the agenda of the Christian Coalition (Christian Coalition 1995, 21–22). *Partial birth abortion* is a political term, not a medical one; the legislation defined such an abortion as one "in which the person performing the abortion partially vaginally delivers a living fetus before killing the fetus and completing the delivery." Because of the vagueness of the bill, it was unclear exactly what procedures would have been banned. This legislation, however, was certainly directed toward late second- and third-trimester abortions, which account for only 1 percent of the abortions performed in the United States (Bonavoglia 1997; Rosenfield 1994). Supporters of the bill rejected amendments to allow the procedure when it would avert serious, adverse health consequences for the woman. President Clinton vetoed the bill in both years (AGI 1996a, 4; Purdum 1996).

Although the 104th Congress was unsuccessful in reinstating the Mexico City policy, anti-abortion politicians were able to effect an 85 percent reduction in U.S. assistance for international family planning. Ironically, these funds were to be used for contraception, not abortion, and without this funding for contraceptive services, it was estimated that there would be many more maternal deaths and induced abortions in the countries affected (AGI 1996c).

The volatility of abortion politics at the federal level is captured somewhat in table 4.2 (p. 76), which shows various federal abortion policies in 1992, 1994, and 1996.

The 105th Congress. In terms of abortion-related issues, the 105th Congress followed in the footsteps of its immediate predecessor. Partial birth abortion amendments remained on the agenda. There was even more clamoring among some conservatives, most notably Representative Chris Smith (R-N.J.), to reinstate the Mexico City policy. Funding for the United Nations Fund for Population Assistance was curtailed.

LIKELY EFFECTIVENESS OF FEDERAL ABORTION POLICY
As the previous sections indicate, abortion policy is quite different from family planning policy. Whereas federal family planning policy emanates from multiple and distinct legislative enactments, federal abortion policy is derived primarily from an ever-changing set of judicial decisions. At any point in time, these judicial rulings, along with certain legislative enactments (e.g., FACE and the

Table 4.2 Changes in Federal Abortion Policies, 1992–96

Policy	1992	1994	1996
Aid to international family planning agencies	Mexico City policy in effect; no funding for IPPF, UNFPA, WHO	Mexico City policy rescinded; funding for IPPF, UNFPA, WHO reinstated	Mexico City policy rescinded; U.S. international aid reduced by 85%
Mifepristone (RU 486)	Import for personal use banned by FDA	U.S. clinical trials favored by FDA	U.S. clinical trials ongoing
Medicaid funding	Hyde amendment in effect; funding available only in case of life endangerment	Hyde amendment in effect; exceptions expanded to include rape and incest	Hyde amendment in effect; exceptions include life endangerment, rape, and incest
Military hospitals	Ban on privately funded abortions in overseas military hospitals except in case of life endangerment	No ban on privately funded abortions in overseas military hospitals	Ban on privately funded abortions in overseas military hospitals except in case of life endangerment, rape, or incest
Fetal tissue research	No federal funding	Research funded by NIH	Executive block on funding for some types of research
Harassment and protests	No provisions	FACE in effect	FACE in effect
Specific procedures	No policy	No policy	Partial Birth Abortion Act vetoed by president
Medical training	No policy	No policy	ACGME requirement for abortion training nullified

Table 4.3 Statutory Coherence Scores for Federal Abortion Policy

STATUTORY VARIABLE	1973	1978	1983	1988	1993	1998
Precise and ranked objectives	1	1	1	1	0	0
Validity of causal theory	1	1	1	1	1	1
Adequate funding	1	0	0	0	0	0
Hierarchical integration	0	0	0	0	0	0
Officials' commitment	0	0	0	0	0	0
Formal access	0	0	0	0	0	0
Total	3	2	2	2	1	1

Hyde amendment) and executive orders (e.g., the gag rule), constitute federal abortion policy. To assess the likely effectiveness of federal abortion policy, we examine how well it has compared over time with Mazmanian and Sabatier's elements of statutory coherence (see table 4.3). We use the same rating and weighting scheme here as we did in assessing federal family planning policy in chapter 3.

Precise and Clearly Ranked Legal Objectives

"Legal objectives which are precise and clearly ranked in importance serve as an indispensable aid in program evaluation, as unambiguous directives to implementing officials, and as a resource to supporters of those objectives" (Mazmanian and Sabatier 1989, 25). Judicial rulings are seldom broad or precise enough to satisfy this criterion. The 1973 *Roe* decision, however, did establish that a woman's right to decide whether to terminate her pregnancy is a fundamental right, part of a "right to privacy" that the Court had recognized in earlier cases. Under *Roe*, only a compelling reason would allow government to interfere with the exercise of a woman's right to choose.

The Court was quite specific about when and under what circumstances government could intervene. During the first trimester of pregnancy, the state could require only that a licensed physician perform the procedure. During the second trimester, the only permissible regulations were those that ensured the safety of the procedure. During the third trimester, the state could restrict or even prohibit abortion "in order to protect fetal life," unless the abortion was necessary to preserve the woman's life or health (Tribe 1992, 11–12).

The trimester framework established in *Roe* remained intact until the 1989 *Webster* decision. Here, the plurality questioned *Roe's* trimester framework, and Justice Sandra Day O'Connor offered the vaguer undue burden standard, which permitted state abortion restrictions not allowed under *Roe*. In the 1992 *Casey* decision, the majority of the Court discarded the trimester framework, replacing it with the more lenient undue burden standard. Under that standard, the

Court upheld even more state abortion restrictions. The precision and clarity of objectives has thus declined over time, a factor exacerbated by permitting more state-to-state variation in policy. This variable received a score of 1 for the period before *Casey* and 0 for the period after.

Validity of Causal Theory

When performed by a skilled clinician, an abortion safely and effectively terminates an unintended pregnancy. The 1973 *Roe* decision noted "the now-established medical fact that until the end of the first trimester mortality in abortion may be less than mortality in normal childbirth" (Tribe 1992, 277). In fact, this was a great understatement, even for the time. Currently, deaths from either abortion or childbirth are rare, and the risk of dying from childbirth is eleven times greater than the risk of dying from abortion. The relative risk for first-trimester abortion is even lower (Gold 1990, 29). This variable received a score of 1 for the entire period.

Adequate Funding

Like many judicial rulings, *Roe* did not consider the cost of its implementation. Instead, this decision established a woman's right to choose to have an abortion. Initially, the Court did not consider whether a woman's ability to exercise this right was contingent upon the availability of funding. In 1977, the Court determined that states did not have to cover abortions through their Medicaid programs unless the abortions were therapeutic (i.e., necessary to protect the woman's life or health). Similarly, public hospitals were not required to provide nontherapeutic abortions. In 1980, the Court upheld the Hyde amendment, which restricted federal Medicaid funding of abortions to medically necessary ones (i.e., those required to save the woman's life). In the same year, it also ruled that states did not have to provide reimbursement for medically necessary abortions. Funding policy thus works counter to established policy for granting access to abortion. This variable received a score of 1 for 1973 and 0 for the remaining period. (Note that the Hyde amendment was originally enacted in 1977.)

Hierarchical Integration

Coordinated action is difficult within a single agency and is particularly challenging among the numerous semiautonomous agencies involved in most implementation efforts. Mazmanian and Sabatier (1989, 27) point out that "the problem is particularly acute in the case of federal statutes which rely on state and local agencies to carry out the details of program delivery in a very heterogeneous system." Federal abortion policy certainly falls under this rubric.

Because of the numerous issues involved (e.g., parental involvement, public funding for low-income women, and violence toward abortion providers), the implementation of federal abortion policy is more organizationally complex than the implementation of many other kinds of policy. Moreover, the states have discretion in many facets of federal abortion policy. There are few opportunities for coordination among organizations and many veto points—that is, opportunities for various actors to impede the achievement of legal objectives (Mazmanian and Sabatier 1989, 27). This variable received a score of 0 for the entire period.

Decision Rules of Implementing Agencies

Other than the trimester framework, *Roe* did not provide decision rules to the states and implementing agencies. This situation is not uncharacteristic of a judicial ruling. Because we had already measured the replacement of the trimester framework by the undue burden standard in terms of precise and clearly ranked objectives, we did not score this variable.

Officials' Commitment to Statutory Objectives

The attainment of legal objectives is unlikely unless officials in the implementing agencies are committed to the achievement of those objectives. A judicial ruling will rarely assign a case to a particular agency, and federal abortion policy is no exception. This variable received a score of 0 for the entire period.

Formal Access by Outsiders

Opportunities for participation by policy supporters outside the implementing agencies are seldom incorporated in judicial decisions. This variable received a score of 0 for the entire period.

CONCLUSION

In 1973, the U.S. Supreme Court established a single, national policy for abortion. Like most judicial decisions, *Roe* was not a model of statutory coherence. As table 4.3 (p. 77) shows, abortion policy has become less coherent over time, permitting more state restrictions on abortion. The effect is more state variation in funding for low-income women, parental involvement requirements, waiting periods, and other restrictions.

Abortion policy at both the federal and state levels remains highly volatile. Table 4.2 (p. 76) indicates how quickly federal abortion policies can change. In the next chapter, we examine state abortion policies and their determinants.

CHAPTER 5

State Fertility Control Policies

THE PRECEDING TWO chapters have shown that the national government provides resources for and determines many of the legal parameters of state fertility control policies. The states, however, have a great deal of leeway in setting both family planning and abortion policies. This chapter discusses the options available to the states, examines state practices and their variation, and analyzes which factors influence the development of state policies.

FAMILY PLANNING

As noted in chapter 3, Titles V, X, XIX, and XX have provided nearly all federal support for family planning since 1975. While these laws give states little choice in which agencies will administer federal funds for family planning services, they do allow for state discretion in other areas. States may decide whether to use specific grant programs for family planning. They also have some choice in setting eligibility levels, in determining the range of services that constitute family planning, and in involving parents in minors' decisions to use birth control. Recently, states have decided how they will approach the option of Medicaid managed care and how family planning services should be accommodated under that option.

Use of Different Funding Sources

State discretion in administering family planning funds varies by federal statute; that is, different policies allow the states and the implementing organizations different amounts of latitude. States may choose whether to spend any of the two block grants—Title V (maternal and child health) or Title XX (social services)—for family planning. All states have Medicaid programs, and under Title XIX, family planning is a required service for the categorically needy (it is an optional service for the medically needy).[1] Title X grants, which are specifically earmarked for family planning services,[2] are federally administered, so the states do not decide whether to use those funds. However, each state has at least one Title X grantee.

Table 5.1 Number of States Using Specific Sources of Federal Funding

YEAR	TITLE V	TITLE X	TITLE XIX[a]	TITLE XX	STATE APPROPRIATIONS
1980	42	50	43	35	25
1981	44	50	43	34	26
1982	37	50	43	28	29
1983	39	50	47	25	37
1985	36	50	43	21	34
1987	32	50	49	19	41
1990	35	50	47	15	41
1992	34	50	46	16	37
1994	36	50	45	16	37

a. Since 1981, when Arizona became the fiftieth state to develop its own Medicaid program, all states have had Medicaid expenditures for family planning. The numbers here are artifacts of data reporting.

Although all states use Title X to fund family planning services, states differ in their reliance on Title X and other funding sources. In 1994, for example, Title X accounted for nearly 44 percent of all public spending for family planning in Arkansas but for only 16 percent in New Hampshire.

All state health departments receive Title V funds, but as table 5.1 shows, only thirty-six states reported spending these monies for family planning services in 1994. California spent no Title V monies for family planning that year, while nearly 32 percent of South Dakota's family planning budget came from maternal and child health funds.

In 1994, forty-five states reported using Title XIX funds for family planning. Because family planning is a required service under the Medicaid program, this number undoubtedly means that five states just did not report their expenditures. Nevertheless, the states do vary greatly in their reliance on Title XIX for financing family planning services. Nearly 68 percent of all public spending for family planning in Arkansas was covered by the Medicaid program. In contrast, Hawaii's Title XIX program accounted for only 16 percent of public family planning expenditures.

Just sixteen states spent Title XX dollars for family planning services in 1994. That year, Title XX accounted for 22 percent of all public spending for family planning in Texas; indeed, Texas's Title XX spending for family planning services represented 42 percent of nationwide family planning expenditures from the social services block grant. In Ohio, on the other hand, Title XX funds constituted less than 1 percent of all public expenditures for family planning.

In 1994, thirty-seven states used their own funds for family planning. In Virginia, where all local health departments are required to offer family planning services, state funds accounted for 55 percent of all public expenditures for family planning. In contrast, in Illinois, state funds accounted for only 2 percent.

Over time, there has been little variation in the number of states using Titles X and XIX for family planning. States' use of both block grants, particularly Title XX, has decreased since the 1980s. The number of states appropriating funds for family planning has increased.

Implementing Organizations

As noted, states have little discretion over which organizations will administer federal funds for family planning. By law, funds from Titles V, XIX, and XX must be allocated to state agencies. Title V funds are awarded only to state health departments. In most states, Title XIX monies go to state welfare departments, although other types of state agencies also administer Medicaid programs.[3] Increasingly, state Medicaid agencies are contracting with managed care organizations, a trend that has serious implications for the provision of family planning services to low-income women. State welfare departments administer Title XX.

Title X has no explicit mandate to allocate funds to a state agency. Title X requires that this categorical program be administered by the Office of Population Affairs within DHHS. OPA delegates decisions about grantees and allocations to family planning consultants in each of the ten regional USPHS offices.[4] Title X grantees include state health departments, state and regional family planning councils, Planned Parenthood affiliates, and community health centers.

The organizational configuration of Title X grantees has changed over time, as has the number of grantees. In 1980, there were 235 Title X grantees nationwide (U.S. DHHS 1980). Under its policy of devolution, the Reagan administration tried to consolidate all Title X grantees within a state into a single grantee, most often the state health department. From the vantage point of the Reagan administration, this policy was quite successful; by 1983, there were just 85 Title X grantees. As noted in chapter 3, Texas had 37 Title X grantees in 1980; by the following year, the Texas Department of Health was the only Title X grantee in the state (Smith 1991).

In spite of this upheaval, some variation in the organizational configuration of Title X grantees in the states has remained. In some states, the health department is not just the only Title X grantee in the state, but also the sole provider of publicly subsidized family planning services; Mississippi is an example of such a "closed system" (see table 5.2). In other states in which the state health department is the only Title X grantee, such as Delaware, the health department not only delivers family planning services itself, but also has diverse contracts with agencies to deliver family planning services. A third arrangement in states in which the health department is the only Title X grantee is that the health depart-

Table 5.2 State Organization of Title X Grantees, 1981 and 1996

ORGANIZATIONAL CONFIGURATION	NO. OF STATES	% OF STATES
Health department: closed system		
1981	11	22
1996	17	34
Health department and grantees with diverse contracts		
1981	12	24
1996	17	34
Health department: grantee administration only		
1981	1	2
1996	1	2
Councils statewide or areawide		
1981	5	10
1996	8	16
Planned Parenthood statewide		
1981	1	2
1996	4	8
Multiple grantees with no central control		
1981	20	40
1996	3	6

Source: Adapted from Dryfoos and White 1980.

ment does not deliver services itself; instead, as in South Dakota, it contracts for all Title X family planning services. In other states, a single statewide or several areawide free-standing family planning grantees serve as the Title X grantees; in Pennsylvania, for example, the four Title X grantees are regional family planning councils, which contract with other agencies to provide services. Another Title X arrangement, used in Wisconsin, is for a Planned Parenthood affiliate to function as the sole state grantee. Other states have multiple grantees; in New Jersey, for example, both the state health department and the New Jersey Planning League are grantees (U.S. DHHS 1991).

Table 5.2 shows the organizational breakdown of Title X grantees in 1981, before the grantee consolidation implemented by the Reagan administration, and in 1996. Very few changes occurred in the configuration of Title X grantees after Reagan's policy was implemented in 1982–84. Before the grantee consolidation, state health departments were the sole state Title X grantees in 48 percent of the states. After that administrative policy was implemented, state health department assumed central control of Title X in 70 percent of the states.

Although these organizational changes have scarcely been studied, we believe that this legacy from the Reagan era has profoundly changed state family planning politics. With central control assumed by a state agency—the state health department—grantees and their contracting agencies have been much less able to engage in political advocacy than were freestanding grantees.

Eligibility

Except for Title X, eligibility for services also varies greatly (see table 5.3). Title X requires that services be provided regardless of income, although grantees are permitted to charge fees on a sliding scale to clients whose incomes are above the federal poverty level[5] (U.S. DHHS 1981). Within applicable categories (e.g., pregnancy or motherhood), all women and children are eligible for Title V services, but, again, states may charge those whose incomes are above the poverty level. Eligibility for Title XX services is completely established by each state.

Medicaid eligibility varies widely among the states. For example, a family with a monthly income of $1,111 is eligible for Medicaid services in Florida, while a family has to be making less than $424 a month to be eligible for Medicaid in Georgia (U.S. GAO 1998). Before the 1996 Welfare Reform Act replaced AFDC with TANF, states *had* to pay for covered medical services for all those eligible for AFDC, for pregnant women who met AFDC income and resource requirements, and for most Supplemental Security Income (SSI) recipients (Andrews and Orloff 1995). State could choose to offer Medicaid benefits to optional groups, such as non-AFDC adolescents and nonpregnant, medically needy adults.

The 1996 Welfare Reform Act increased the variation among states in Medicaid eligibility. Medical coverage through Title XIX is no longer automatic for families who receive cash assistance from TANF (Kaiser Family Foundation 1998). For the nation as a whole, TANF has contributed to declining Medicaid enrollments. By 1997, an estimated 675,000 low-income people had become uninsured as a result of welfare reform, and the majority were chil-

Table 5.3 State Discretion by Source of Federal Family Planning Funds

	DISCRETION AVAILABLE TO THE STATES			
ISSUE	TITLE V	TITLE X	TITLE XIX	TITLE XX
Use of Funds for Family Planning	Yes	No	No	Yes
Eligibility	Yes	No[a]	Yes	Yes
Range of Clinical Services	Yes	No	Yes	Yes
Education and Counseling	Yes	No	Yes	Yes
Parental Involvement	Yes	No	No	Yes

a. States do have discretion about how much to charge for services and how to organize their sliding-fee scales.

dren under age nineteen (Klein 1999). Clearly, this trend affects funding for family planning services.

Federal waivers of the original statutory requirement that Medicaid enrollees could choose their medical providers have permitted states to restructure their entire Medicaid delivery systems, as well as to expand eligibility for family planning services. Texas, for example, uses primary care case management and capitated systems to provide Medicaid services.[6] As part of its waiver, Texas has agreed to extend family planning services to all women of childbearing age who have lost Medicaid eligibility (U.S. DHHS 1995, 1996). Medicaid waivers have been used more in the 1990s than ever before; we discuss them in greater detail later in this chapter.

Range of Clinical Services

The range of services that constitute family planning varies by source of funding and by the state in which services are provided. Title V does not define clinical services, and the range of services offered is thus left to the discretion of individual states. Unlike Title V and the other two federal funding sources, Title X is quite specific about the minimum set of services that grantees must offer. Although these required services are quite extensive, some grantees offer more than the minimum.[7] Title X regulations require that grantees adhere to its clinical guidelines for *all* the family planning services they deliver even if there are other funding sources, such as Medicaid or state appropriations (U.S. DHHS 1981).

Family planning services are not defined per se in the Title XIX statute or regulations. Nevertheless, the federal government provides guidance to the states on this point. The Senate report that accompanied the Medicaid legislation in 1965 emphasized as categories of service "those who voluntarily choose not to risk an initial pregnancy" and "families with children who desire to control family size" (U.S. DHHS 1988, 4270). In addition, the Medicaid manual for the states specifies that they may limit their definition of Medicaid family planning services to "those services which either prevent or delay pregnancy," or they may define the term more broadly to include services for the treatment of infertility (U. S. DHHS 1988, 4270).

Title XX's definition of family planning is very broad and permits states that use these funds for family planning a great deal of leeway. For example, states can choose to provide social services only and still comply with the following definition:

> Family planning services are those educational, comprehensive medical or social services or activities which enable individuals, including minors, to determine freely the number and spacing of their children and to select the means by which this may be achieved. These services

and activities include a broad range of acceptable and effective methods and services to limit or enhance fertility, including contraceptive methods (including natural family planning and abstinence), and the management of infertility (including referral to adoption). Specific component services and activities include preconceptional counseling, education, and general reproductive health care including diagnosis and treatment of infections which threaten reproductive capability [Federal Register 1993].

Education and Counseling

Education and counseling are generally considered important components of family planning services. While individual patient counseling is a standard component of most medical family planning services, more extensive or innovative educational strategies are usually lacking. Theoretically, of course, any grant mechanism that does not strictly define family planning could be used to fund a variety of educational interventions. In fact, however, Titles V, X, XIX, and XX and state appropriations seldom fund any educational services beyond routine contraceptive counseling. Because Title V is a block grant given to maternal and child health bureaus in state health departments, it adheres for the most part to a medical or public health nursing model of delivering care, emphasizing clinical services and one-to-one counseling. Medicaid reimbursements for family planning counseling are related almost exclusively to contraceptive use. Title XX expenditures for family planning usually mimic Medicaid reimbursements, and state appropriations usually fund existing patterns of care.

Even Title X, which does require that family planning services include education and counseling, is restricted in practice. Although OPA and the USPHS regional offices require grantees to submit information about their educational activities beyond routine patient counseling, fiscal allocations to the grantees are based predominantly on the number of patients receiving clinical family planning services. Thus, there is little incentive for grantees to expend resources for education and counseling.

Parental Involvement

All states allow minors to receive contraceptive care without parental consent or notification, either explicitly or implicitly. By law, minors in twenty-four states may consent to receiving contraceptive services. In all other states, no specific legislation addresses this situation, but no state has a law mandating that parents be notified when their minor children receive contraceptive services or that they give their consent for these services. State law and provider behavior are not necessarily the same, and health care providers in states without applicable legislation may impose their own parental involvement requirements (Donovan 1992). To promote the use of family planning services among sexually active minors, two of the federal sources of family planning funds address this point. Title X stipulates that services must be provided without regard to age, and Title XIX has a supremacy clause, which states that this federal law allowing confidential family planning services supercedes any restrictive state laws that may be enacted. As Medicaid enrollment in managed care has expanded, however, one of the concerns is that confidentiality of services for minor patients may be compromised.[8] The other statutes are silent on this important aspect in the delivery of publicly funded family planning services.

Medicaid Managed Care

Medicaid accounts for nearly one out of every two dollars of public monies spent for family planning (see chap. 6). The structure of state Medicaid programs is therefore particularly important for fertility control. In addition to specifying that Medicaid programs be administered by state agencies, the original Medicaid statute allowed for managed health care (i.e., a prepaid health plan). However, the 1965 legislation also required that states adhere to "freedom-of-choice" provisions. By ensuring that Medicaid enrollees could obtain care from the provider of their choice, these provisions prevented states from mandating enrollment in managed care plans (Gold and Richards 1998, 144). One of the most common types of managed care organizations is the health maintenance organization (HMO), which is "a prepaid medical practice delivering a comprehensive set of health services to enrollees for a fixed fee (capitation) paid in advance" (Patel and Rushefsy 1995, 140).

The freedom-of-choice provisions have been modified. In 1981, the Omnibus Budget Reconciliation Act established section 1915 of the Social Security Act, which allowed states to waive the freedom-of-choice provisions and to require enrollment in managed care plans. These provisions were called "section 1915 waivers" (Gold and Richards 1998, 144). Under Medicaid managed care arrangements, providers have contracts with state Medicaid agencies and act as gatekeepers for all health care services for enrollees, determining what services shall be provided and which may be reimbursable outside the plan. In addition, in 1982, DHHS began using its authority under section 1115 of the Social Security Act to permit states to develop large Medicaid demonstration programs that mandated managed care arrangements and broadened eligibility. However, the section 1115 waivers were rarely used until the Clinton presidency (Gold and Richards 1998; Rosenbaum et al. 1997; Salganicoff and Delbanco 1998).

In 1986, Congress amended the Medicaid statute to require states with managed care plans operating under section 1915 waivers to "restore the right of patients to choose their own family planning providers" (Gold and Richards 1998, 145). In so doing, Congress was responding to the concerns of both patients and providers. In many states with section 1915 waivers, Medicaid beneficiaries had continued to seek family planning services from traditional, community family planning providers, even though these services were "out-of-plan"—that is, nonreimbursable. Among their reasons for doing so were "the need for confidentiality, patient preference and comfort, and the need to avoid the delays imposed by the managed care system" (Rosenbaum et al. 1994). Family planning providers, who had lost much of their Medicaid revenue to managed care organizations, confirmed that many Medicaid patients still sought their now-nonreimbursable family planning services. In 1987, Congress extended the freedom of choice of family planning providers to enrollees in all federally qualified HMOs participating in Medicaid, "regardless of whether the enrollment in the HMO was part of a section 1915 mandatory demonstration on a voluntary basis" (Rosenbaum et al. 1997, 1197).

Congress did not extend the freedom-of-choice requirements to section 1115, so Medicaid managed care demonstration projects authorized under this provision are not required to offer the freedom to choose family planning service providers (Rosenbaum et al. 1997). Interestingly, however, many states volunteered to retain this freedom of choice. Of the fifteen statewide section 1115 waivers that have been approved, ten have retained enrollees' freedom of choice of family planning providers, "even though they are not mandated by federal law to do so" (Gold and Richards 1998, 146).

In addition to other problems, Medicaid managed care lacks uniform definitions for family planning services and contraceptive supplies. Thus, individual states and managed care organizations within those states have different definitions and standards. There is little uniformity concerning specific services for which out-of-plan family providers may be reimbursed or how providers unauthorized to furnish services should refer patients back to managed care plans for treatment (Rosenbaum et al. 1997). Some managed care plans require patients to have prior authorization before going out-of-plan, effectively nullifying the freedom-of-choice guarantee. As stated earlier, patient confidentiality is also a concern, particularly for adolescent patients (Gonen 1997).

In spite of these problems, Medicaid managed care is expected to grow. The Balanced Budget Act (BBA) of 1997 permitted states to mandate managed care enrollment for most Medicaid beneficiaries without having to seek a federal waiver (Kaiser Family Foundation 1998).

ABORTION

As discussed in chapter 4, Supreme Court decisions, along with executive and legislative developments, have given states latitude in establishing abortion policies. States may not, however, use federal funds to pay for abortions, except when the lives of Medicaid-eligible women are endangered or when their pregnancies are the result of incest or rape. States *must* pay for abortions under those circumstances. States may require parental involvement in the abortion decision of an emancipated minor, but only if a judicial bypass is available. States may also require a waiting period.

Funding

In 1980, in *Harris* v. *McRae*, the Supreme Court upheld the Hyde amendment, which limited Medicaid funding of abortions to those necessary to save a pregnant woman's life. In another 1980 decision, the Court ruled that states do not have to pay for other medically necessary abortions for Medicaid patients. In 1993, Congress expanded the longstanding Hyde amendment to provide Medicaid coverage of abortion when pregnancy results from rape or incest (AGI 1993k).

As of January 1999, twenty-nine states and the District of Columbia were in compliance with the 1993 federal law, funding abortion for Medicaid-eligible women in cases of life endangerment, rape, or incest. Two states—Mississippi and South Dakota—were in violation because they refused to fund in cases of rape or incest (NARAL 1999). Five states not only funded abortion in cases of rape, incest, and life endangerment, but also under some other health circumstances.[9] Only fourteen states funded abortions for Medicaid-eligible women in *most* circumstances.[10]

In 1976 and 1977, before the Hyde amendment was first enacted, all fifty states were funding most abortions requested by Medicaid recipients. Table 5.4 (p. 90) shows that this figure dropped to sixteen in 1981, the year after the *Harris* v. *McRae* decision upheld the Hyde amendment. In the years since, the figure has varied only slightly as a result of state court rulings and legislative actions.

Parental Involvement

As indicated in chapter 4, the Supreme Court has ruled repeatedly on the parental involvement issue. In *Hodgson* in 1990, the Court ruled that states may require that both parents be notified of a minor's abortion as long as a judicial bypass is provided for minors who do not want to inform their parents. In 1992, in its *Casey* decision, the Court held that states may require all minors to obtain the consent of one parent or a judge. Not surprisingly, state policies and practices differ widely concerning parental consent for or notification of a minor's abortion.

Thirty states currently enforce laws that prevent a minor from obtaining an abortion without parental consent or notification; another nine states have parental involvement laws but do not enforce them (see table 5.5, p. 91).[11] Of the thirty states that enforce such laws, twenty-four permit a minor to obtain an abortion without parental consent or notice but only if she secures a court order waiving the requirement. Two states, Idaho and Utah, "do not have a judicial or other bypass provision allowing a minor to secure a court order in lieu of noti-

Table 5.4 States Funding Abortions for Medicaid Recipients in Most Circumstances

YEAR	NO. OF STATES	CHANGES
1973	47	*Roe* v. *Wade* decision was handed down on 22 January.
1974	48	Wyoming began funding.
1975	49	New Hampshire began funding.
1976	50	West Virginia began funding.
1977	50	First Hyde amendment was enacted.
1978	20[a]	
1979	19[a]	Idaho stopped funding.
1980	46	Injunction against Hyde amendment was effective until 19 September when *Harris* v. *McRae* decision was handed down. Kentucky, North Dakota, Rhode Island, and South Dakota did not fund.
1981	16[a]	
1982	15	Georgia stopped funding.
1983	15	
1984	15	
1985	16	Vermont started funding.
1986	14	Colorado and Pennsylvania stopped funding.
1987	14	
1988	14	
1989	13	Michigan stopped funding.
1990	13	
1991	13	
1992	13	
1993	13	Alaska, California, Connecticut, Hawaii, Maryland, Massachusetts, New Jersey, New York, North Carolina, Oregon, Vermont, Washington, and West Virginia are funding.
1994	13	
1995	17	Idaho, Minnesota, Illinois, and New Mexico started funding.
1996	17	Montana started and North Carolina stopped funding.
1997	16	Idaho stopped funding.
1998	14	Alaska and Illinois stopped funding.
1999	14	

a. As of 1 January.

fying her parents." Delaware, Maine, Maryland, and West Virginia permit a minor to obtain an abortion without parental notice if a physician or health professional waives the requirement. In Maine, for example, "a minor may obtain

Table 5.5 States Requiring and Enforcing Parental Involvement in Minors' Abortions

YEAR	NO. OF STATES WITH LAWS	NO. OF STATES ENFORCING	NOTES
1991	35	15	Alabama, Arkansas, Indiana, Louisiana, Massachusetts, Michigan, Minnesota, Missouri, North Dakota, Ohio, Rhode Island, South Carolina, Utah, West Virginia, Wyoming enforce.
1992	33	17	Georgia and Nebraska begin to enforce.
1993	35	21	Kansas, Maryland, Tennessee, Wisconsin begin to enforce.
1995	35	24	Kentucky, Mississippi, Pennsylvania begin to enforce.
1996	36	27	North Carolina adds restriction and enforces. Delaware and Idaho begin to enforce.
1997	38	28	Iowa and Maine add restriction; Iowa enforces.
1998	39	30	Virginia adds restriction.South Dakota and Virginia enforce.
1999	39	30	

Source: NARAL 1991–93, 1995–99.
Note: No report was issued in 1994.

an abortion without parental consent if a physician has secured the written consent of the minor and the minor is mentally and physically competent to give consent" (NARAL 1999, xv). At least ten states allow a minor to obtain an abortion without parental involvement if she declares that she is a victim of abuse, neglect, rape, or incest.[12]

There are other variations in state law. Under certain circumstances, eight states permit a minor to notify specified adults other than her parents.[13] Connecticut does not require parental involvement, but it does require that before obtaining an abortion, a minor receive counseling that includes the possibility of consulting her parents (NARAL 1999, xv).

Waiting Periods
Nineteen states have laws prohibiting a woman from obtaining an abortion until a specified time after she has received a state-mandated lecture or other infor-

Table 5.6 Mandatory Waiting Periods for Abortion

STATE	MINIMUM WAITING PERIOD	ENFORCED	ENJOINED OR NOT ENFORCED
Delaware	24 hours		X
Idaho	24 hours	X	
Indiana	18 hours	X	
Kansas	24 hours	X	
Kentucky	24 hours	X	
Louisiana	24 hours	X	
Massachusetts	24 hours		X
Michigan	24 hours		X
Mississippi	24 hours	X	
Montana	24 hours		X
Nebraska	24 hours	X	
North Dakota	24 hours	X	
Ohio	24 hours	X	
Pennsylvania	24 hours	X	
South Carolina	1 hour	X	
South Dakota	24 hours	X	
Tennessee	48–72 hours[a]		X
Utah	24 hours	X	
Wisconsin	24 hours	X	
Total (19 states)		14	5

Source: NARAL 1999.

a. A woman may not obtain an abortion until the third day after her initial consultation.

mational materials (see table 5.6). Fourteen states currently enforce these mandatory waiting periods (NARAL 1999). Before the *Casey* decision in 1992, only two states permitted this type of restriction.

Other Restrictions

Many other state restrictions on abortion exist. Indeed, we identified over twenty different state abortion policies. Except for laws designed to prevent violent protests at clinics, all these policies were formulated for the purpose of reducing the incidence of abortion (Meier et al. 1996). These restrictive policies are listed in table 5.7 (pp. 94–95), along with a brief explanation of each, the total number of states that have such restrictions, and the number of states that have passed these restrictions since 1982. We will refer to the latter again in chapter 6 when we analyze policy outputs.

EXPLAINING THE VARIATION IN STATE POLICIES

Although all states are subject to the same federal policy parameters, they have considerable discretion in determining their own fertility control policies; the result has been variation in state family planning and abortion policies. In this section, to gain insight into the process of fertility control policymaking, we analyze state policy variation. First, we review research that has been conducted in this policy area. Previous research has examined state abortion policies, but to date, no empirical analysis has examined why state family planning policies differ so much or whether the same factors that influence state abortion policies also shape state family planning policies. Based on that literature review, we present our general hypotheses. Next, we describe our dependent and independent variables, both conceptually and in terms of our data, and present more specific hypotheses. The lack of data, particularly for family planning policy, presents a challenge to researchers in this policy area. Finally, we discuss our findings and their implications for state fertility control policymaking.

Previous Research

State Family Planning Policies. Four principal factors explain the paucity of research on state family planning policies. The first is that before 1985, Title X was the predominant source of public funding for family planning, and advocates and researchers focused their attention on expanding or maintaining it.[14] The other funding sources (Titles V, XIX, and XX and state appropriations), which allowed the states greater discretion, received short shrift. The quantitative analyses that were conducted in the 1970s and 1980s focused largely on family planning's impact on fertility (Cutright and Jaffe 1976; Anderson and Cope 1987) or its cost effectiveness (Forrest and Singh 1990a,1990b).

The second factor is a lack of data—a situation that has deteriorated over time. Two government reports containing detailed information on state family planning policies were published in the 1970s (AGI 1974, 1978). Although these reports did not present quantitative data, the categories they employed (e.g., eligibility and range of services) were clear enough that data coding would have been relatively easy. During the 1970s and early 1980s, state family planning expenditures and numbers of family planning patients served were published annually. However, the federal government has not collected family planning patient data on an ongoing basis since 1981 (McFarlane and Meier 1993b).

The third factor is that funding to support studies of family planning issues at the state level has been limited, even from the Office of Population Affairs, which has the mandate to support this type of research. As noted in chapter 3, Title X has not been reauthorized since 1985; Title X programs have been fund-

Table 5.7 State Abortion Policies

Type of Policy	Explanation	Total No. of States	No. of States Enacting Since 1982
Conscience clause	Allows physicians not to perform abortions if they are opposed to abortion	36	4
Fetal experimentation	Prohibits experiments using material from aborted fetuses and bans abortions for the purpose of experimentation	30	6
Postviability requirement	Establishes when viability occurs and regulates abortions after viability	30	11
Postviability care	Requests postabortion care for a viable fetus	30	2
Anti-abortion memorial	Requests that Congress ban abortion	25	2
Feticide	Outlaws killing of a fetus	10	7
Fetal disposal	Regulates disposal of aborted fetuses	11	4
Abortion-specific informed consent	Prohibits abortion without the pregnant woman's "informed consent," which requires that she receive anti-abortion lectures or materials approved by the state[a]	20	11
Informed consent of minors	Applies the informed consent law to minors rather than requiring parental consent	2	2
Parental consent	Requires minors to obtain consent for an abortion from parents or the courts	22	16
Parental notification	Requires that a minor's parents be notified before an abortion is performed	21	13
Spousal consent	Requires the husband's consent for an abortion	8	3
No wrongful life/ wrongful birth policy	Prohibits lawsuits whereby a person argues that he or she should not have been born (wrongful life) or parents allege that had they been informed correctly, they would have had an abortion (wrongful birth)[b]	8	8

Private insurance	Permits restricted access to abortion or no abortion coverage in private health insurance policies	11	8
State insurance	Bans abortion coverage in health insurance of state workers	1	1
Public facilities	Bans the use of public facilities in performing abortions	6	6
Fetal pain	Requires physician to inform the pregnant woman that the fetus feels pain and that anesthesia is available	1	1
Gender selection	Bans abortion performed because of parents' gender preferences	2	2
Physician-only	Stipulates that only licensed physicians may perform abortions	6	6
Reporting requirement	Stipulates that all abortions be reported to a state agency	20	20
Clinic violence	Prohibits violence toward or harassment of abortion clinics and workers	9	9
Waiting period	Specifies a period that must pass between the request for an abortion and the time the procedure is performed	6	6
Right to life	Makes it illegal to kill a fetus in the womb unless certain conditions are met and/or requires the physician to give any fetus born alive during an abortion a chance to live	12	12

a. *Informed consent* has a different meaning for other medical procedures.

b. Banning wrongful life suits has not generated great controversy, but pro-choice advocates "often believe that proscribing wrongful birth suits prohibits physicians from recommending tests, such as amniocentesis (which may detect a fetal abnormality), that a woman may have undergone had she known of their existence" (Halva-Neubauer 1993, 188–89).

ed by continuing resolution ever since. This lack of funding, along with Title X's mission to fund family planning services, has meant that research has not been a priority for OPA.

The fourth factor in accounting for the lack of research on state differences in family planning is the disciplinary backgrounds of many of the researchers. Sociologists with other specialties, demographers, public health analysts, and psychologists are unaccustomed to viewing state policies as dependent variables. The availability of only expenditure data (as opposed to patient data) as an output measure does not lend itself to familiar analyses in these disciplines.

State Abortion Policies. In the years immediately following the 1973 *Roe* v. *Wade* ruling, the numerous Supreme Court decisions that addressed abortion largely prohibited state governments from intervening in a woman's right to choose abortion. When the Court handed down its *Harris* v. *McRae* decision in 1980, funding became the major exception to the Court's upholding the right to choose. It was not until the 1989 *Webster* decision that other state abortion restrictions were allowed to stand.

During this sixteen-year period, research on state-level abortion policies was not plentiful. In 1980, Hansen published a seminal article that examined abortion politics at both the national and state levels, but she did not look specifically at state policies. Because her most recent state-level data were from 1976—before Medicaid funding restrictions were permitted—analyzing determinants of state policies would not have been possible.

After the *Webster* decision in 1989, research on state abortion policy burgeoned. For the most part, however, this work did not analyze the determinants of abortion policy. Halva-Neubauer (1990) categorized state attempts to restrict abortion after the *Roe* decision. The result was an interesting dependent variable, but no analysis was performed on it. Goggin and Wlezien (1993) identified twenty-four different forms of abortion policy that have been codified into state laws. From those, they developed a cumulative measure of state abortion policy in 1988. The utility of this index is limited, however, because it gives the same weight to all abortion restrictions.

Several scholars have analyzed the effect of women legislators on state abortion policies. Hansen (1993) showed that electing more women to state legislatures reduced the number of abortion restrictions adopted. Indeed, she found evidence of a threshold effect—that is, when women account for more than 20 percent of the legislators, fewer restrictions are enacted. Berkman and O'Connor (1993) found that Democratic women legislators, even in states with a small percentage of women in the legislature, had a disproportionate effect on blocking abortion restrictions.

Some scholars have looked at the relative importance of other factors in determining abortion policies. In examining the relative impact of public opinion and interest groups on state abortion policies, Cohen and Barrilleaux (1993) found that when abortion opinion is narrowly decided on an issue or leans slightly in one direction, pro-life interest groups generally prevail. In 1995, Segers and Byrnes edited a volume of case studies on state abortion policies. Wetstein (1996) reported that the variance in state abortion policies on parental involvement and Medicaid funding could be explained by social, economic, religious, and opinion factors.

General State Policies. The literature on general state policies also offers theoretical guidance for examining the variation in state fertility control policy. Hwang and Gray (1991, 278) argue that state policies can be grouped into two types: redistributive policies and developmental policies. A substantial literature supports the proposition that redistributive policies are determined primarily by political forces (e.g., interest groups and political parties), whereas developmental policies are largely determined by socioeconomic forces (e.g., industrialization and affluence).

In addition to these two broad clusters of state policy, a third policy type—morality policy—exists at the state level. We mentioned in chapter 1 that state governments have a long tradition of enacting morality policies (Gusfield 1963); these include the regulation of alcohol, gambling, drug use, and Sunday closings. State morality policies are largely the result of the competition between religious forces and citizen groups (Meier and Johnson 1990; Morgan and Meier 1980), political forces, and the demand for the "immoral" good.

Salience and Complexity. The notion that an issue's salience and complexity determine its politics was discussed in chapter 1 (see table 1.2, p. 16). At the beginning of the twenty-first century, abortion is a highly salient issue in the American states, while family planning vacillates between being highly salient and moderately salient. Neither family planning nor abortion is a technically complex issue.

Most fertility control issues, then, are decided by hearing room politics in which the major participants are politicians, citizen groups, and journalists. Because abortion policies are consistently salient and portrayed as noncomplex, they are nearly always determined by hearing room politics. When family planning issues are less salient, street level politics may also operate, meaning that lower-level bureaucrats and family planning providers also participate. Although these two groups may make the day-to-day operating decisions, hearing room politics determine broader policy decisions.

General Hypotheses

Both family planning funding and abortion funding are redistributive policies, so *we expect that they are largely determined by interest groups and other political forces.* Given the higher salience of abortion, *we expect that forces identified in the hearing room scenario* (e.g., citizen/advocacy groups and political forces) *affect state abortion policies more than they affect state family planning policies.* Because interest groups and political forces change, a corollary is that *state family planning policies should be more stable over time than are state abortion policies.*

We have already pointed out that not all abortion policies are subject to exactly the same political forces. *We expect that interest groups affect parental involvement policies more than they affect abortion funding policies,* because the former are more exclusively a morality issue than the latter.

Dependent Variables

Family Planning Funding. One of the most important decisions states have to make concerning family planning is how many sources of public funds to use for birth control services. As already noted, states have no discretion in whether they will use Title X; this categorical program is federally administered, and funds are awarded to all fifty states. Similarly, all states use Title XIX funds for family planning.[15] States do have discretion in whether to use Titles V and XX or their own appropriations for family planning. States also decide *how much* of those funds will be used for family planning.

The dependent variable here is the number of discretionary sources of family planning funds that a state uses. This variable was coded 0 if no discretionary source is used, 1 if only one source is used, 2 if two sources are used, and 3 if three sources are used.

Abortion Funding. State policies on funding abortions generally fall into three groups. First, several states pay for abortions for all women who are covered by Medicaid; these states are termed *voluntary-unrestrictive.* Second, courts in several states have ruled that the state must cover abortions for Medicaid-eligible women if the state also covers pregnancies; these states are termed *court order–unrestrictive.* Third, all other states restrict the use of public funds for abortions for Medicaid-eligible women to cases of life endangerment of the mother or other specific circumstances.[16] To measure this variable, we employed a two-point scale, coding 1 if the state is unrestrictive (voluntary or not) and 0 if the state restricts funding of abortions for Medicaid-eligible women.[17]

Parental Involvement in Abortion. State policies regarding parental involvement in abortion fall into one of six groups, another ordinal measure. If a state has no policy regarding parental consent for or notification of a minor's abortion, this variable was coded 0. A state policy was coded 1 if the state requires counseling for the teenager seeking an abortion, 2 if the law requires notification of at least one parent, and 3 if the law requires notifying both parents. A state policy was coded 4 if consent by one parent is required before the procedure can be performed, 5 if the state requires the consent of both parents and the law provides for a judicial bypass, and 6 if the law requires the consent of both parents and makes no provision for judicial bypass.

Independent Variables

Advocacy Groups. Family planning advocacy groups operate in many states. In most cases, these organizations lobby on behalf of the providers of family planning services. However, there is no complete count or list of these groups. If those data were available, we would expect that states with family planning advocacy groups would be more likely than states without such groups to use multiple sources of funds for family planning.

Advocacy groups exist on both sides of the abortion issue. Perhaps the most visible pro-choice advocate is the National Abortion Rights Action League (NARAL). Our measure of NARAL strength (obtained directly from the organization) is the number of NARAL members in the state per 1,000 population. Because pro-life groups were unresponsive to requests for state membership information, we used two surrogates for pro-life strength: the percentage of the state population that is Catholic and the percentage of the population that belongs to Christian fundamentalist churches.[18] Both groups are associated with right-to-life activities. The Catholic Church in particular has been extremely active; all 180 U.S. dioceses operate separate offices for right-to-life activities (Moore 1989, 912). *We expect that NARAL membership has been inversely related to the restrictiveness of state policies toward abortion funding and parental involvement.* Similarly, *we expect that the percentages of the population who belong to Catholic or fundamentalist Christian churches have been directly related to the restrictiveness of state policies regarding abortion funding.*

Pro-choice advocates uniformly support publicly subsidized family planning services, while many of the pro-life groups oppose family planning. *We expect that NARAL membership has been directly related to the use of public funds for family planning* and *that the percentages of the population who are Catholic or belong to fundamentalist Christian faiths have been inversely related to the number of discretionary funding sources that the state uses for family planning services.*

Political Forces. Political variables affecting state family planning policies should be the same as those affecting state abortion variables. In other words, with very few exceptions, the same groups that favor or disfavor support for family planning would also favor or disfavor support for abortion. We included four independent political variables: Democrats, party competition, conservative strength, and New Deal liberalism.

The Democrats measure is simply the percentage of Democrats in both houses of the state legislature for the decade of the 1980s; for Minnesota with its nonpartisan legislature, we used the distribution of the partisan vote for members of Congress.[19] Given the platforms of each major political party, *we expect that the greater the percentage of Democrats, the more funding sources of family planning a state will have used, while its policy toward funding abortions and parental involvement will have been less restrictive.*

Political scientists generally hypothesize that greater party competition increases public expenditures because political parties try to create or expand programs (especially redistributive programs) to satisfy voters. Therefore, *we expect that the greater the party competition, the more funding sources of family planning a state will have used.* In an area as controversial as abortion, however, one may expect a reversal of this relationship (Colby and Baker 1988). With less party competition (or issue salience), elected officials are more likely to allow the professional judgment of public health officials or bureaucrats to determine policies. Party competition was calculated in the traditional way by subtracting 50 from the percentage Democratic and subtracting the absolute value of this figure from 100 (see Bibby et al. 1990). *We hypothesize that party competition has been directly related to the restrictiveness of state policies on funding abortion and to requirements for parental involvement.*

We used two measures of ideology designed to tap conservative strength and the ability to appeal to traditional (i.e., New Deal) Democrats on the abortion issue. Conservative strength is a measure of state electoral conservatism developed by Holbrook (1984); it is the sum of conservative coalition scores for all members of Congress from a state. New Deal liberalism is a measure developed by Rosenstone (1983) to measure how well state policies adhere to economic liberalism, as opposed to social liberalism (see Holbrook-Provow and Poe 1987). *We expect that states' conservative strength and New Deal liberalism have been inversely related to the number of sources of family planning funding and directly related to the restrictiveness of state policies on abortion funding and parental involvement.*

Demand. We measured demand for family planning and abortion by using four demographic surrogates related to unwanted pregnancy and abortion rates in the general population. These surrogates are percentage of the population that resides in urban areas, percentage of females in the labor force, percentage of the population that is black, and percentage of the population that is Hispanic.[20] Henshaw and Silverman's (1988, 162) assessment of abortion patients showed that nonwhite women, Hispanic women, employed women, and women living in urban areas are more likely to have had an abortion. For parental consent, we added another measure of need or demand, the teenage birth rate. *We expect that the percentages of black women, Hispanic women, employed women, and urban women have been directly related to the number of sources of family planning funds used by a state. We expect that each of these variables has been inversely related to the restrictiveness of state policies on funding abortions and requiring parental involvement in minors' abortion decisions.*

Related Policies. Hofferbert and Urice (1985) argue that states adopt policies similar to related policies. These related policies create a policy environment that frames the policy issue under consideration. Family planning and abortion are certainly related. Because they are redistributive, funding policies for family planning and abortion should be related to state welfare policy as well.

Our measure of welfare policy is state Medicaid generosity, a factor measure developed by Colby and Baker (1988) to assess state Medicaid programs in terms of benefits provided and population covered. Medicaid generosity reflects a state's commitment to redistributive policy. *We expect that the generosity of a state's Medicaid program has been directly related to the number of sources of family planning funds used in the state. We also expect that the generosity of the state's Medicaid program has been inversely related to the restrictiveness of state policy on funding abortions.*

Family planning policy is measured by the per capita expenditures from all public funding sources for family planning. If family planning programs are successful, the number of unplanned pregnancies should decline. With a decline in unplanned pregnancies, the demand for abortion should also drop. To allow sufficient time for family planning programs to have an impact on funded abortions, this variable was lagged by two years. A well-funded family planning program could be perceived as an alternative to funding abortions. Because family planning services can reduce the demand for abortion, *we expect that public funding for family planning has been inversely related to abortion funding policy.*

Public family planning programs serve mostly young, unmarried women, so state support for family planning represents a recognition of sexual activity in this population. Because both family planning and parental involvement policies should be influenced by state morality politics, *we expect that state support for family planning has been inversely related to parental involvement for minors seeking abortions.*

Another policy related to parental involvement is abortion funding policy. *We expect that states that fund abortion have been less likely to require or to enforce parental involvement.*

Findings

We specified several hypotheses in which the independent variables are likely to overlap. Thus, collinearity could have been a problem. To avoid this problem, we reestimated models after deleting statistically insignificant variables. Only the final model is presented here. When regression is the technique used, tolerance coefficients are reported.

Family Planning Funding. The results for our final model of the number of sources of family planning funds are shown in table 5.8 (p. 102). The percentage of the state's population that belonged to NARAL was omitted from the final model because it was not significant. The two pro-life measures were positively associated with more sources of family planning, the opposite of what we hypothesized.

In terms of political forces, two of our hypotheses were supported. States with greater party competition and more Democrats were positively associated

Table 5.8 Determinants of States' Use of Multiple Sources of Public Family Planning Funds

INDEPENDENT VARIABLES	SLOPE	T-VALUE
Advocacy groups		
Catholics	.035	3.18
Fundamentalists	.025	2.13
Political forces		
Democrats	.017	1.70
Party competition	.045	3.27
New Deal liberalism	.360	2.36
Demand		
Black population	.021	1.34
R^2	.35	
Adjusted R^2	.26	

with the use of more sources of public funds for family planning. Contrary to our hypothesis, New Deal liberalism was also positively associated with more sources of family planning funding. Only one of our measures of demand, the percentage of the state's population that is black, was associated with the use of more sources of public funds, but this association was weak.

Abortion Funding. To examine our two-point abortion funding scale, we used logit analysis. Table 5.9 presents the results of the logit analysis to predict which states would fund abortions. Many of our independent variables were not directly related to abortion funding policy. In fact, with only four independent variables—percentage of Catholics, NARAL membership, party competition, and conservative strength—were state policies accurately predicted. The model correctly predicted forty-seven states in 1985, forty-seven in 1987, and forty-nine in 1990. The incorrectly predicted states were North Carolina in all three years,[21] Michigan in 1985 and 1987, Colorado in 1985, and Maine in 1987.

Abortion funding policy is clearly a function of citizen groups and political forces, exactly what one would expect in a highly salient but noncomplex policy area. Table 5.9 also presents impact coefficients that show the change in probability of funding abortions for a one standard deviation change in the independent variable holding all other independent variables constant at the mean. These coefficients show that NARAL membership is the strongest single determinant of abortion funding policy. The other three forces are relatively equal in 1990; this represents an increased impact of party competition over the coefficients for 1987 and 1985. The indicators of demand for abortion had little impact on funding policy.

Table 5.9 Determinants of State Abortion Funding Policy

INDEPENDENT VARIABLES	1985	IMPACT	1987	IMPACT	1990	IMPACT
Advocacy groups						
% Catholic	−.192	.54	−.157	.41	−.259	.47
	(.086)*		(.071)*		(.120)*	
NARAL membership	4.294	.65	3.799	.57	7.003	.81
	(1.427)*		(1.305)*		(2.942)*	
Political forces						
Party competition	−.115	.30	.118	.29	−.268	.51
					(.138)**	
Conservative strength	−.073	.56	−.068	.50	−.104	.55
	(.029)*		(.027)*		(.047)	
Model chi-square	37.97		35.40		42.53	
% correctly predicted	94.0		94.0		98.0	
Proportionate reduction in error	78.6		78.6		92.3	

$^*p < .05.$ $^{**}p < .10.$

Parental Involvement. The variables that predict family planning and abortion funding policies explain very little of the variance in state parental involvement policies. We added two policy measures—family planning expenditures and abortion funding policy—to the equation. We also added a need variable—the teen birth rate. The results are still very modest, as shown in table 5.10.

Table 5.10 Determinants of Parental Involvement Policies

INDEPENDENT VARIABLES	SLOPE	T-SCORE
Political forces		
New Deal liberalism	−.868	2.53
Demand for abortion		
Black population	.062	1.76
Teen birth rate	.044	1.57
Related policy forces		
Family planning expenditures	−.953	2.38
Abortion funding	−.969	1.67
R^2	.24	
Adjusted R^2	.16	

Table 5.11 Determinants of Enforced Parental Involvement Policies

INDEPENDENT VARIABLES	SLOPE	T-VALUE
Advocacy groups		
Catholics	.049	3.01
NARAL membership	−.741	2.90
Political forces		
Party competition	−.071	4.92
Demand		
Teen birth rate	−.056	3.32
Other policy		
Family planning funding	−.440	1.75
R^2	.55	
Adjusted R^2	.49	

Parental involvement policies are adopted by conservative states with large black populations; they are also associated with states that do not spend money on family planning and have restrictive abortion funding policies. Since such states have slightly higher teen pregnancy rates, these states can be characterized as states with weak fertility control policies. Overall, however, the level of explained variance is low, and these findings should be considered at best tentative.

We extended this analysis by examining only those states with effective parental involvement policies—that is, those states that actually enforce these policies. The results of that analysis appear in table 5.11, where a pattern of morality politics is more evident. Interest group forces are active, with a positive relationship for the Catholic population and a negative relationship for NARAL membership. Enforced parental consent policies also exist in states with low levels of party competition. These states have lower levels of family planning funding and lower levels of teen pregnancy as well. This finding suggests that symbolic parental consent policies occur where needs are high but that enforced policies occur in states with lower levels of need.

CONCLUSION

Although the federal government establishes policy parameters, the states have a great deal of discretion in determining their own fertility control policies. Consequently, family planning and abortion policies vary greatly among the states. For example, states decide whether to use specific sources of public funds for family planning, what services to provide along with contraception, and who is eligible for services. They also decide whether to fund abortions for low-income women and whether parents must be involved in minors' decisions to terminate pregnancies.

The dynamics of state policymaking vary for different types of fertility control policies. Advocacy groups and political forces explain states' decisions to fund abortions, which, as we have noted, is exactly what one would expect in a highly salient but noncomplex policy area. It is worth emphasizing that NARAL membership is the strongest single determinant of abortion funding policy.

Even though parental involvement policies address abortion, the politics involved appear to differ from those of abortion funding policy. One major difference here is that most states (thirty-nine) have parental involvement laws, while only fourteen states fund abortion. Whereas advocacy groups help explain state decisions on abortion funding, they do not explain the presence of parental involvement laws.

Fewer states, but still most (thirty), enforce parental involvement in a minor's decision to have an abortion. At this juncture in policymaking, advocacy groups and political forces have a greater role in whether parental involvement law is enforced. Again, NARAL in particular appears to be very important. On the political front, states with more party competition tend to shy away from this controversial area.

The determinants of family planning policy differ from those of abortion policy. Here, policy choices are made in the bureaucracy. Making quiet bureaucratic decisions about which sources of public funds to use for family planning would not be possible if this were as salient an issue as abortion funding.

CHAPTER 6

The Outputs of Fertility Control Policies

THIS CHAPTER EXAMINES the immediate effects, or outputs, of fertility control policies. The first section discusses available data. Incomplete data have been a major issue in assessing family planning policy outputs, because for most of the 1980s and 1990s, the number of publicly subsidized family planning patients is unknown. On the other hand, there are two sets of national estimates of the number of abortion procedures for this period. The second section of this chapter examines the statutory or policy coherence hypothesis in terms of policy outputs. Here, we look at the interstate distribution of public family planning funds and at trends in national abortion data. The third section analyzes the determinants of state policy outputs. Because state family planning policies and abortion policies are so fragmented, we consider their outputs separately. In the final section, we examine the efficacy of state restrictions in curbing a particular policy output: state abortion rates.

AVAILABLE DATA
Family Planning Data
Number of Patients. The most direct measure of family planning performance is the number of patients served each year (Bogue 1970). From 1968 to 1981, the federal government collected or financed the collection of data on publicly subsidized family planning. Until 1977, all federally supported family planning clinics were required, and other clinics were encouraged, to participate in the National Reporting System for Family Planning Statistics (NRSFPS). As part of a budget-cutting move in 1977, the Carter administration converted this 100 percent reporting system to a sample system. The administration of NRSFPS was also decentralized, thus weakening the uniformity and quality of these patient data (Dryfoos and Doring-Bradley 1978).

In 1981, as part of the massive Reagan cutback of the National Center for Health Statistics, NRSFPS was terminated altogether. There was a privately funded patient data collection effort in 1983, but no national family planning patient data were collected again until 1994 (see table 6.1).[1] The 1994 patient

Table 6.1 Number of Patients Served by Publicly
Subsidized Family Planning

YEAR	PATIENTS (IN THOUSANDS)
1968	863
1969	1,070
1970	1,410
1971	1,889
1972	2,612
1973	3,089
1974	3,282
1975	3,924
1976	4,083
1977	4,215
1978	4,453
1979	4,486
1980	4,644
1981	4,609
1982	—
1983	4,966
1984	—
1985	—
1986	—
1987	—
1988	—
1989	—
1990	—
1991	—
1992	—
1993	—
1994	6,600

Sources: AGI 1981b (1968, 1970–79 data); AGI 1983a (1969,
1980, 1981 data); AGI 1984 (1983 data); Frost 1996 (1994 data).

data were collected in a one-shot survey rather than as part of an ongoing monitoring system (Frost 1996).

Family Planning Expenditures. Both national and state-level expenditure data are available by source of funding for most fiscal years between 1976 and 1994. Table 6.2 (p. 108) shows these expenditures. It is noteworthy that expenditures of the national family planning program (Title X) decreased by more than 12 percent between fiscal 1981 and fiscal 1982. Indeed, a decade passed before actual expenditures surpassed the 1982 levels.

Actual expenditures, of course, do not take into account the rising costs of providing services. Table 6.3 (p. 109) shows real public family planning expen-

Table 6.2 Public Expenditures for Family Planning Services (in millions of dollars)

Year	Title V (Maternal and Child Health)	Title X (Family Planning)	Title XIX (Medicaid)	Title XX (Social Services)	State Appropriations	Total
1976	20.2	89.5	37.6	30.1	22.3	199.7
1977	24.1	106.4	46.0	39.4	21.6	237.5
1978	19.4	129.7	35.9	54.4	32.1	271.5
1979	20.3	127.6	48.6	60.8	48.3	305.6
1980	20.8	153.1	69.6	55.0	48.6	347.1
1981	22.2	152.2	90.1	60.5	49.8	374.8
1982	16.6	118.1	94.2	46.2	53.1	328.2
1983	19.1	117.1	108.8	37.9	57.7	340.6
1985	23.1	133.5	137.1	40.1	63.9	397.7
1987	31.0	130.7	137.8	35.3	50.0	384.8
1990	27.1	111.8	190.0	34.3	139.8	503.0
1992	29.3	110.4	319.2	29.8	155.5	644.2
1994	34.1	151.1	332.4	33.6	161.9	713.1

Sources: Doring-Bradley 1977 (1976 data); AGI 1979a, 1979c (1977 data); AGI 1980a, 1979a (1978 data); AGI 1981b, 1981d, 1981c (1979 data); Nestor 1982 (1980, 1981 data); AGI 1983a (1982 data); Gold and Nestor 1985 (1983 data); Gold and Macias 1986 (1985 data); Gold and Guardado 1988 (1987 data); Gold and Daley 1991 (1990 data); Daley and Gold 1993 (1992 data); Sollom, Gold, and Saul 1996 (1994 data).

Note: Expenditure data were not collected for 1984, 1986, 1988, 1989, 1991, and 1993.

Table 6.3 Public Expenditures for Family Planning Services, Adjusted for Inflation (in millions of dollars)

Year	Title V (Maternal and Child Health)	Title X (Family Planning)	Title XIX (Medicaid)	Title XX (Social Services)	State Appropriations	Total
1976	38.8	172.1	72.3	57.9	42.9	384.0
1977	42.3	186.7	80.7	69.1	37.9	416.7
1978	31.4	209.9	58.1	88.0	51.9	439.3
1979	30.1	189.0	72.0	90.1	71.6	452.8
1980	27.8	204.4	92.9	73.4	64.9	463.4
1981	26.8	183.6	108.7	73.0	60.1	452.2
1982	17.9	127.7	101.8	49.9	57.4	354.7
1983	19.0	116.4	108.2	37.7	57.4	338.7
1985	20.4	117.6	120.8	35.3	56.3	350.4
1987	23.8	100.5	105.9	27.1	38.4	295.7
1990	16.6	68.7	116.7	21.1	85.9	309.0
1992	15.4	58.1	167.9	15.7	81.8	338.9
1994	16.2	71.6	157.5	15.9	76.7	337.9

Note: Adjustment for inflation was made using Medical Care Price Index (U.S. Bureau of the Census, *Statistical Abstract*, 1998, table 772, p. 489), 1982–84 = 100.

ditures for this period using 1980 dollars as a constant. The adjustment for medical care inflation reveals a pronounced decline in the capacity of the public sector to fund family planning services after 1981, one from which the national program has still not recovered. In real dollars, expenditures for family planning were higher in 1981 than they were in 1994, the most recent year for which expenditure data are available.

As discussed in chapter 5, the states differ widely in how they have used different sources of public funding. Overall, Medicaid has become the largest source of public funding for family planning, although there is considerable variation here. For example, Medicaid accounts for 71 percent of all public spending for family planning in Missouri and for only 16 percent in West Virginia. Similarly, Pennsylvania spends no state funds for family planning, but state funds provide nearly 50 percent of public funds for family planning in California (Sollom, Gold, and Saul 1996).

Dividing state family planning expenditures by their respective target populations permits a comparison of states' family planning efforts. The conventional target population for subsidized family planning services is "women at risk"[2]—that is, low-income, sexually active women who are not currently pregnant or trying to become pregnant (Dryfoos 1973; Torres, Forrest, and Eisman 1981; AGI 1988d). As can be seen in table 6.4, there are great differences among the states in public expenditures per woman at risk. In 1994, state family planning expenditures ranged from $40.17 in Vermont to $5.24 in Rhode Island.

Unfortunately, women-at-risk figures are estimated only periodically and are not available an annual basis. Time-series analysis, however, requires data for each year. In several analyses, in this chapter and in chapter 7, we have used total state population—which is available each year—as a proxy for women at

Table 6.4 1994 State Family Planning Expenditures per Woman at Risk and per Capita

	PER WOMAN AT RISK	PER CAPITA
Alabama	$30.45	$3.60
Alaska	8.84	1.15
Arizona	7.40	0.99
Arkansas	18.15	1.96
California	20.56	2.83
Colorado	9.72	1.38
Connecticut	20.28	2.84
Delaware	24.34	3.18
Florida	28.34	3.30
Georgia	18.49	2.46
Hawaii	14.87	1.92

Table 6.4 *(continued)*

	PER WOMAN AT RISK	PER CAPITA
Idaho	12.37	1.41
Illinois	12.59	1.65
Indiana	8.78	1.12
Iowa	16.84	1.90
Kansas	12.07	1.42
Kentucky	28.32	3.26
Louisiana	6.32	0.75
Maine	36.77	4.66
Maryland	23.35	3.16
Massachusetts	15.94	2.41
Michigan	18.92	2.48
Minnesota	19.49	2.52
Mississippi	31.58	3.57
Missouri	27.10	3.34
Montana	26.63	2.88
Nebraska	12.24	1.43
Nevada	23.21	3.40
New Hampshire	27.46	3.97
New Jersey	13.02	1.85
New Mexico	26.45	3.33
New York	39.10	5.53
North Carolina	24.25	3.08
North Dakota	21.17	2.38
Ohio	15.77	2.00
Oklahoma	21.59	2.39
Oregon	22.38	2.75
Pennsylvania	15.72	2.08
Rhode Island	5.24	0.74
South Carolina	32.50	4.01
South Dakota	10.01	1.10
Tennessee	15.58	1.91
Texas	27.99	3.63
Utah	13.95	1.78
Vermont	40.17	5.42
Virginia	30.82	4.05
Washington	16.80	2.22
West Virginia	28.28	2.94
Wisconsin	17.45	2.18
Wyoming	29.21	3.21

risk in order to standardize state family planning expenditures. The correlation between total family planning expenditures per woman at risk and total per capita expenditures is .97 for 1994. Therefore, little error results from using per capita data.

Abortion Data

Abortion data in the United States come from two sources: the Centers for Disease Control and Prevention (CDC) and the Alan Guttmacher Institute (AGI). The CDC abortion surveillance system involves cooperative relationships with vital statistics bureaus at state health departments.[3] Through this system, CDC is able to generate annual estimates of abortions performed in each state. The Alan Guttmacher Institute collects its abortion data directly from abortion providers. AGI's estimates are considered to be more complete abortion counts than CDC's, but they are not done every year. We used AGI's abortion data for the years in which they were collected. To provide estimates for the years when AGI did not provide state estimates (1983, 1986, 1989, 1990, 1993, and 1994), we used the Meier and McFarlane (1994) method of estimating abortion rates.

The estimation procedure is as follows. First, we calculated the ratio of abortions reported to CDC in 1983 to those reported in 1982. In this step, we recognized that the CDC data were biased because of underreporting (Jones and Forrest 1992), but we assumed that this bias was consistent from year to year. We interpreted this ratio as the annual rate of growth in each state for 1983. These abortion estimates were converted into rates. We then verified these rates by comparing them with later AGI data, making any corrections necessary based on a set of specific decision rules. We employed the same procedure to calculate rates for the other years in which AGI did not collect data.

Table 6.5 shows the annual number of abortions performed in the United States from 1973 to 1996. The absolute number of abortions remained fairly constant from 1980 to 1992, after which there was a decline. The abortion rate has followed a similar pattern, while the abortion ratio has declined very gradually over the same period.

STATUTORY COHERENCE
Family Planning

In chapter 3, we discussed the statutory coherence hypothesis; that is, *effective implementation is a function of a policy's structure*, or its *statutory coherence*. In that chapter, we also calculated the statutory coherence scores for each of the four federal statutes that fund family planning services. Title X showed the most statutory coherence (5), followed by Title XIX (1) and then by Title V (0) and Title XX (0).

Table 6.5 Number of Reported Abortions, Abortion Rate, and
Abortion Ratio

YEAR	ABORTIONS (IN THOUSANDS)	RATE[a]	RATIO[b]
1973	744.6	16.3	193
1974	898.6	19.3	220
1975	1,034.2	21.7	249
1976	1,179.3	24.2	265
1977	1,316.7	26.4	286
1978	1,409.6	27.7	292
1979	1,497.7	28.8	296
1980	1,553.9	29.3	300
1981	1,577.3	29.3	301
1982	1,573.9	28.8	300
1983	(1,575.0)	(28.5)	(304)
1984	1,577.2	28.1	297
1985	1,588.6	28.0	297
1986	(1,574.0)	(27.4)	(294)
1987	1,559.1	26.9	288
1988	1,590.8	27.3	286
1989	(1,566.9)	(26.8)	(27.5)
1990	(1,608.6)	(27.4)	(280)
1991	1,556.5	26.3	274
1992	1,528.9	25.9	275
1993	(1,500.0)	(25.4)	(274)
1994	(1,431.0)	(24.1)	(267)
1995	1,363.7	22.9	260
1996	1,365.7	22.9	261

Source: Reproduced with the permission of The Alan Guttmacher Institute from
Henshaw, S. K., "Abortion Incidence and Services in the United States, 1995–1996,"
Family Planning Perspectives, 1998, 30(6): 263–70, 287, table 1.

Note: Figures in parentheses are for years when AGI did not collect abortion data. These
figures were estimated by the interpolation of numbers of abortions for the preceding and
succeeding years.

a. Number of abortions per 1,000 women aged fifteen to forty-four.

b. Number of abortions per 1,000 pregnancies ending in abortion or live birth.

Within most federal policies, there is an inherent assumption, if not an
explicit mandate, that implementation should occur evenly across jurisdictions
(e.g., the states). In fact, the equitable distribution of statutory benefits can be
considered a condition of effective implementation. For example, the effective
implementation of pollution control policy would imply that similar standards

had been enforced throughout the target area. Similarly, the effective implementation of a redistributive social welfare policy would imply that all eligible persons had access to the program's benefits.

If interjurisdictional variation is a function of statutory coherence, then *we would expect that Title X would show the least variation in family planning outputs among the funding statutes, followed by Title XIX and then by Titles V and XX.*

To account for the respective size of each state population, we measured the policy outputs as annual family planning expenditures per woman at risk. We employed the coefficient of variation, a statistic that permits the comparison of the variances of populations with different means, to examine state variation in spending.[4]

We found that the data support the statutory coherence hypothesis (see table 6.6). Title X expenditures per woman at risk show the least state variation, followed by Title XIX (since 1979) and then by Titles V and XX. In other words, states are most alike in how they spend Title X funds, and they differ most in terms of the block grants. After 1982, the state variation in total public family planning expenditures (not shown in table 6.6) increased because a greater proportion of state family planning expenditures emanated from more discretionary federal grants and state appropriations than in the pre-Reagan era.

Abortion

In chapter 4, we found that the statutory coherence of national abortion policy has declined since the 1973 *Roe* decision (see table 4.3, p. 77). Allowing several years for start-up time for abortion providers after that decision, table 6.5 (p. 113) shows that both the number of abortions and abortion rates increased until 1981, the year after the Supreme Court's *McRae* decision allowed states not to pay for most abortions for Medicaid-eligible women. The number of abortions, abortion rates, and abortion ratios declined again within a few years of the *Webster* (1989) and *Casey* (1992) decisions.

The annual abortion data and the statutory coherence scores are in the same direction, but certainly factors other than statutory coherence have influenced abortion trends. For example, more effective contraceptive use may have decreased abortion rates. In the final section of this chapter, we rigorously examine the effects of state restrictions on state abortion rates.

DETERMINANTS OF STATE POLICY OUTPUTS

In chapter 5, we investigated the politics of fertility control policymaking in the states. Here, we examine the determinants of state policy outputs. For family planning, we look at expenditures from each grant type. For abortion, we also examine public spending. *We expect that advocacy groups, political forces, demand, and related policies influence the outputs of fertility control policies.* Because abortion is a more salient issue than family planning, *we expect that advocacy groups*

Table 6.6 Coefficients of Variation for State Family Planning Expenditures per Woman at Risk

Year	Title V (Maternal and Child Health)	Title X (Family Planning)	Title XIX (Medicaid)	Title XX (Social Services)	State Appropriations
1976	99.0	35.8	140.8	148.5	150.4
1977	104.5	34.7	134.8	112.3	184.3
1978	97.3	33.2	104.1	120.0	230.0
1979	97.5	31.6	96.4	105.7	196.7
1980	118.0	31.0	76.0	108.7	274.9
1981	142.7	23.4	76.0	109.8	268.3
1982	122.8	28.7	75.3	118.8	219.1
1983	104.6	28.6	73.1	135.0	135.5
1985	105.1	33.2	83.8	144.0	145.1
1987	132.0	29.4	81.7	156.8	121.3
1990	166.2	27.1	77.9	106.2	104.2
1992	107.2	44.2	55.5	176.8	139.1
1994	127.3	36.7	54.8	190.1	116.1

*and political forces influence public abortion expenditures more than they influence
public spending for family planning.*

Family Planning Expenditures

State spending for family planning is an amalgam of federal grants and state
appropriations. Nationally, federal monies dominate family planning funding.
In 1994, fully 77 percent of reported expenditures were from federal funds
(Sollom, Gold, and Saul 1996, 169). Each pertinent federal grant, however, has
its own political dynamics. For example, state-level advocacy groups have little
influence over Title X allocations, but they can push state agencies to allocate
more Title V and XX funds for family planning, and they can also encourage
state legislators to appropriate state funds for family planning.

Nationally, as we have already noted, the largest source of public family
planning funds is the Medicaid program. Many of the important Title XIX decisions (e.g., eligibility and range of services) are made at the state level. Because
this source of family planning funds is driven by its own dynamic, predicting
total state spending for family planning is difficult.

In most policy areas, funding for a previous year is a good predictor of funding for the current year, but state family planning expenditures are volatile. Table
6.7 shows the relationship between family planning expenditures in 1990 and
1994. The very modest correlation of .44 between per capita family planning
expenditures at the state level in these years is extremely low for a continuing
policy program. The correlation for Medicaid is an even lower .36, illustrating
that Medicaid funding and its volatility are a primary cause of this fluctuation.

Dependent Variables. The dependent variables analyzed here are those over
which the states exercise some control: family planning expenditures from state
funds per capita, block grant (Titles V and XX) expenditures per capita, and
Medicaid (Title XIX) expenditures per capita.

Table 6.7 Correlation Coefficients for State Family Planning Expenditures, 1990 and 1994

PROGRAM	CORRELATION COEFFICIENTS
All family planning	.44
Title XIX	.36
Title X	.62
Title V	.84
Title XX	.64
State funding	.74

Note: Measures are in expenditures per capita.

Table 6.8 Hypothesized Relationship between Independent Variables and State Family Planning Expenditures

INDEPENDENT VARIABLES	MEASURES	HYPOTHESIZED RELATIONSHIP
Advocacy groups	NARAL membership	Direct
	% Catholic	Inverse
Political forces	% Democratic legislators	Direct
	Party competition	Direct
	Conservative strength	Inverse
	New Deal liberalism	Direct
Demand	% female population that is black	Direct
	% female population that is Hispanic	Direct
	% female population that is employed	Direct
	% female population that is urban	Direct
Related policies	Prior year's family planning expenditures (incrementalism)	Direct
	Federal funding	Direct
	Medicaid generosity	Direct

Independent Variables. The independent variables are much the same as in chapter 5: advocacy groups (NARAL membership per 1,000 state population, percentage of the state's population that is Catholic), political forces (percentage of Democrats in both houses of the state legislature, party competition, conservative strength, New Deal liberalism), demand (percentages of female population that are black, Hispanic, employed, urban), and related policies (federal funds, state funds, Medicaid generosity). Table 6.8 shows the hypothesized relationship between each independent variable and state family planning expenditures.

Findings. Table 6.9 (p. 118) shows the regression results for per capita family planning expenditures from state appropriations. Catholics, NARAL membership, and Democrats are significant determinants of state funding for family planning. An examination of the regression diagnostics revealed that New York state was an overly influential case. Column 2 controls for New York. Here, the impact of federal funds and Catholics becomes negligible, while the impact of previous state expenditures becomes significant. Apparently, state support for family planning is incremental.

Our model for family planning expenditures from the block grants (Titles V and XX, not shown in table 6.9) yielded an R^2 of .18. The only significant predictors of these meager results are New Deal liberalism and conservative strength. The results for Medicaid family planning spending per capita (also not

Table 6.9   Determinants of 1994 Family Planning
Expenditures from State Appropriations

INDEPENDENT VARIABLE	COLUMN 1	COLUMN 2
Catholics	−.017	−.007
	(3.20)	(1.46)
NARAL membership	.451	.277
	(4.56)	(3.08)
Democrats	.014	.008
	(4.08)	(2.55)
Federal funds	−.106	—
	(1.67)	—
State funds 1990	—	.030
	—	(5.10)
New York	1.096	.517
	(2.48)	(1.45)
R^2	.49	.68
Adjusted R^2	.43	.63

Note: Figures in parentheses are *t*-scores.

shown) are somewhat better, but overall the model explains only 30 percent of the variation. The only positive and significant determinant is NARAL membership. Contrary to our hypotheses, the percentage of women living in urban areas and Medicaid generosity are negatively related to Medicaid spending.

Discussion. Given the moderate salience and noncomplexity of family planning as a public issue, we predicted that advocacy groups and political forces would influence state family planning spending. Here, we analyzed three types of discretionary state spending: state appropriations, block grants, and Medicaid. Advocacy groups, political party, and incrementalism are important determinants of family planning expenditures from state funds.[5] Apparently, however, advocacy groups and political forces have little influence on state decisions to spend block grant funds for family planning, but NARAL, which advocates primarily for pro-choice positions, is a significant determinant of Medicaid expenditures for family planning.

Publicly Funded Abortions

In this section, we examine the determinants of the actual outputs of state abortion funding policies.

Dependent Variables. We used two dependent variables to assess the outputs of state abortion funding policies for low-income women. The first, the funded abortion rate, is the number of abortions funded per 1,000 women aged

Table 6.10 Determinants of Funded Abortion Rate

INDEPENDENT VARIABLES	1985		1987		1990	
	SLOPE	STANDARD ERROR	SLOPE	STANDARD ERROR	SLOPE	STANDARD ERROR
Advocacy groups						
% Catholic	—	—	—	—	0	.0016**
Political forces						
Party competition	—	—	.0063	.0019	—	—
New Deal liberalism	−.0959	.0354*	−.0681	.0281*	−.0955	.0243*
Demand for abortion						
% black	.0086	.0034*	.0140	.0031*	.0040	.0017*
% Hispanic	.007	.0037**	.0058	.0028*	.0077	.0019*
Related policies						
Family planning expenditures	—	—	−.0672	.0348**	—	—
Abortion funding policy	.5588	.0625*	.6174	.0483*	.6430	.0366*
R^2	.76		.87		.93	
Adjusted R^2	.74		.85		.93	
F	36.45		46.58		113.19	

Note: Dependent variable is logged funded abortions per 1,000 women aged fifteen to forty-four.
$*p < .05.$ $**p < .10.$

fifteen to forty-four. The second, the funded abortion ratio, is the number of abortions funded per 1,000 live births.[6] Because both variables are highly skewed, a log transformation of each was used in the regression analysis.[7]

Independent Variables. We used the same independent variables as in chapter 5 to assess what impact abortion funding policy has on program outputs. To those independent variables, we added a dummy variable coded 1 if the state funded abortions in a particular year and 0 if it did not.

Findings. Table 6.10 presents the determinants of the number of abortions funded per 1,000 women aged fifteen to forty-four. The regression models perform well, explaining 76 percent of the variation in 1985, 87 percent in 1987, and 93 percent in 1990. A state's current abortion funding policy is the major influence on the funded abortion rate, but several other factors also influence that rate. In 1987, family planning expenditures are negatively associated with the funded abortion rate. In all three years, demand variables are important; the percentages of the population that are black and Hispanic are both positively related to abortion funding rates. Political factors also have some direct impacts

Table 6.11 Determinants of Funded Abortion Ratio

INDEPENDENT VARIABLES	1985		1987		1990	
	SLOPE	STANDARD ERROR	SLOPE	STANDARD ERROR	SLOPE	STANDARD ERROR
Advocacy groups						
NARAL membership	—	—	—	—	.0896	.0369*
Political forces						
Party competition	—	—	.0048	.0020*	—	—
New Deal liberalism	−.1308	.0714**	−.0690	.0293*	−.0561	.0248*
Demand for abortion						
% black	—	—	.0104	.0032*	.0037	.0022**
% Hispanic	—	—	.0059	.0030**	.0123	:0025*
Related policies						
Abortion funding policy	1.4450	.1256	1.6285	.0507*	1.6058	.0520*
R^2	.81		.97		.98	
Adjusted R^2	.80		.97		.98	
F	64.38		265.50		403.76	

Note: Dependent variable is logged funded abortions per 1,000 live births.
*$p < .05$. **$p < .10$.

on the funded abortion rate. In all three years, New Deal Liberalism is negatively related to the funded rate; party competition is positively correlated with the funded rate in 1987, an unexpected relationship. Striking in their absence are the advocacy group variables. Only the percentage of the population that is Catholic is related to funding policy, and only for 1990. A reasonable conclusion from this table is that advocacy group forces have little impact on the funded abortion rate.

Table 6.11 presents the determinants of the funded abortion ratio (number of abortions funded per 1,000 live births). The results here are generally similar to those in table 6.10. A state's policy on funding abortions for Medicaid-eligible women is the major determinant of the funded ratio. Demand factors continue to play a role, with positive impacts for the black and Hispanic populations in 1987 and 1990. Of the advocacy groups and political forces, only New Deal liberalism has a consistently negative impact on funding. Party competition again has an unexpectedly positive impact in 1987, and in 1990, NARAL membership is positively related to the funding ratio. The models predict very well, explaining 81 percent of the variation in 1985, 97 percent of the variation in 1987, and 98 percent in 1990.

Discussion. The determinants of state abortion funding policy, discussed in chapter 5, differ from factors associated with abortion funding levels. Once the policy to fund abortions is established, demand for abortions becomes a factor, even though demand has no impact on adopting a policy. On the other hand, advocacy groups, important in setting policy, have little impact on funded abortion levels.

The relationship of party competition to abortion funding policies and funded abortion rates and ratios merits discussion. Party competition is negatively related to the decision to fund abortions but positively correlated with the number of abortions funded. One explanation for this is that abortion funding policy is a combination of a morality issue and a redistributive issue. As a morality issue, competitive political systems should influence politicians to avoid funding abortions. Once abortion is funded, however, the number of abortions funded is influenced by the responsiveness of the political system to "have-nots." This explanation is consistent with the long-held theory that competitive party systems benefit the poor and the minorities. After passage, therefore, abortion funding should be considered a welfare issue rather than a morality issue. The consistently negative relationship between New Deal liberalism and levels of funded abortions also supports the notion of abortion funding as a welfare issue because New Deal liberals are economic liberals but social conservatives.

ABORTION POLICY RESTRICTIONS

Abortion funding policies are only one type of restriction exercised by the states. In this section, we examine a wide range of policy decisions that states made during the 1980s and early 1990s and analyze their effects on state abortion rates.

As noted in chapter 4, the Supreme Court's 1973 *Roe* v. *Wade* decision held that state governments could not regulate abortions performed in the first trimester of pregnancy and could regulate but not prohibit abortions in the second trimester. With subsequent court decisions (*Maher* v. *Roe* in 1977; *Harris* v. *McRae* and *Williams* v. *Zbaraz* in 1980), states gained control over whether to fund abortions for Medicaid-eligible women. The Court's rulings in *H.L.* v. *Matheson* in 1981 and *City of Akron* v. *Akron Center for Reproductive Health* in 1983 also gave states control over certain aspects of parental involvement in minors' abortions. The Court, however, uniformly struck down other restrictions on abortion until 1989, when it issued its *Webster* decision (McFarlane 1993).

Webster v. *Reproductive Health Services* is regarded as a pivotal case because the Supreme Court reversed its previous trend and upheld several state abortion restrictions. In turn, states responded with a wide array of restrictions, including waiting periods, postviability requirements, and abortion-specific "informed consent" (Halva-Neubauer 1990). In addition to permitting these new restrictions, the *Webster* decision allowed states to enforce a number of restrictions that were already on the books.

Here, we focus on whether state restrictions during an eleven-year period both before and after the *Webster* decision actually reduced the incidence of induced abortion. Abortion restrictions, like restrictions in other public policies, attempt to limit citizens' access to a good or a service (Blank, George, and London 1994; Medoff 1988; Meier and McFarlane 1993a, 1993b). Two general approaches are commonly used. First, a policy can seek to alter a person's decision calculus by either increasing the cost of a good or service or decreasing the benefits and, in the process, reduce demand. Second, a policy can attempt to restrict the supply of the good or service that is available. Most state abortion policy restrictions follow one or both of these general approaches.

Methods

The literature contains numerous models predicting state levels of abortion (Blank, George, and London 1994; Gohmann and Ohsfeldt 1993; Hansen 1980, 1993; Medoff 1988). Because virtually all these models are cross-sectional, they must control for all other factors that affect the incidence of abortion to provide a precise estimate of the impact of legal restrictions.

These models risk the possibility of showing that states with low abortion rates are the states that adopt subsequent restrictions. As a result, spurious findings are possible because omitted variables could be correlated with the adoption of restrictions. Because individual states' abortion rates are fairly stable (Blank, George, and London 1994; Hansen 1993), an obvious solution is simply to incorporate the abortion rate for the previous year into the models. This strategy indirectly controls for all factors that affect past abortion rates and forces additional independent variables to explain changes from past rates rather than the overall levels of state abortion rates. Because the passage of a law is a new event, it should predict future changes in the level of abortions if it has any impact on abortions.[8]

Design

We used a pooled time-series analysis of state abortion rates from 1982 to 1992 to determine the impact of state policies. Pooled time-series designs permit an assessment of relationships both across time and across states. First, we introduced a base model of abortion determinants in the fifty states to represent the factors influencing the level of abortions before the *Webster* decision. Second, we added to this model a series of measures that represent the states' efforts to restrict abortions. Third, because some restrictions were enjoined by the courts and therefore were not implemented, we replicated the analysis using only those restrictions that were actually enforced by the states.

Dependent Variable: State Abortion Rates

Our dependent variable is the number of abortions performed per 1,000 women aged fifteen to forty-four. We used AGI data for all years except 1983, 1986, 1989, and 1990, when AGI did not provide state estimates (Henshaw and Van Vort 1988, 1990, 1994). For these years, we used the Meier and McFarlane (1994) method of estimating abortion rates, described earlier in this chapter. The estimation of abortion rates for these years has two benefits: it permits the use of sophisticated pooled time-series techniques, and it allows a precise model to estimate the exact year when laws should have an impact. We used abortion rates by state of occurrence because they should be more sensitive to changes in law than are rates by state of residence, since women can travel across state lines to obtain an abortion.

A Model of Abortion Determinants

Our initial model-building strategy was to identify variables that would affect either the demand for abortion or the supply of abortions. We then tested and evaluated each of these factors while controlling for the previous year's abortion rate. We found four significant determinants.

Two of these are essentially indicators of the demand for abortion: the percentage of the population that is black and the rate of abortions funded for Medicaid-eligible women. Other factors that we considered, which did not significantly affect abortion rates in the presence of controls for past abortion rates, were unemployment, religion (percentages of Catholics and Christian fundamentalists), educational levels, proportion of the population aged eighteen to forty-five, income, female participation in the labor force, percentage of the population that is Hispanic, live birth rates, access to contraceptive technology, and marriage and divorce rates (Powell-Grinder and Trent 1987). Blacks have a substantially higher rate of abortions than do nonblacks, so changes in the black population are likely to affect abortion rates (Henshaw, Koonin, and Smith 1991). Funding abortions for Medicaid-eligible women quite logically increases the number of abortions performed because it removes one barrier to demand—namely, cost (Blank, George, and London 1994; Hansen 1993; Meier and McFarlane 1994). The measures are the percentage of blacks in the state population (taken from the U.S. Bureau of the Census) and the number of abortions funded per 1,000 women aged fifteen to forty-four[9] (Gold and Daley 1991; Gold and Guardado 1988; Gold and Macias 1986; Gold and Nestor 1985).

The other two significant determinants are related to the supply of abortions: urbanism and the number of abortion providers. Abortion rates are higher in urban areas simply because most providers are located in cities; 98 percent of abortions are performed in metropolitan areas (Henshaw and Van Vort 1990). The shorter the distance a pregnant woman has to travel to obtain an

Table 6.12 Determinants of Abortion, 1982–92

INDEPENDENT VARIABLE	MODEL 1		MODEL 2		MODEL 3	
	SLOPE	T-SCORE	SLOPE	T-SCORE	SLOPE	T-SCORE
Lagged abortion rate	.940	74.06	.935	72.74	.940	73.95
Black population	.018	2.23	.020	2.48	.018	2.23
Urban population	.022	3.35	.024	3.66	.020	2.99
Abortion providers	.037	3.42	.039	3.55	.039	3.50
Funded abortion rate	.230	1.94	.234	1.97	.249	2.07
Enforcement statement	—	—	−1.102	1.79	—	—
Enforced laws	—	—	—	—	.010	.28
Nonenforced laws	—	—	—	—	.094	1.12
R^2		.975		.975		.975
F		4202.96		3517.15		2999.31
Autocorrelation						
First order		−.01		−.01		−.01
Second order		−.04		−.04		−.05
White test						
5, 6, and 7 degrees						
of freedom		1.54		1.58		1.81
Probability		.91		.95		.97
No. of cases		550		550		550

Note: Dependent variable is abortions per 1,000 women aged fifteen to forty-four.

abortion, the more likely she is to have one (Shelton, Brann, and Shultz 1976). Abortion providers are not distributed uniformly in the United States. Where providers are lacking, women must either travel to another locality or carry the pregnancy to term. Although providers and urbanism are somewhat collinear, they are distinct enough to be used in the same model. The measures are the percentage of the population living in urban areas (taken from the U.S. Bureau of the Census) and the number of abortion providers per 1 million population[10] (Henshaw and Van Vort 1988, 1990, 1994).

We also considered a wide variety of political factors that might create a political climate either more or less favorable to abortion. These factors were the percentage of female legislators, the percentage of Democratic legislators, measures of elected officials' positions on abortion, required sex education in schools, state spending on Aid to Families with Dependent Children, and public spending for family planning. None of these factors added any predictive power to the base model.

The base model is shown as model 1 in table 6.12. Several aspects of the model are noteworthy. First, the fit of the model (97.5 percent of total variation) is good. Second, the dominant factor in the model is the past abortion rate. The other factors are related to abortion rates in the direction predicted by past research; that is, abortion rates are related positively to black population, urban population, the availability of providers, and the funded abortion rate. Third, pooled models are often susceptible to serious problems of autocorrelation (where the error terms are correlated) and heteroscedasticity (where the error terms are not constant for all values of the independent variables), both of which can distort the results (Greene 1993; Maddala 1992; Schroeder, Sjoquist, and Stephan 1986; Stimson 1985). We tested for autocorrelation by estimating the amount of first-order and second-order serial correlation. The residuals for each state were used to estimate autocorrelation one state at a time, and then these results were pooled. We assessed heteroscedasticity with the White test, using the entire pool. As shown by the diagnostics in the table, neither problem affects model 1. The lack of autocorrelation and heteroscedasticity is largely a function of lagging the dependent variable. Thus, by building in a state's past abortion rate, we controlled not only for unmeasured determinants of past rates, but also for two serious statistical problems.

What the States Did
We identified twenty-three different policy actions either enforced or unenforced that might have influenced the number of abortions. Except for laws designed to prevent violent protests at clinics, all policies were intended to reduce the incidence of abortion. By examining the Alan Guttmacher Institute's *Legislative Record*, we were able to determine the year each law went into effect and whether it remained in effect. We counted only laws adopted after 1982. With the notable exceptions of funding prohibitions and parental involvement requirements, nearly all state abortion restrictions adopted after *Roe* but before *Webster* would not have been enforceable. Before *Webster*, the U.S. Supreme Court struck down most state restrictions. However, these restrictions may have had other effects, such as discouraging women in those states from seeking abortions. Such effects should be incorporated in our model by the inclusion of prior years' abortion rates.

To make sure this assumption of nonenforceability did not affect our results, we replicated this analysis with all laws passed after *Roe* (Halva-Neubauer 1990) and obtained identical results. Except as noted below, each variable was coded 1 if the state had the law and 0 if it did not in a given year. (Changing the coding of all laws to dichotomous variables did not affect the results.) These laws are shown in table 5.7 (see pp. 94–95).

Although not all these laws place a burden on either the physician or the patient, we opted to be inclusive in our analysis rather than assuming that some laws would have no impact. Because we tested each law separately, each law received its own opportunity to influence abortion results. Thus, the impact of a law designed to reduce abortions was not diluted statistically by the presence of other laws.

The Impact of These Laws

Our strategy of analysis was to enter each law into the base equation separately and determine whether it was related significantly to state abortion rates. With twenty-three laws (variables) and a .05 level of significance, one would expect to find at least one significant relationship by chance alone; none were significant, however. We then entered all the variables into the base model simultaneously to determine whether they might have an impact jointly rather than as individual items. The joint F-test for significance was .85, with a probability of .67 (degrees of freedom = 23, 520). In short, none of the twenty-three policy actions either separately or together had any effect on the rate of abortions in the states that adopted these laws.

Not all the laws passed by the states remained on the books; many were passed in an attempt to determine how far the Supreme Court would let states go in regulating abortion. Some laws were challenged immediately in court, and enforcement of the law was enjoined pending the result of the court case. Laws that are passed but not enforced can still have an effect if an individual does not know about the injunction or the lack of enforcement. Even so, perhaps a better test would be to assess only those laws and policies that were not enjoined from enforcement. This does not mean that the laws were actually enforced (e.g., that consent from both biological parents was obtained before a minor underwent an abortion procedure), but only that there were no legal barriers to enforcement.

The results of assessing only the laws that were not enjoined were the same as the results for all laws. Not a single policy action had a significant negative impact on the abortion rate. One new enforcement-related item came close, however. If the state passed a law saying that it would enforce its abortion laws, that action had a negative impact with a probability of .07, barely missing our criterion for statistical significance (see model 2, table 6.12, p. 124). The model suggests that the adoption of an enforcement law results in a decrease of 1.1 abortions per 1,000 women, all other things being equal. Given the large number of variables tested, the minuscule improvement in prediction, and the failure to meet the .05 level of significance in this case, we are skeptical about this finding. Such a pattern could occur easily by chance at least once in examining almost fifty possible relationships; in fact, it would occur twice by chance alone. We also tested all the nonenjoined laws jointly and found that as a group they, too, did not affect abortion rates (F-test = .65, probability = .90).

One last possibility exists: that the impact of these laws occurs at the margins and that each of these impacts is rather small. A series of small impacts, however, could have a significant cumulative effect. In other words, what is important is not a specific restriction that a state imposes on abortion, but the total number of restrictions that it imposes. Any one restriction might not dissuade a woman from obtaining an abortion, but several at once might do so. To test this possibility, we summed the number of laws passed and not enjoined by each state. The total ranged from zero to thirteen. As another symbolic test, we also summed the laws passed but enjoined. The results of these tests are presented as model 3 in table 6.12 (p. 124). Not only is the impact of the restrictions not statistically significant; in both cases, the relationship is positive rather than negative. We find no evidence that state restrictions on abortions reduce the overall incidence of abortion.

Parental Involvement

While our findings are similar to Wetstein's (1995) national-level results, they stand in contrast to other reports that find an impact for some laws—notably, those involving parental involvement (see Cartoof and Klerman 1986; Ohsfeldt and Gohmann 1994; Rogers et al. 1991). These studies examined abortion rates for specific age groups (and only for single states in Cartoof and Klerman and in Rogers et al.). Only Cartoof and Klerman were able to control for past abortion rates (but not for other factors, such as providers). Because our study used an elaborate pooled design for all fifty states and controlled for the previous year's abortion rates, we believe our test is more rigorous and our findings more representative of the impact of abortion restrictions on the incidence of abortion.

To investigate the question of parental involvement further, we conducted several additional analyses. In our data set, parental notification was correlated negatively with abortion rates (parental consent was uncorrelated with abortion rates). This negative correlation disappeared when previous abortion rates were entered into the equation. We were able to find one ordinary least squares model that showed an impact for parental notification when the only other variables in the model were providers, percentage of the population that is urban, percentage that is black, and the funded abortion rate. This model, however, displayed severe autocorrelation problems (Rho = .82), which can cause nonsignificant relationships to appear significant. When we corrected the autocorrelation problem with an error components analysis (Greene 1993, chap. 16), parental notification declined to statistical insignificance. Similarly, when we conducted a least squares dummy variables model that specified a fixed intercept for each state, parental notification was statistically insignificant. Finally, a simple first-order autoregressive model with a correction for heteroscedasticity also resulted in an insignificant effect for parental notification. We conclude that even in a favorable model (i.e., a model with few controls and without a lagged dependent variable), when appropriate procedures are conducted to correct for problems inherent in pooled time-series analysis, parental involvement laws have no impact on overall state abortion rates.[11]

As a final test of whether parental involvement policies have an impact on the incidence of abortions, we predicted 1996 abortion rates by using AGI's 1992 abortion estimates and adding in parental involvement laws or just those parental involvement laws that were enforced. Despite the long lag time (four years should be plenty of time for any policy change to generate an impact), abortion rates in states with parental involvement laws (enforced or not) were no different from abortion rates in states without parental involvement laws. In short, using a wide variety of appropriate tests, we could find no evidence that parental involvement laws reduce the incidence of abortion.

Discussion

By allowing certain abortion restrictions to stand, the *Webster* decision encouraged states to enforce and enact more such restrictions. Our analysis of twenty-three separate policy actions over an eleven-year period found no evidence that these policies, either individually or aggregated, had an appreciable impact on states' abortion rates.

Although our findings are important, they do not refute the possibility that state policies can affect the rate of induced abortions. Indeed, our base model includes a restriction that can reduce a state's abortion rate—that is, a restriction on funding abortions for low-income women. The measure used in our model is the funded abortion *rate* (the number of abortions funded per 1,000 women aged fifteen to forty-four), which is a direct *outcome* of a state's funding policy. Every 100 abortions funded by the state resulted in an increase of 23 abortions. (The relationship is not 1.0 because many abortions are paid for with private funds if public funds are not available.) As noted in chapter 4, state funding restrictions were found to be constitutional a decade before the *Webster* decision.

Also important is the relationship between the number of providers and the abortion rate. Our model underscores Henshaw and Van Vort's (1994) suggestion that the national decline in abortion rates from 1989 to 1992 may be due to a decline in the number of abortion providers, particularly hospitals.

Other possible effects of post-*Webster* restrictions may not be captured by our outcome measure of state abortion rates. While state restrictions may not affect the annual abortion rates, these restrictions may delay abortions for some women (see Rogers et al. 1991). Although legal abortion is generally a safe procedure, the earlier an abortion is performed, the safer it is (Gold 1990). Women who delay abortion procedures face higher risks of morbidity and mortality.

Another possible effect of state abortion restrictions is that women living in states with restrictions may travel to states with more permissive abortion laws (Gold 1990). Our dependent variable, however—abortion rates by state of occurrence—should be more sensitive to this factor than abortion rates by state of residence would be. Yet because our analysis showed no effect of the restrictions with this more sensitive measure, we doubt whether these restrictions significantly altered existing patterns of travel.

In sum, the post-*Webster* restrictions did not have the immediate effects that pro-choice advocates feared and pro-life supporters anticipated. As Justice Blackmun predicted, *Webster* encouraged states that were so inclined to enact restrictions that would serve as test cases. Since 1989, rulings in other Supreme Court cases—*Hodgson* v. *Minnesota* (1990), *Ohio* v. *Akron Center for Reproductive Health* (1990), and *Planned Parenthood of Southeastern Pennsylvania* v. *Casey* (1992)—have upheld more state restrictions. Among the four restrictions upheld by the *Casey* decision was a twenty-four-hour waiting period. This restriction has been enforced and enacted in many states, and some anecdotal analysis suggests that it has an effect (Althaus and Henshaw 1994).

CONCLUSION

The measurement of state policy outputs is hampered by data availability. A major issue for family planning is incomplete data; there is no ongoing reporting system for the numbers of patients served. Therefore, we have relied on expenditure data to measure outputs. For abortion procedures, there are two sets of state estimates for the number of abortions performed. The annual figures from CDC are widely recognized to be an undercount, while the more complete AGI data are not collected each year.

Outputs from both family planning policy and abortion policy lend support to the statutory coherence hypothesis. The most coherent policy, Title X, produces the most evenly distributed spending for family planning throughout the states. While the same type of analysis could not be performed on abortion policy, trend data suggest that as abortion policy has become more restrictive, the annual number of abortions has decreased.

Because abortion is a more salient issue than family planning, we expected that advocacy groups and political forces from the hearing room scenario (Gormley 1986) would influence abortion policy outputs more than they would the outputs of family planning policy. Our findings from analyses of state family planning expenditures and funded abortion levels did not support this notion. Advocacy groups and political forces explained very little of the variance in state funded abortion rates and ratios, although these factors did explain a significant amount of the variance in family planning spending from state funds and Medicaid. What appears to be happening is that abortion funding policy is set in the hearing room scenario, influenced greatly by advocacy groups and political forces. Once the policy is decided, however, demand or need determines policy outputs. Such a pattern is consistent for a policy as it moves from a political to a bureaucratic environment. Once authorized to fund abortions, bureaucrats try to match funding with need. The modest results from the analysis of state family planning expenditures, as well as data issues, preclude us from drawing more comparisons between the respective dynamics of family planning and abortion funding policy outputs.

A pressing question regarding fertility control policy outputs is the effect of the numerous state abortion restrictions. We found no evidence that abortion restrictions, other than those that prohibit public funding, affect state abortion rates. We realize that this finding may be only a short-term effect; in the long run, abortion providers may not locate in states with certain restrictions.

CHAPTER 7

The Impact of Fertility Control Policies

THE PRECEDING CHAPTER discussed the policy outputs of family planning and abortion policies. In this chapter, we turn to the long-term effects, or impacts, of these policies. The first section reviews empirical work relevant to policy impacts. Because that body of work lacks a recent assessment of the health impacts of fertility control policies, the second section analyzes how publicly funded family planning and abortion affect public health. While the findings are reassuring to fertility control advocates, they do not provide sufficient guidance to legislators, who must vote on the four different statutes that fund family planning. Therefore, the third section analyzes whether different grant types or statutes are equally cost-effective in terms of producing health impacts. This analysis is guided by propositions from the intergovernmental grants literature, as well as by the Mazmanian and Sabatier model of policy implementation.

PREVIOUS STUDIES OF THE EFFECTS OF FERTILITY CONTROL POLICIES
Family Planning
The benefits of family planning are well known. By assisting people in planning their fertility and decreasing the incidence of unintended pregnancies, family planning services can reduce the number of abortions and unwanted births. Among the various studies that have evaluated the impact of publicly funded family planning services is one by Cutright and Jaffe (1976). Analyzing data from 1969 and 1970, these authors concluded that the U.S. family planning program reduced the fertility of low-income women by helping them prevent unwanted and mistimed births. In an analysis of 1980 data, Anderson and Cope (1987) documented that public family planning programs actually lowered fertility in areas that had such programs. Grossman and Jacobowitz (1981) and, subsequently, Corman and Grossman (1985) reported that organized family planning services reduced both infant and neonatal mortality rates.

Forrest and Singh performed cost-benefit analyses for the United States as a whole (1990b) and for California in particular (1990a). Their studies showed that for every dollar of public funds spent to provide contraceptive services, an average of $4.40 was saved in public-sector costs. The savings were more for states with relatively generous health and social service benefits. For example, in California, every dollar spent on family planning services resulted in a savings of $7.70.

A more recent study by Forrest and Samara (1996) examined the impact of publicly funded contraceptive services. The authors estimated that if publicly funded family planning services had not been provided in 1987, an additional 1.3 million unplanned pregnancies would have occurred. Moreover, 623,000 of these pregnancies would have ended in induced abortion, which would have increased the number of abortions nationally by 40 percent. Through the Medicaid program, federal and state governments would have spent far more on expenses associated with unplanned births and abortions. Forrest and Samara (1996, 188) estimated that for every dollar spent to provide publicly funded contraceptive services, an average of $3.00 was saved in Medicaid costs alone for pregnancy-related health care and medical services for newborns. This is a conservative estimate, since the study did not consider other substantial costs, such as the costs of welfare programs.

Abortion

A number of studies have looked at the impact of legalizing abortion. Grossman and Jacobowitz (1981) found that increased access to legal abortion was the most important factor in the large decreases in U.S. neonatal mortality from 1964 to 1977; the second most important factor was subsidized family planning services for low-income women. In a subsequent study, Corman and Grossman (1985) reported that increased availability of abortion was by far the most important factor in the decline in black neonatal mortality. For whites, however, abortion availability was only the fifth leading contributor to lower neonatal rates.

Abortion affects neonatal mortality by reducing the number of unwanted births. Women with unwanted pregnancies are less likely to receive early prenatal care, which may be associated with low birth weights (Joyce and Grossman 1990; Weller, Eberstein, and Bailey 1987; Marsiglio and Mott 1988; Currie, Nixon, and Cole 1993). By reducing unwanted births, access to abortion is indirectly associated with earlier prenatal care and higher birth weights. Both reduce neonatal mortality.

Not only does legalizing abortion have an impact on public health; the provision of public funding for abortion is cost-effective. A 1984 study by Torres et al. (1986) showed that in states where public funds were not available to pay for abortions for low-income women, more money was spent to provide benefits to women on Medicaid. This study found that for every dollar used to pay for abortions for low-income women, more than four dollars was saved in medical and social welfare costs over the next two years.

FERTILITY CONTROL FUNDING AND PUBLIC HEALTH IMPACTS

As noted earlier, the empirical literature lacks a recent assessment of whether public funding for fertility control actually produces public health benefits. This section addresses that question by analyzing the impacts of state funding policies for abortions and family planning during the period 1982–88.[1]

Whether pregnancies are intended or unintended is important for health outcomes. Obviously, women who have unintended pregnancies are more likely to seek induced abortions, but intended status is also important for pregnancies that are carried to term. Women whose pregnancies are planned are more likely to receive adequate prenatal care than are women experiencing unplanned pregnancies (Institute of Medicine 1995; Joyce and Grossman 1990; Weller, Eberstein, and Bailey 1987; Marsiglio and Mott 1988). Women with unintentional conceptions are more likely to smoke and drink alcoholic beverages during pregnancy (Institute of Medicine 1995). Smoking in particular is a risk factor for low birth weight and infant mortality (Shiano and Behrman 1995). In sum, *we expected that increasing the percentage of intended births reduces prenatal problems and results in healthier babies.*

Dependent Variables

State abortion rates (the number of abortions per 1,000 women aged fifteen to forty-four) are from the Alan Guttmacher Institute (Henshaw and Van Vort 1988, 1990). To provide estimates for 1983 and 1986, when AGI did not collect data, we used the Meier and McFarlane (1994) procedure described in chapter 6.

All other dependent variables are from the U.S. National Center for Health Statistics (1982–88). The measures are the teen birth rate (number of births per 1,000 women aged fourteen to nineteen), the percentage of babies with low birth weight (less than 2.5 kilograms), the percentage of premature births (less than thirty-seven weeks of gestation), percentage of births with no prenatal care or late prenatal care (defined as starting after the first trimester of pregnancy), the infant mortality rate (number of deaths among infants less than twelve months old per 1,000 live births), and the neonatal mortality rate (number of deaths among infants less than twenty-eight days old per 1,000 live births).

Independent Variables

The two major independent variables of interest are policies that fund abortions for Medicaid-eligible women and policies that fund family planning services for low-income women. The measure of abortion funding policy is the funded abortion rate (the number of publicly funded abortions in the state per 1,000 women aged fifteen to forty-four) (Meier and McFarlane 1993a, 1993b). The per capita family planning measure includes all federal (Titles V, X, XIX, XX) and state funds.[2]

Public policies on funding abortions and family planning are not the only factors that influence maternal and child health; numerous socioeconomic factors do as well. Precise estimates of the impacts of abortion funding and family planning policies on maternal and child health require that these other factors be included as control variables. For example, teen pregnancy rates and children born into poverty (a risk factor for child morbidity) are higher among blacks than among whites. Black women are also less likely than white women to receive adequate prenatal care (U.S. National Center for Health Statistics 1993). In addition, Henshaw et al. (1991) found that the abortion rate is 2.7 times higher for nonwhites than for whites, and Marsiglio and Mott (1988) found that blacks are much more likely than whites to have an unwanted birth. Hispanics also have higher abortion rates than do non-Hispanics (Henshaw and Silverman 1988). These relationships necessitated including both black and Hispanic population percentages in our model.[3]

States with fewer low-income women have fewer birth-related problems (Joyce 1987). Income is also related to abortion rates. Medoff (1988) found that women's participation in the labor force increases the demand for abortions (but see also Henshaw and Silverman [1988]). For these reasons, our model includes per capita income and the percentage of females in the labor force.[4]

The model also includes a proxy measure of a state's pro-life attitudes: the percentage of the state's population that is Catholic (Quinn et al. 1982). The Catholic Church has actively supported right-to-life groups and opposes abortion and most birth control methods (Meier and McFarlane 1993a, 1993b). We expected a negative relationship between the proportion of Catholics in a state and the rate of abortions.

The final control variable is access to abortion providers. Because we expected a positive relationship between access to providers and the abortion rate, our model includes the percentage of a state's population living in counties with large providers of abortion—that is, facilities that provide 400 or more procedures per year (Henshaw 1995).

Methods

The analysis is a pooled time series of all fifty states from 1982 to 1988. We examined the effects of abortion and family planning funding policies, as well as the effects of the control variables, on each of the dependent variables. As noted in chapter 6, a pooled time-series design is often plagued by problems of auto-correlation and heteroscedasticity (Hsiao 1986; Pindyck and Rubinfeld 1991). Although the current data set is cross-sectionally dominant, preliminary analysis revealed that first-order autocorrelation was the major problem. This problem dictated that all models be estimated using generalized least squares–autoregressive moving average models without forced homoscedasticity.[5] After initial model estimation, residuals were examined to determine if significant fixed effects were omitted from the model. As would be expected, individual states often deviated greatly from the model. To control for such influences, we added a series of state-dummy variables to the equations.[6] The note to table 7.1 (p. 137) lists the state dummies for each regression model.

Findings

The regression results for all variables appear in table 7.1. Because our concern is the impact of abortion funding and family planning expenditures, we do not interpret the coefficients for the control variables here. Most of these coefficients are statistically significant and in the direction predicted by previous research.

Abortion Rates. Our model predicts state abortion rates fairly well, yielding an R^2 of .89. Both policy impacts are as might be expected. A per capita increase of one dollar in family planning expenditures is associated with 1.046 fewer abortions per 1,000 women, consistent with the notion that effective family planning policies reduce the need for abortions. Similarly, each additional abortion funded by a state increases the number of abortions by .42.

Maternal and Child Health. The remainder of table 7.1 reveals a generally good level of prediction for the child and maternal health indicators (R^2 in all cases is greater than .69). Although there is no significant relationship between family planning funding and teen birth rates or premature births, family planning funding is significantly related to all other indicators. All other things being equal, each additional family planning dollar spent per capita by a state is associated with .049 percentage points fewer babies with low birth weight, .261 percentage points fewer births to mothers with late or no prenatal care, .159 fewer infant deaths, and .134 fewer neonatal deaths per 1,000 live births.

The public funding of abortions has somewhat different results. All other things being equal, an increase of one funded abortion per 1,000 women of childbearing age is associated with .673 fewer births per 1,000 teenage women. It is also associated with .024 percentage points fewer babies with low birth weight,[7] .027 percentage points fewer premature births, and .263 percentage points fewer births to women who have late or no prenatal care.

Two comments about the size of these coefficients are in order. First, publicly funded abortions are associated with a major drop in births to teen mothers—as many as .67 teen births for every abortion funded. Second, although many other impacts of abortion and family planning funding appear modest, even small changes in these variables can have a major impact.

Using the equations generated in table 7.1, we estimated the impact of publicly funded abortions and family planning expenditures in each state. To esti-

Table 7.1 Effects of Funding Policies and Control Variables on Abortion Rates and Maternal and Child Health: Pooled Estimates, 1982–88

				DEPENDENT VARIABLE			
INDEPENDENT VARIABLE	ABORTION RATE	TEEN BIRTH RATE	% LOW BIRTH WEIGHT	% BIRTHS PREMATURE	% BIRTHS WITH LATE OR NO PRENATAL CARE	INFANT MORTALITY RATE	NEONATAL MORTALITY RATE
Family planning funding per capita	-1.046 (5.47)	-.026 (.11)	-.049 (2.02)	.045 (1.03)	-.261 (1.88)	-.159 (2.29)	-.134 (2.29)
Funded abortion rate	.420 (4.76)	-.673 (7.81)	-.024 (2.73)	-.027 (2.83)	-.263 (7.56)	-.011 (.70)	.003 (.25)
% of population that is black	.110 (3.44)	.385 (10.87)	.105 (35.00)	.175 (39.08)	.069 (3.85)	.138 (21.33)	.130 (24.34)
% of population that is Hispanic	.394 (10.06)	.842 (25.15)	.022 (6.01)	.039 (9.59)	.457 (13.09)	-.006 (.79)	-.019 (4.10)
% of population that is Catholic	-.027 (1.24)	-.617 (24.86)	-.005 (2.48)	-.011 (2.96)	-.185 (13.13)	.001 (.16)	.018 (4.88)
Per capita income (in thousands)	-.217 (3.32)	.407 (5.41)	.009 (.99)	.058 (4.58)	.052 (1.16)	-.191 (9.48)	-.158 (9.43)
% of females in labor force	.076 (1.60)	-.255 (4.95)	-.059 (11.47)	.016 (1.60)	-.050 (1.39)	-.042 (4.06)	-.046 (5.84)
% of population with geographic access to abortion	.225 (17.57)	-.020 (2.14)	.003 (2.79)	-.006 (3.67)	-.003 (.49)	.005 (2.14)	.006 (3.23)

Buse R^2	.89	.79	.79	.84	.74	.69	.69
Adjusted R^2	.88	.78	.78	.83	.72	.67	.67
Rho	.40	.50	.60	.56	.71	.26	.29

Note: Coefficients are unstandardized regression coefficients; *t*-scores are listed in parentheses. Fixed effects for the equations above were estimated for the following states. *Abortion rate:* Arkansas, Connecticut, Delaware, Florida, Georgia, Idaho, Indiana, Kentucky, Maine, Maryland, Massachusetts, Mississippi, Nevada, New Mexico, North Carolina, Rhode Island, South Carolina, South Dakota, Utah, West Virginia, Wyoming. *Teen birth rate:* Colorado, Iowa, Kentucky, Louisiana, Maryland, Minnesota, Mississippi, New York, Oklahoma, Rhode Island, Utah, Virginia, Washington. *Low birth weight:* Alaska, Colorado, Hawaii, Nevada, Washington, Wyoming. *Premature births:* Connecticut, Hawaii, Kentucky, Maryland, Minnesota, Rhode Island, Washington, West Virginia, Wyoming. *Late prenatal care:* Arkansas, Iowa, Minnesota, New Mexico, New York, South Carolina, South Dakota, Utah, Oklahoma, Virginia, West Virginia. *Infant mortality:* Alaska, Arkansas, Illinois, Louisiana, South Dakota, Wyoming. *Neonatal mortality:* Alabama, Arkansas, Delaware, Illinois, Louisiana, Mississippi, New Hampshire, Washington.

Table 7.2 National Totals for Abortion Funding, 1982–88:
Impact on Number of Abortions and Birth Status

INDICATOR	STATES THAT FUND	STATES THAT DO NOT FUND
Number of abortions	+563,866	−503,778
Births to teenage mothers	−151,907	+136,499
Low birth weights	−21,255	+18,453
Premature births	−23,928	+20,760
Late or no prenatal care	−232,570	+201,907

Note: Figures do not include the District of Columbia.

mate the impact of state abortion funding policies, we multiplied the regression coefficients in table 7.1 by the actual funded abortion rate. We then translated the results from rates per 1,000 women or percentages to actual numbers. For states that did not fund abortions, we estimated what would have happened if the state had funded abortions. With all other state-level factors remaining the same, the mean funded abortion rate for states that actually funded abortions (4.97 per 1,000 women) was used for these states. These numbers suggest the impact of not funding abortions.[8]

Table 7.2 shows the national estimates. In states that funded abortions for one or more of the seven years under analysis, there were approximately 564,000 more abortions (an annual average of 80,557), 152,000 fewer births to teenage mothers (an annual average of 21,714), 21,500 fewer babies with low birth weight (an annual average of 3,000), 24,000 fewer premature births (an annual average of 3,429), and 232,500 fewer births to mothers who had late or no prenatal care (an annual average of 33,286) than there would have been in the absence of public funding for abortions. States that did not fund abortions had about 504,000 fewer abortions (an annual average of 72,000), 136,500 more births to teenage mothers (an annual average of 19,500), 18,500 more babies with low birth weight (an annual average of 2,643), 21,000 more premature births (an annual average of 3,000), and 202,000 more births to mothers with late or no prenatal care (an annual average of 28,857) than they would have had if those states had funded abortions for low-income women. The cumulative impact of funding or not funding abortions for Medicaid-eligible women over this time period was substantial.

Table 7.3 estimates the impact of 1982–88 family planning funding on abortions, low birth weight, late or no prenatal care, infant deaths, and neonatal deaths. We generated these estimates by calculating the actual amount spent per capita in each state and then transforming the predicted rates into raw numbers. The total number of abortions prevented (670,500) suggests that an absence of family planning funding would probably have increased the number of abortions during this seven-year period by about 6 percent nationally. Family

Table 7.3 National Totals of Benefits from Family Planning
Funding, 1982–88

INDICATOR	50-STATE TOTAL	AVERAGE ANNUAL 50-STATE TOTAL
Decline in low birth weights	20,025	2,861
Decline in late or no prenatal care	106,867	15,267
Decline in infant deaths	6,498	928
Decline in neonatal deaths	5,476	782
Decline in number of abortions	670,384	95,769

planning funds were also associated with 20,000 fewer babies with low birth weight and 107,000 fewer births to mothers who had late or no prenatal care. These two impacts likely explain family planning's impact on infant and neonatal mortality; family planning funding was associated with 6,500 fewer infant deaths and 5,500 fewer neonatal deaths. Although these numbers are dwarfed by the national totals for neonatal and infant deaths, they represent a significant spillover benefit, given that family planning is not directly targeted at infant mortality but at unwanted pregnancies.

Discussion

This analysis links public funding for abortion and family planning to public health benefits. States that fund abortions for low-income women have substantially fewer teen births and about one-fourth fewer cases of inadequate prenatal care than states than do not fund abortions. Because maternal age of less than twenty years and inadequate prenatal care are both risk factors for premature birth and low birth weight,[9] it is not surprising that abortion funding was associated with a modest reduction in each.

Publicly subsidized family planning services also produce public health benefits, though the dynamics are somewhat different from those of publicly funded abortion. Family planning funding is associated with fewer babies with low birth weight and fewer births to mothers with late or no prenatal care, and both these impacts reduce neonatal and infant mortality. In contrast to abortion funding, however, family planning expenditures show almost no effect on teen birth rates. Even though both abortion and family planning policies address unwanted fertility, their respective public health outcomes differ. These differences may be explained by clientele, delivery systems, and funding mechanisms.

Clientele. The characteristics of abortion and family planning patients contribute to different outcomes. Women having abortions are predominantly young, single, and of modest means (Gold 1990). More than half of all abortion patients are nulliparous (i.e., have not previously given birth) and have not previously experienced induced abortions (Henshaw, Koonan, and Smith 1991).

Many family planning patients are also young, single, and poor (Frost 1996; Frost and Bolzan 1997). However, we believe that during the period under analysis, it is likely that a greater proportion of teenage family planning patients had already experienced a live birth or a previous pregnancy than had teenage abortion patients. With the cutbacks in public funds for family planning during the 1980s, family planning clinics focused on serving existing patients. For the most part, there was no outreach to new patients and teenagers (Dryfoos 1989). Such a difference in parity would explain why family planning funding hardly affected the teen birth rate. However, without adequate patient data systems, we can only engage in suppositions.

Delivery Systems. Differences in the delivery of abortion and family planning services also contribute to their respective impacts on maternal and child health. For the most part, family planning clinics provide more continuous care and are more integrated with other health services than are abortion providers. When a woman receives services at a family planning clinic, she is expected to be a continuing patient. Moreover, a family planning patient has entered a health care delivery system where she will receive maternal and child health services or be referred to another health care provider as needed. In contrast, because most abortions are performed in clinics where abortion is the main service provided (Henshaw 1991), referral patterns are unlikely to be as well established as in a family planning clinic. A woman who receives an abortion is thus far more likely to receive only a single health service.

Family planning services are also more geographically accessible than are abortion services. Publicly subsidized family planning services are delivered through 3,119 provider agencies operating at 7,000 sites (Frost 1996), whereas 93 percent of abortions are provided in 1,339 nonhospital facilities. Family planning services are offered in nearly every county in the United States, while 32 percent of metropolitan areas and 86 percent of nonmetropolitan counties lack an abortion provider[10] (Henshaw 1998). This difference in the availability of services means that a woman seeking an abortion is far more likely than a woman seeking contraception to receive services outside her county or state of residence. This situation decreases the likelihood that an abortion patient will be successfully referred to another health care provider.

Funding Mechanisms. A third difference between abortion and family planning services is how they are financed. The states that fund abortions do so through state Medicaid programs, a fee-for-service funding mechanism whereby patients go to a health care provider for a single service. In contrast, even though Medicaid is now the largest single contributor to the national family planning effort, most family planning providers receive funds from a variety of public sources (Gold and Daly 1991). If the family planning agency receives *any* Title X funds, then it must provide an array of services, including appropriate referrals for other health services.

IMPACTS FROM DIFFERENT FAMILY PLANNING POLICIES

The preceding analysis examined the public health benefits of funding family planning and abortion services from 1982 to 1988, assessing the degree to which public expenditures for family planning and abortion improved maternal and child health, including unwanted fertility. While these findings are important, they do not provide sufficient guidance for policy design because the differential impact of various funding sources was not assessed.

The theoretical literature can provide guidance here. In political science, the Mazmanian and Sabatier model of policy implementation posits that program impacts are actually a function of policy construction. In public finance economics, the Gramlich typology of intergovernmental aid focuses on a single characteristic of distributive public policy and indicates that different grant forms produce different outputs.

Mazmanian and Sabatier's Policy Implementation Model

This model considers factors that affect program impacts. Indeed, Mazmanian and Sabatier hypothesize that both program outputs and outcomes are functions of policy construction (Mazmanian and Sabatier 1981, 1983, 1989). More specifically, a policy's *coherence* is directly related to the likelihood that statutory goals will be achieved (McFarlane 1989). The seven conditions for statutory coherence were discussed in chapter 3 (see fig. 3.1, p. 56).

Gramlich's Typology of Intergovernmental Grants

The single characteristic of distributive public policy on which the Gramlich typology focuses is the grant form used to allocate funding. Federal aid is divided into three types of grants: types A, B, and C (see table 7.4). Open-ended, matching grants, which reduce the relative prices of designated public goods and

Table 7.4 Intergovernmental Grant Mechanisms

GRANT TYPE	GRANT MECHANISM	PROCESS	EMPIRICAL RESULTS	EXAMPLES
Type A	Open-ended, matching	Reduces relative prices of grant-aided goods and services	Usually less additional spending than size of grant	AFDC, Medicaid
Type B	Closed-ended, unconditional	Changes income of subnational community; redistributive	Some tax reduction and expenditure increase, less than for type A	Revenue-sharing and block grants
Type C	Closed-ended, conditional	Requires expenditures for certain goods or services	Local spending roughly equal to size of grant	Title X

Source: Gramlich 1977.

Table 7.5 Statutes Authorizing Federal Funding for Family Planning: Grant Characteristics, Administrative Mechanisms, and Grant Type

STATUTE	GRANT CHARACTERISTICS AND ADMINISTRATIVE MECHANISMS	GRANT TYPE
Title V of Social Security Act (Maternal and Child Health and Crippled Children Act)	Closed-ended formula grants matched by the states; administered by state health departments	Type B
Title X of Public Health Service Act (Family Planning Services and Population Research Act)	Categorical legislation with project grants; may or may not be state agency–administered	Type C
Title XIX of Social Security Act (Medicaid)	Reimbursement of providers for services rendered to eligible clients; state agency–administered	Type A
Title XX of Social Security Act (Block Grant to the States for Social Services)	Block grant to state welfare departments; allocation based on state's population size	Type B

services for subnational governments, are *type A* grants; Medicaid is an example. *Type B* grants are closed-ended, nonrestrictive grants (e.g., revenue-sharing and block grants), which essentially raise the incomes available to lower levels of government but not the relative prices facing them. *Type C* grants are closed-ended, categorical grants, which provide monies for very specific purposes, thus altering both the relative prices and incomes facing the subnational governments that receive them (Gramlich 1977).

Gramlich discussed the differential performance of each type of grant. Federal open-ended, matching grants (type A) awarded to subnational governments, usually the states, generally result in somewhat less additional spending on the designated goods and services than the size of the grant. Type B grants stimulate more local spending, but the expenditure increase for these grants is less than for type A. Typically, the federal government establishes rather tight controls over the way type C grant money can be spent, so it is not surprising that categorical grants stimulate subnational spending by roughly the same amount as the grant (Gramlich 1977).

Empirical research showed that functional spending—meaning expenditures for specific program areas—varied by the type of intergovernmental grant. Gramlich encouraged researchers to extend their work on the outputs (e.g., expenditures) of federal grants to include the outcomes of such programs. Because all three grant types are employed by multistatutory federal policy, family planning affords such an opportunity.

The studies discussed earlier in the chapter did not explicitly consider whether different sources of funding might yield different cost-benefit ratios. That savings may differ by source of funding is suggested by a Los Angeles study (Radecki and Bernstein 1989) showing that family planning services funded by Medicaid were almost twice as expensive as those provided by publicly supported family planning clinics. A high proportion of the Medicaid services were delivered as part of the general practice of medicine rather than through specialized clinics; presumably almost all the publicly supported family planning clinics had at least some Title X money.

Whether different statutes or different kinds of grants are equally cost-effective is an important question for both policymakers and advocates. In an earlier study (Meier and McFarlane 1996), we showed that a dollar expenditure on family planning by Title X had more impact on maternal and child health in 1982–88 than did a dollar spent by a combination of the other sources of public family planning funds. In this section, we extend that work, examining whether family planning statutes that employ different grant mechanisms produce the same impacts (see table 7.5).

Hypotheses

Because it is a categorical program and a type C grant, *we expect that Title X is the most effective federal family planning statute in terms of producing desired impacts. We also expect that Title XIX,* an entitlement program and a type A grant, *is more effective in producing fertility and health benefits than are Titles V and XX,* the block grants (type B).

Dependent Variables

Unintended Pregnancies. As noted earlier, whether a pregnancy is intended or unintended is important for health outcomes. Women with intended pregnancies have higher rates of prenatal care, as well as lower behavioral risk factors for successful gestation. Although annual state data on unintended pregnancies do not exist, an increase in unintended pregnancies affects two measures for which data are available: the birth rate and the induced abortion rate.[11] We believe these are valid proxies. More than half of all unintended pregnancies end in induced abortions (Forrest 1994),[12] and 44 percent of all births in the United States are the result of unintended pregnancies (Institute of Medicine 1995). Our measures are the birth rate (number of births per 1,000 population) and the abortion rate (number of abortions per 1,000 women aged fifteen to forty-four).[13]

Maternal and Child Health. We used a single indicator of maternal and child health: infant mortality. Both the social science and biomedical literatures have documented that infant mortality is an important indicator of a population's

Table 7.6 Descriptive Statistics for All Variables

VARIABLE	MEAN	STANDARD DEVIATION
Dependent variable		
Birth rate	15.92	2.11
Abortion rate	22.25	9.73
Infant mortality	10.07	1.65
Independent variable		
Family planning funding per capita		
Title X	.58	.19
Title XIX	.59	.46
Titles V and XX	.22	.22
State funding	.27	.38
Control variable		
% of population that is black	9.53	9.14
% of population that is Hispanic	5.11	7.26
% of population that is Catholic	18.68	13.28
Per capita income (in thousands)	14.39	3.42
% of females in labor force	56.08	4.87
Funded abortion rate	1.39	3.00
% of population with geographic access to abortion	27.71	27.70

health status and well-being (Singh and Yu 1995). The infant mortality rate is the number of deaths among infants less than one year of age per 1,000 live births in that year.[14] The means and standard deviations for all variables are shown in table 7.6.

Independent Variables

Family Planning Funds. As discussed earlier, states may use four sources of federal funds for publicly subsidized family planning services. The best source of data for family planning funds is the Alan Guttmacher Institute, but, as noted in chapter 6, AGI does not collect data for every year. Because Title X funds are categorical—that is, specifically earmarked for family planning—an alternative source of annual data is available: the U.S. Domestic Programs Data Base (Bickers and Stein 1994). We relied on this source for total Title X funds per state for each year and on AGI data for the other sources of federal funding. When data were missing, we called the state agencies responsible for Title X implementation. In most cases, we had to follow up with calls to other state agencies, such as the welfare department or the health department. If the state agencies did not know the amounts of specific annual expenditures or when follow-up was unsuccessful, we interpolated to estimate missing data.[15] We converted these expenditure data to per capita expenditures in 1982 constant dollars. Since our concern was the relative impact of the various types of grant programs, we included per capita measures of Title X (type C), Title XIX (type A), and the combined total for Title V and Title XX (type B). Because some states also appropriate money for family planning expenditures, we included state funding as a separate category.

Control Variables. Unintended pregnancy rates and infant health are obviously influenced by a variety of forces besides family planning efforts. To get a precise estimate of the impact of the individual family planning policies, we controlled for these other forces. Perhaps the most important single influence on both unintended fertility and infant health is poverty.

About 14.5 percent of the U.S. population lives in poverty, and in this country, poverty and race are intertwined. The racial breakdown here is that 11.6 percent of whites, 33.3 percent of blacks, and 29.3 percent of Hispanics live in poverty (U.S. Bureau of the Census, *Statistical Abstract*, 1994, table 730). The racial composition of a state's population can affect the dependent variables in several ways. Overall, nonwhite women experience higher fertility rates than do white women (U.S. Bureau of the Census, *Statistical Abstract*, 1994, table 92). Consistent with higher rates of unintended pregnancy among women in poverty, unintended pregnancy is much more common among blacks than among whites (Institute of Medicine 1995). As noted earlier, black women are less likely than white women to receive adequate prenatal care, the percentage of children born into poverty is higher among nonwhites, and the abortion rate among nonwhites is 2.7 times higher than among whites (Sable et al. 1990; U.S. National Center for Health Statistics 1993; Henshaw 1992). For these reasons, our model includes measures of the percentages of the population that are black and Hispanic.[16]

More direct measures of poverty are per capita income and female participation in the labor force. The latter is related to a wide variety of improvements in maternal and child health (McFarlane and Meier 1992; Medoff 1988). We included both variables as controls in our model.[17]

Religion can have an indirect effect on pregnancy rates, as well as on maternal and child health. However, accessing annual information by state on religion in the United States is difficult; only for Catholicism is such information available. The official position of the Catholic Church is opposition to the use of artificial birth control. Though Catholics are just as likely as non-Catholics to use modern contraceptives (Goldscheider and Mosher 1991), the presence of Catholics in a state signifies at least monetary support for the Catholic Church. The Catholic Church supports a well-organized, national pro-life or anti-abortion effort that works in every diocese and congressional district. For the most part, this effort does not distinguish family planning from abortion; the Catholic Church is opposed to both (McKeegan 1992). Hence, our measure is the percentage of the state population that is Catholic (Garand, Monroe, and Meyer 1991).

Birth rates, abortion rates, and even maternal and child health are affected by the access of low-income women to abortion (Meier and McFarlane 1994). Several states fund all or most abortions for Medicaid-eligible women; other states rarely fund any abortions except in the most extreme circumstances. Our model includes each state's funded abortion rate.

The final control variable included in our model is geographic access to abortion. The first measure here is the number of abortion facilities in a state; the second is the percentage of a state's population living in counties with large providers of abortion (i.e., facilities in which 400 or more abortions are performed each year).

Methods

The analysis is a pooled time series of all fifty states from 1982 to 1991. Each dependent variable was examined as the result of the seven control variables, as well as of per capita family planning spending by Title X, Title XIX, the combined total of Titles V and XX, and state programs. Although the data set is cross-sectionally dominant, preliminary analysis revealed that first-order autocorrelation was the major problem. This problem dictated that all models be estimated using generalized least squares-autoregressive moving average models without forced homoscedasticity. After the initial estimation of these models, residuals were examined to determine if significant fixed effects were omitted from the model. As would be expected, individual states often deviated greatly from the model. To control for such influences, we incorporated a series of state-dummy variables into the equations.[18] In the case of abortion rates, the number of fixed effects was so large that we estimated the model with an error components procedure (Judge et al. 1985).

Findings

The impact of family planning expenditures on pregnancies (birth and abortion rates) and on infant mortality is shown in table 7.7. Because all family planning measures are in dollars per capita, the relative impact of the family planning programs can be compared directly. We do not interpret the coefficients for the control variables here because our concern is the impact of family planning funds rather than the determinants of fertility or maternal and child health.

Table 7.7 shows that every dollar spent by Title X in a state is associated with a decline of .594 births per 1,000 population. This impact is much larger than the size of the impact for other family planning funds. Title XIX has an impact of −.215, and Titles V and XX have an impact of −.317. State expenditures have an unexpectedly positive relationship with the birth rate. The reason for this is that state expenditures are highly skewed; most such expenditures occur in a few states with relatively high birth rates.

Table 7.7 Impact of Family Planning Expenditures and Control Variables on Birth Rate, Abortion Rate, and Infant Mortality

	DEPENDENT VARIABLE		
INDEPENDENT VARIABLE	BIRTH RATE	ABORTION RATE[a]	INFANT MORTALITY
Family planning funding per capita			
Title X	−.594	−3.162	−.544
	(2.19)	(2.13)	(1.88)
Title XIX	−.215	−1.128	−.315
	(2.96)	(3.27)	(2.29)
Titles V and XX	−.317	.089	−.417
	(2.20)	(.07)	(2.29)
State funding	.258	−.467	−.445
	(2.72)	(.90)	(3.77)
Control variable			
% of population that is black	.021	.096	.127
	(2.89)	(1.43)	(20.99)
% of population that is Hispanic	.147	.212	−.006
	(16.59)	(2.67)	(.90)
% of population that is Catholic	−.025	.005	−.006
	(4.75)	(.10)	(1.14)
Per capita income (in thousands)	−.016	−.104	−.189
	(1.10)	(1.40)	(11.90)
% of females in labor force	.023	−.148	−.045
	(1.98)	(1.98)	(4.14)
Funded abortion rate	−.039	.082	.002
	(1.84)	(.81)	(.10)
% of population with geographic access to abortion	−.003	.237	.047
	(1.09)	(8.57)	(1.91)
Buse R^2	.64	.26	.67
Adjusted R^2	.627	.24	.66
Rho	.62	.80	.34
Hausman specification test	2.64	2.54	1.06

Note: Coefficients are unstandardized regression coefficients; *t*-scores are listed in parentheses. Fixed effects controls for birth rate are Alaska, Florida, Hawaii, Idaho, Louisiana, North Dakota, South Dakota, Utah, West Virginia, Wyoming; for infant mortality, they are Alaska, Arkansas, Delaware, Illinois, South Dakota, Utah.

a. Abortion rate estimated with error components.

The equations for the abortion rate show a much different impact. Only Title X and Title XIX have significant impacts. The results are consistent with our hypotheses. The impact of Title X on the state abortion rate is nearly three times the impact of Title XIX. The infant mortality results show a somewhat more balanced impact. An increase of one dollar in Title X expenditures is associated with a .544 drop in the infant mortality rate. This impact is larger than the impacts for state funds (–.445), Title V and XX (–.417), and Title XIX (–.315).

Overall, our first hypothesis is consistently confirmed. Title X, the categorical grant program, is associated with the largest declines in the birth rate, abortion rate, and infant mortality. Our second hypothesis receives somewhat mixed confirmation. Title XIX consistently has a significant negative relationship with the birth, abortion, and infant mortality rates; it is the only program other than Title X that does. Title XIX does not, however, consistently have the second strongest impact; only for the abortion rate is that the case. Overall, however, the conclusion must be that Title XIX is the second most effective program. Finally, even the block grants, Titles V and XX, are associated with declines in the birth rate and infant mortality—not as strong as those for Title X but positive for public health nonetheless.

Discussion

The results of this analysis have implications for both policy and theory. By supporting our hypotheses, these findings corroborate Gramlich's observations about intergovernmental aid and extend empirical tests to program impacts. This analysis corroborates the findings in the second section of this chapter, demonstrating again that public family planning funds reduce unintended fertility and that these funds contribute to increased infant survival in the states. Our most striking results, however, are the differential impacts of the various federal family planning policies.

For every measure of maternal and child health or unintended fertility that we examined, Title X, the categorical program, was far more cost-effective than any of the other federal authorizations or state appropriations. We also found that the expenditure of a Medicaid dollar for family planning usually had a greater impact than did an outlay of a dollar from the block grants.

Program impacts do vary by grant mechanism, and those differences are consistent with our hypotheses. The most cost-effective way to fund family planning services, which does reduce unintended pregnancy and promote infant health, is through the categorical grant mechanism. The second best alternative is probably to use the type A grant, in this case, the Medicaid program.[19] Although block grant expenditures for family planning certainly produce benefits, they are the least cost-effective of the three grant types.

These findings also corroborate the statutory coherence hypothesis from the Mazmanian and Sabatier model of policy implementation. In chapter 3, we derived measures from Mazmanian and Sabatier's seven prescriptive criteria for effective policies (i.e., statutory coherence) and calculated statutory coherence scores for each of the four federal family planning statutes (see table 3.4, p. 61). The statutory coherence hypothesis would have predicted our findings about the impacts of different grant types.

CONCLUSION

This chapter has demonstrated that fertility control policies have positive and long-term health effects. All the policies that we examined produced positive impacts; nevertheless, the type of policy or funding mechanism employed does matter. While our findings lead directly to policy prescriptions, fertility control politics are unfortunately not as straightforward.

Public funds for both abortion and family planning contribute to improved health status, but differences in the public health outcomes of each present a strong argument for a more integrated approach to the delivery of both services. The fact that so many young women initiate family planning *after* an unwanted pregnancy certainly calls for a greater and more effective family planning effort. Recognizing that there is and will continue to be a demand for abortion, family planning providers need to be able to refer patients for this procedure and then integrate them back into family planning services. For many young and low-income women, family planning clinics *are* their health care delivery system. A political maneuver like the gag rule makes no sense from a public health standpoint; it simply deters integrated health care, which itself promotes good health outcomes.

In terms of producing positive health impacts, Title X is the most cost-effective way to fund family planning services. This finding will not surprise those familiar with publicly subsidized family planning services. Although there are no national data on service unit costs, a Los Angeles study (Radecki and Bernstein 1989) did show that Medicaid family planning services were almost twice as expensive as those delivered by Title X subsidized clinics. At half the price, a Title X dollar could certainly produce a greater impact. Furthermore, when a Title X grantee has other funding sources for family planning, Title X guidelines prevail. This regulation magnifies the impact of Title X.

Our second analysis supported hypotheses from Gramlich's typology of intergovernmental grants, as well as Mazmanian and Sabatier's statutory coherence hypothesis. Title X, which employs the most cost-effective grant mechanism, also has the highest statutory coherence score. Similarly, Title XIX, with the second most cost-effective mechanism, has the second highest statutory coherence score.

Are the three different grant types and statutory coherence measuring the same phenomena? To a large extent, the answer is affirmative. For example, categorical grants are more likely than type A and type B grants to have clear mandates and monitoring requirements, both of which are elements of statutory coherence. Block grants, by definition, usually have the least statutory prescription embedded in their authorizations. In general, statutory coherence provides more detail about the inner workings of a program, although the type of grant mechanism may be the single most important variable.

Ironically, the relative importance of Title X, the most efficient and effective way to fund family planning services, has diminished over the years. In 1982, Title X accounted for 43 percent of all federal expenditures for family planning and for just 27 percent in fiscal year 1994. Medicaid's proportion of federal family planning funding increased from 34 percent to 60 percent during the same period. The block grants (Titles V and XX) decreased from 23 percent of total federal family planning expenditures to 12 percent. Obviously, the federal government is not employing the most cost-effective mechanism to fund family planning services.

This trend, of course, is the result of politics, not policy analysis. During the 1980s, with a conservative presidency greatly influenced by the Christian Coalition (McKeegan 1992), Title X simply was not allowed to expand so that it could cover the needs of low-income women and keep up with inflation (McFarlane and Meier 1993b). In fact, Title X began the 1980s with a 25 percent cut, a result of Reagan's retrenchment efforts. Throughout the decade and the early 1990s, anti-abortion activists argued that Title X and Planned Parenthood of America fostered abortion and teenage promiscuity (McKeegan 1992).[20] Although many members of Congress were skeptical, they also feared the power of the anti-abortion movement and the Christian Coalition. As a result, Title X has not been reauthorized since 1985.

CHAPTER 8

Conclusion

THIS BOOK HAS traced the development and implementation of fertility control policies in the United States. We contend that the demand for fertility control is universal and that Americans are no exception in this regard. Because fertility control involves sexuality, morality politics come into play and may create poorly structured and unworkable policies. Our study has shown that the structure of laws matters in terms of both policy outputs and outcomes.

We began by looking at the history of fertility control. Abortion and family planning have been practiced throughout the ages and in every human society. Organized efforts to regulate and restrict abortion and family planning are not new. Indeed, a widely accepted explanation of why medieval witch-hunts occurred posits that they were attempts to curtail fertility control (Heinsohn and Steiger 1982).

In American history, public policy toward fertility control has been cyclic. In 1800, contraception and abortion were legal. During the course of the nineteenth century, both were outlawed, a situation that persisted until 1965 for contraception and 1973 for abortion. In both cases, legalization came about because of judicial decisions, not legislative actions, and long after public opinion supported a change in policy.

In concurring with the *One Package* decision in 1937, Judge Learned Hand recognized the reluctance of American elected officials to address such a delicate matter as birth control. He commented that legislative action might come "long after a majority would repeal [birth control restrictions], if a poll were taken" (*United States* v. *One Package* [86 F. 2d 737]). The history of fertility control, as it turns out, reveals a great deal about American politics in general and morality politics in particular.

Fertility control involves fundamental values relating to highly personal topics, such as sexuality, marriage, bodily integrity, and the definition of life. We have argued that morality politics influence both policy development and implementation.

In morality politics, advocates frame issues starkly, thus obfuscating their complexity. Issue frames, such as "sanctity of life" and "legal but discouraged," are attempts to simplify an issue and set the agenda in ways that benefit one side or the other. This scenario certainly plays out not only in abortion politics, but also in many family planning issues. Simple, value-laden, readily understood messages attract politicians and citizen groups, who appreciate their potential for wide appeal and often use them as "sound bites."

As with other morality issues, public pronouncements about fertility control frequently diverge from the private behavior of many, if not most, citizens. Politicians often confuse the public pronouncements of advocacy groups with actual public opinion. This confusion may lead lawmakers to support policies that are more extreme than the actual preferences of their constituents. An example is the bipartisan support for the Personal Responsibility and Work Opportunity Reconciliation Act of 1996. This so-called Welfare Reform Act states that the expected standard for sexual activity is a "mutually faithful monogamous relationship in the context of marriage" and that one should attain self-sufficiency before engaging in sexual activity. Recent sexual exposés imply that these are not necessarily standards that policymakers apply to themselves.

Morality politics also affect the implementation of fertility control politics. In this atmosphere of fundamental values and extreme positions, politicians find it hard to compromise, much less to design coherent fertility control policies. This lack of coherence has consequences. Both policy implementation theory and our own empirical findings tell us that the structure of a policy affects the likelihood of successful implementation.

Although abortion and family planning often share the same political winds, American family planning policy is separate from abortion policy. For the most part, abortion policy emanates from U.S. Supreme Court decisions, although in recent years, the Court has devolved more power to the states. Abortion policy is multifaceted and mostly regulatory, but one important redistributive element is whether states decide to fund abortions for low-income women.

Federal family planning policy in the United States is redistributive and consists largely of subsidizing services for the poor. Through the Food and Drug Administration, the federal government does regulate which contraceptive devices are allowed on the market for all women, but this regulatory process has not been a focus of this book. Our analysis of family planning has concentrated on the four federal statutes and state appropriations that fund birth control services for low-income women. With four federal statutes, three grant types, and fifty states, this is not only a complex case in policy implementation, but also an interesting one, both substantively and theoretically.

In the course of examining abortion and family planning policies, we used several well-known analytical models. These models of policy development, policy implementation, and intergovernmental transfers have yielded valuable insights into the dynamics of fertility control policies. In turn, we believe that this substantive policy area has validated and extended these models.

In terms of policy development, the "hearing room politics" of abortion predicted the decisions of forty-seven to forty-nine states (depending on the year) on whether to fund abortions for low-income women. Our explanations of state family planning policies are not as dazzling, but Gormley's model and the theory of morality politics allow for that deficiency as well: family planning is not as salient or value-laden a public issue as abortion.

In looking at both policy outputs and impacts, we turned to Mazmanian and Sabatier's well-known model of policy implementation, as well as Gramlich's typology of intergovernmental grants. In terms of family planning outputs, our major challenge was material, not theoretical. As noted in chapter 6, data on the number of patients served by public family planning funds have not been collected on an ongoing basis since 1981. Similar, but less severe, data issues are associated with abortion.

Our findings demonstrate that both abortion and family planning funds produce significant public health benefits. Often, these positive effects do not come to light in policy debates because topics associated with fertility control are too narrowly framed as morality issues. What is theoretically interesting about these findings is that the different grant types and statutes produced impacts in the same relative proportions as the Mazmanian and Sabatier and the Gramlich models predicted. What is substantively important is that the health impacts have been quantified for each grant type. Our hope is that these analyses will inform future policy debates.

POLICY IMPLEMENTATION OVER TIME

Although we set the stage with a long-term historical view, our focus has been on contemporary fertility control policies and politics. When possible, our analyses have taken up to a twenty-five-year perspective; thus, we have been able to see the development and implementation of policies over time.

In their treatise on policy implementation, Mazmanian and Sabatier also examine this process over time. They acknowledge the difficulty of "any implementation effort that goes against strongly held beliefs, long-standing practices, and potent political forces," especially considering "our rather fluid political system with its multiplicity of possible veto points." They observe that "there seems to be no routine or 'natural' progression to implementation." Policy implementation "may begin slowly or quickly, pick up or lose momentum, or pass through several cycles" (Mazmanian and Sabatier 1989, 276–77).

Mazmanian and Sabatier point out that the relative importance of factors in the implementation process changes in the long run. In the short run, "effective implementation is especially dependent upon the strength of the original statute" in terms of such variables as the clarity and consistency of policy directives, assignment to a sympathetic agency (or having a sympathetic official head of the program), and formal access for supportive constituencies. In the long run, Mazmanian and Sabatier (1989, 277) postulate that changing socioeconomic conditions and the ability of supportive constituency groups to maintain their organized presence are probably more important than the statutory variables.

We do not view the long- and short-term influences on implementation as discrete. Instead, we see all these factors as part of the same process. Over time, supportive constituency groups attempt to maintain favorable statutory conditions. At the same time, antagonistic constituency groups pressure the executive branch and legislators to alter or undermine those statutory conditions. Depending on the issue and its tractability, changing socioeconomic conditions can work for or against statutory changes.

Undermining Policy Implementation

The same factors that contribute to effective policy implementation can be turned around to undermine policy implementation. By juxtaposing the conditions of effective implementation, or statutory variables, with the signs of undermining a policy, table 8.1 illustrates this point. In chapter 3, we discussed the antipathy of the Reagan administration and many of its supporters toward family planning, particularly Title X. Although the administration did not have the congressional votes to terminate Title X, it was successful in weakening it.

The steps taken to undermine Title X were antithetical to policy coherence. If precise and clearly ranked objectives increase the likelihood that policy goals can be achieved, then the construction of conflicting objectives and ambiguous definitions will have the opposite effect. For example, by defining family planning so broadly that it included "natural family planning methods, adoption, infertility care and general reproductive health care, abstinence and contraception" (U.S. DHHS 1988, 2925), Title X lost focus and did not have priorities or clearly ranked objectives.

If the incorporation of a valid causal theory contributes to policy success, then amending a policy to include an inadequate theory will detract from policy success. The requirement that family planning programs include abstinence as a contraceptive method was such a ploy, since there was no evidence that family planning programs had been successful in discouraging sexual activity among their clients (Institute of Medicine 1995). Such a mandate consumed resources (e.g., staff time, client attention) that could have been better expended elsewhere.

Money is obviously a critical factor for program success. Not surprisingly, the Reagan administration vigorously pursued budget cuts for Title X, as well as for other federal programs that funded family planning (see table 3.2, p. 43;

Table 8.1   Statutory Variables for Effective Policy Implementation
and Signs and Examples of Undermining a Policy

STATUTORY VARIABLE	SIGNS OF UNDERMINING A POLICY	EXAMPLES OF UNDERMINING A POLICY (1981–92)
Precise and clearly ranked objectives	Construction of conflicting objectives and ambiguous definitions	Defining family planning as including adoption, infertility, and abstinence
Adequate causal theory incorporated into policy	Amendment of policy to include programs not based on adequate causal theory	Promotion of abstinence
Adequate funds provided to implementing organizations	Low budgetary requests for authorizations and appropriations	Budget cuts of 1981; no reauthorization of Title X since 1985
Few veto points in the implementation process; sanctions or inducements to overcome resistance	Requiring more decision points; reducing sanctions or inducements	Consolidation of many grantees under state health departments; favorable match for family planning eliminated
Decision rules biased toward achievement of statutory objectives	Developing decision rules that contradict statutory objectives	Regulations requiring parental involvement in minors' decisions to use contraceptives (e.g., squeal rule)
Implementation assigned to supportive organizations and individuals	Assigning policy implementation to an individual or agency that disagrees with policy goals	Appointment of a DASPA in fundamental disagreement with program goals
Participation of supportive outsiders encouraged	Participation of critical outsiders encouraged and of supportive outsiders discouraged	DASPA and staff meeting regularly with pro-life groups; not informing family planning advocates of new initiatives

table 6.2, p. 108). Both federal budget cuts and devolving authority to the states were part of a strategy to terminate or at least to curtail many social service and health programs.

If the number of veto points is inversely related to policy success, then increasing the number of veto points should undermine the national program. If providing policy inducements contributes to achieving statutory goals, then eliminating those inducements should detract from the program's ability to achieve its goals. By consolidating Title X grantees under state health departments, more decision makers (e.g., state health directors) were introduced into the implementation process. Adding more organizational veto points is the opposite of what Mazmanian and Sabatier would prescribe for effective implementation.

If the formal decision rules (e.g., regulations) of implementing agencies are consistent with statutory goals, then there is a greater likelihood of effective implementation. Conversely, if decision rules contradict or obfuscate statutory goals, then implementation will certainly be rendered less effective. The "squeal rule," issued by the Reagan administration, is an example of the latter. This regulation required that parents be notified when their minor children obtained family planning services from a Title X–funded clinic (McKeegan 1992). The squeal rule contradicted the intent of Title X, which stated that family planning services would be provided to women *in need* without regard to age. (The term *women in need* was changed to *women at risk* in 1981.)

Overestimating the importance of implementing officials who are committed to statutory goals is hard. Policy framers, however, usually find it difficult to write this assurance into legislation or a judicial opinion. By virtue of the power to make political appointments, the executive branch has leverage here. Supportive officials can be appointed to implement policies favored by the administration. Conversely, officials who disagree with policy goals can be put in charge of disfavored programs. During the Reagan-Bush years, each deputy assistant secretary for population affairs (the political appointee in charge of the Office of Population Affairs, which administers Title X) was adamantly anti-abortion and usually anti–family planning. For example, Marjory Mecklenberg, Reagan's first DASPA, had helped start the National Right to Life Committee (Gorney 1998; McKeegan 1992).

If statutory provisions or the current administration encourages the participation of supportive outsiders, then there is a greater likelihood of effective implementation. However, if an administration is antagonistic toward a policy, it can contribute to its demise by encouraging the participation of those opposed to the policy. The agency head—in this case, the political appointee—can affect which constituency groups have access to policy implementation. During the Reagan-Bush years, the various political appointees in the Office of Population Affairs met regularly with pro-life groups, while family planning advocates were largely shut out of this process.

Policy Cycles and Scenarios

Although there is no uniform pattern to a policy's life cycle, Mazmanian and Sabatier identify four general patterns: the Effective Implementation Scenario, the Gradual Erosion Scenario, the Cumulative Incrementalism Scenario, and the Rejuvenation Scenario. With the exception of the last, each scenario shows a policy implementation pattern over a twenty-five-year period.

The Effective Implementation Scenario characterizes many policies that "address a rather limited and well-defined set of problems and seek moderate changes in the status quo." Typically, policy advocates mobilize enough support to pass a statute that "establishes a new agency with substantial jurisdiction over the problem area." The initial agency staff is strongly committed to the program. Even if the original staff members leave, effective policy implementation continues because of the limited nature of the problem, strong public and advocacy group support, and continued backing from legislators (Mazmanian and Sabatier 1989, 278).

The Gradual Erosion Scenario characterizes the course of events for many policies that mandate significant behavioral change. Usually, the principal implementing agency is given extensive powers, but it must work through state and local governments to carry out the policy; there is thus ample room for interpretation and even defiance. Over time, the policy's supportive constituency may wither, "while opposition is vociferous, well organized, and persistent." In the short run, an able fixer—that is, a supportive public official who may be from any of the three branches of government (executive, legislative, judicial)— may be able to thwart efforts to weaken the policy (Bardach 1977). In the long run, conformity of the policy outputs with statutory objectives does decline and thus there is erosion in policy impacts (Mazmanian and Sabatier 1989, 279–80).

The Cumulative Incrementalism Scenario begins with a poor statutory base—that is, a weak policy that lacks statutory coherence. Over time, there is "a continual process of fine tuning, goal specification, constituency development, and an enhanced administrative apparatus which gradually brings a program into greater accord with the policy's intent." A federal agency usually directs state and local government agencies to produce this cumulative process. Even the gradual prodding of subnational units requires external monitoring of their activities, the development of increasingly precise indicators of their performance, the presence of a fixer, and an external support constituency. Mazmanian and Sabatier (1989, 280–81) point out that if all these conditions are present, even demanding statutory objectives can be achieved over time.

The last pattern, the Rejuvenation Scenario, combines two elements from the other scenarios: a poor statutory base from the Cumulative Incrementalism Scenario and a poor start-up from the Gradual Erosion Scenario. Mazmanian and Sabatier describe a longer time horizon for the Rejuvenation Scenario, thirty-five years instead of twenty-five. Within a few years, policy proponents may strengthen the statutory base, and initially they may dominate agency staffing. Eventually, unsympathetic public officials, such as presidential appointees or members of Congress, undermine their efforts. The agency administering the policy then settles into a long period of quiet and generally ineffectual activity. After a decade or more, changing socioeconomic conditions increase the number of proponents who try to strengthen the policy's statutory base. During this period of reform, the agency administering the policy becomes more aggressive in the pursuit of statutory objectives. "After several years, however, declining support and rising opposition means that the agency must again pursue more cautious policies, although the agency is not nearly as ineffectual as it was during the long period of inactivity" (Mazmanian and Sabatier 1989, 281–82).

Gradual Erosion or Rejuvenation?

Clearly, abortion and family planning policies are related. Both address unintended pregnancy, and we have demonstrated that public funding for family planning reduces the abortion rate. Moreover, both types of policies face many of the same constituency pressures. Nevertheless, family planning and abortion have had separate implementation patterns. We believe that federal family planning policy most closely resembles the Rejuvenation Scenario, while the course of national abortion policy up through the end of the twentieth century is best described by the Gradual Erosion Scenario.

Family planning policy began with a poor statutory base. In 1965, the Office of Economic Opportunity began to fund family planning services as part of the War on Poverty. OEO did not get specific statutory authority to include family planning until 1967, the same year that Congress added favorable family planning provisions to Titles IV-A and V.

The statutory base was strengthened in December 1970, when Congress passed Title X of the Public Health Service Act. Title X, the Family Planning Services and Population Research Act (PL 572), provided not only direct categorical funding for family planning services, but also an organizational structure for coordinating other sources of public funding for family planning. Dr. Louis Hellman, a well-respected obstetrician-gynecologist with a great commitment to family planning, was named DASPA. During the first few years that the legislation was in place, there was a flurry of activity to initiate and monitor programs in all fifty states. Congress strengthened the statutory base by adding family planning incentives to both Titles IV-A and XIX.

The downward slope in program support began between the fifth and tenth years of the policy cycle. Even though Congress was supportive, Nixon and Ford did not support strong federal mandates in domestic spending. In terms of organizational changes made by the administration and political appointments above the DASPA, the Carter years were also not particularly favorable for family planning, and the Reagan and Bush administrations were largely antagonistic toward it.

The 1992 election of Bill Clinton signaled a change for federal fertility control policy. Clinton submitted higher budgetary requests for Title X than had been the case for well over a decade. Political appointees, among them the surgeon general and the DASPA, were able to strengthen program implementation, including a one-shot, but long overdue, collection of patient data. However, the spillover of the contentiousness of abortion politics to family planning deliberations, as well as the 1994 election of the 104th Congress, meant that Title X was once again not reauthorized. Once again, the Office of Population Affairs had to pursue more cautious policies, although it was far more effective than it had been during the long period of executive disfavor.

In 1973, the *Roe* v. *Wade* decision legalized abortion across the nation. Being case law, *Roe* was not a particularly coherent policy. For example, no implementing agencies were created to monitor the quality of services provided or even to count the number of procedures. No money was allocated so that low-income women would have access to this service.

Mazmanian and Sabatier's description of the Gradual Erosion Scenario, in which the constituency supporting the policy gradually withers while the opposition becomes "vociferous, well organized, and persistent," is reminiscent of federal abortion policy. The *Roe* decision enervated the right-to-life movement. Within five years of that decision, the Hyde amendment effectively denied federal funding for abortions for low-income women, and although that amendment was for a while enjoined, the Supreme Court upheld it in 1980. In the short run, pro-choice abortion policy had at least one able fixer on the U.S. Supreme Court: Harry Blackmun, who, along with several other justices, was able to thwart opponents' efforts to weaken the *Roe* decision. Over time, the Court's composition changed, so that within less than two decades of *Roe*, the fixer's influence had diminished. Parental involvement was upheld, along with waiting periods and viability testing. These policy changes changed policy outputs. Fewer counties (2,042) had abortion providers in 1996 than in 1992 (2,380) or 1982 (2,908), meaning that 86 percent of American counties had no abortion provider (Henshaw 1998).

The fervor of the pitched battle continues in both legislative and judicial chambers. While a handful of pro-choice and pro-life groups have acknowledged the complexity of unintended pregnancy in their attempt to find some common ground (Gorney 1998), the abortion issue is usually framed in absolute moral terms. These simplistic frames make civil discourse, much less compromise, very difficult. The emergence of the partial birth abortion legislation at both the national and state levels represents yet another attempt to frame a complex issue in stark terms.

Our theory suggests that future fertility control policy, particularly abortion policy, will be a continuation of the past. The structure of morality politics is such that if they remain salient, the pattern of politics and policy will be very predictable. The politics will continue in the "no compromise" mode with little effort at fine-tuning policies to make them more effective. Both sides will continue a quest for the idea frame that will change the debate so that they have an advantage. Simplicity will continue to override complex issues, and actual policy analysis will contribute only at the margins, if at all.

POLICY RECOMMENDATIONS

Policy analysis is concerned not just with how things are, but also with how they might be. Several of our findings have implications for the design of effective public policy, and this section details our recommendations. As students of the political process, we are under no illusion that our policy recommendations are feasible at the current time. Still, policy analysts need to place their findings on the record so that if political realities change, advocates of reform will have an agenda to push.

To be effective, fertility control policies must be realistic. Policymakers must recognize the sequential steps in human reproduction: sexual intercourse, conception, and gestation and parturition (see fig. 1.1, p. 5). Abstinence forgoes sexual intercourse. Contraceptives prevent conception. Abortion terminates pregnancy. Although there are separate demand curves for sex, contraception, and abortion, all are related. What happens in one step affects sequential steps.

Don't Count on Abstinence

Public policies that promote abstinence are largely ineffective. Abstinence disallows sexual intercourse between women and men, and we maintain that the demand for sex is relatively inelastic. Our review of the history of fertility control did not identify a single population in which abstinence-only was an effective, long-term method of fertility control. Most Americans at risk of unintended pregnancy are beyond their teenage years, and many are married (Institute of Medicine 1995, 255). Public policy that promotes contraceptive use is far more efficacious than policy that promotes abstinence.

Most public abstinence messages are aimed at adolescents, and recent drops in teenage pregnancy rates have led politicians on both sides of the aisle to credit abstinence policies. There are, however, several problems with this conclusion. First, only about 20 percent of the decline in teenage pregnancy rates can be attributed to an increase in abstinence among teens (Saul 1999). Second, as Kirby (1997) has pointed out, there is little reason to believe that organized programs caused this change:

> Even though abstinence-only programs may be appropriate for many youths, especially junior high and middle school youths, there does not currently exist any published scientific research demonstrating that they have actually delayed (or hastened) the onset of sexual intercourse or reduced any other measure of sexual activity. Thus, at the present time, it is not known whether or not abstinence-only programs delay intercourse.

Moreover, many of the variables associated with teenage sexual activity (e.g., how many years of school an adolescent's mother has completed) are outside the scope of public policy. Third, we do not have enough reliable evidence for a sufficient period of time to conclude that such a change is permanent (Donovan 1998, Saul 1999).

Additional gains from the abstinence messages are unlikely. Individuals with relatively elastic demand curves for sex who are receptive to the abstinence message will forgo or delay sexual activity, but others are unlikely to be receptive to further abstinence appeals.[1] Abstinence can be part of a fertility control policy, and we certainly support learning more about its dynamics. Abstinence, however, cannot be the cornerstone of an effective fertility control policy.

Promote Contraception

Because most people of reproductive age are sexually active, we believe that fertility control policy should focus on contraception: contraceptive knowledge, contraceptive development, and contraceptive services.

Contraceptive Knowledge. Public policy should have a role in promoting contraceptive knowledge. Unfortunately, most Americans know more about the side effects of contraceptive methods than about their efficacy. More accurate knowledge would effectively lower the perceived price of birth control and increase the demand for contraception, which we maintain is quite elastic. Moreover, there is ample precedent for disseminating other health messages (e.g., regarding tobacco, illegal drugs, child immunizations, and AIDS transmission). It is time to shed the legacy of Comstockery.

Contraceptive Development. Public policy should continue to support contraceptive development. The decline in teenage pregnancy since the 1980s illustrates the importance of new methods. In 1988, neither Depo-Provera, the contraceptive injectable, nor Norplant, the contraceptive implant, was available in the United States. By 1995, one in ten sexually active teenage women at risk of unintended pregnancy was using one of these methods. Researchers at the Alan Guttmacher Institute have concluded that about 80 percent of the decline in overall pregnancy rates was due to improved contraceptive use (Saul 1999).

Contraceptive development should also include the dissemination of knowledge. Emergency contraception provides a dramatic example. Emergency contraceptives are methods of preventing pregnancy after unprotected sexual intercourse[2] (Trussell et al. 1997; Hatcher et al. 1998). "It has been calculated that each year the widespread use of emergency contraception could prevent over 1 million abortions and 2 million unintended pregnancies that end in childbirth" (Glacier 1997, 1058). Although this technology has been available for years, it has been underutilized. While every year 2 to 3 percent of American women of reproductive age have induced abortions, only 1 percent report ever having used emergency contraception (Grimes 1997). Within the last few years, there has been significant movement toward making emergency contraception more available in the United States. As recently as 1997, however, a public health editorial stated, "Women don't know about it, clinicians don't talk about it, regulators don't label it, policymakers don't endorse it, and pharmaceutical companies don't market it" (Cates and Raymond 1997). Clearly, there is a role for public policy in contraceptive development and dissemination.

Contraceptive Services. Public policy should promote the access of all Americans to contraceptive services. Unintended pregnancy rates in the United States are high compared with those in many Western European countries, not because Americans are more sexually active, but because Americans are less effective contraceptors (Jones et al. 1989). Public policy can improve this situation.

The implementation of family planning policy is targeted toward low-income and teenage women.[3] Given limited resources, this is an appropriate focus because these women face far more obstacles in obtaining contraception than do women who have greater means (including private health insurance). Consequently, low-income and teenage women have higher rates of unintended pregnancy and abortion (Abma et al. 1997; Gold 1990).

The current public family planning effort is woefully inadequate, and morality politics have made the delivery of family planning services more cumbersome. For example, Public Law 35 states that Title X grantees "shall encourage familiy [sic] participation," and Public Law 78 requires Title X grantees to certify that they encourage family participation. Some grantees even require minors to sign a separate form documenting that they have been given this directive information, a requirement that may discourage sexually active adolescents from seeking contraceptive care.

In 1994—the most recent year for which patient data are available—an estimated 40 percent of the 16.5 million low-income and teenage women at risk of unintended pregnancy received publicly subsidized family planning services (AGI 1997a). Another way of looking at the inadequacy of the public effort is that in 1994, total public expenditures for family planning were $713.1 million. The average public expenditure per woman at risk was $21.51, only a small fraction of the annual cost of providing contraceptive services.

How much it costs to provide family planning depends on the source of funding. We have demonstrated that Title X is a far more cost-effective way to fund family planning than through less direct means, such as Medicaid or Title V (see chap. 7).[4] We also maintain that categorical funding does not lead to fragmented health services; it just requires cost accounting.

Despite sustained political efforts to make it less coherent, Title X is the policy that best meets the criteria established by policy scholars for a successful implementation. As a focus of morality politics, however, Title X has not been reauthorized since 1985. We favor a long-term reauthorization of Title X with funding levels that are at least high enough to meet the demand for contraception (i.e., for women at risk). A long-term authorization is important because the management of the Title X program needs to be distanced from politics rather than being the daily focus of morality politics.

While we favor the expansion of Title X, we also believe that the program can be improved. Effective programs tend to be those with precise and clearly ranked goals, ample resources, and the discretion to apply expertise to the problem. Policy scholars also tell us that the management of effective programs should reduce the number of veto points or implementing agencies. Given that guidance, we recommend that Title X grants once again be competitive so that other agencies can vie with state health departments for the best way to deliver services. Title X also needs to support an adequate reporting system so that policy outputs are known.

We recommend that Title X's redistributive function remain preeminent as policymakers address whether Title X or another public policy should include persons other than "women at risk." We realize that Title X's original mandate was "to assist in making voluntary family planning available to all persons desiring such services" (PL 572). As we have already noted, however, low-income and teenage women have far more limited access to contraception than do women of greater means, and their unintended pregnancy rates are much higher.

While we are most concerned about redistributive efforts, we support regulatory initiatives for contraceptive access. Current data show that substantial numbers of women who are not low-income have unintended pregnancies (Abma 1997). Despite their higher incomes, timely access to contraception can still be problematic for these women, even those who have private insurance (Gold and Richards 1996; Gonen 1997). Recently, much attention has focused on the fact that private health insurance often does not cover contraceptives while other prescription drugs, such as Viagra, are covered (Goldberg 1999).

Be Realistic about Abortion

Abortion is a painful issue. No one likes it. Women who elect to terminate a pregnancy do not make this decision lightly. Most report that more than one factor influenced their decision. Among these factors are conflicting responsibilities, economic circumstances, and unstable relationships (Torres and Forrest 1988). Such complex factors ensure that the demand curve for abortion is highly inelastic.

Outlawing abortion would not change its price elasticity; it would only change the price. When abortion was illegal in the United States, many women took the risk of having an unsafe procedure, often performed by poorly trained, if not incompetent, operators. Abortions often failed, and maternal mortality was high. Evidence from Romania (Legge 1985) and other countries suggests that restrictions on access to abortion consistently generate efforts to circumvent the restrictions. These efforts may be as mild as traveling to countries that permit abortion on demand or as severe as abandoning unwanted children. Any policy that does not have the impact it is intended to have and in the process generates major, negative second-order consequences must be considered a failure.

Banning abortion would without question generate a black market in the service. Legal abortions in nearby countries would service some of the demand. As pharmaceutical methods became more effective, entrepreneurs in other countries would offer to sell such drugs through the mail (the thriving, but illegal, market in Viagra demonstrates how easily this could be done).

Given the inelasticity of the demand curve for abortion, the way to reduce the number of abortions is to decrease the incidence of unintended pregnancy. Contraceptive policies that prevent unintended pregnancy can reduce the demand for abortion in the United States. Our family planning research has shown that funding for contraceptives is negatively and significantly related to the incidence of abortions. If fertility control policies are to work, that means being realistic about sexual activity. Here, of course, is where morality politics come into play.

Symbolic Politics: Is There a Way Out?

In short, we favor public policies that would prevent most unintended pregnancy and, when necessary, would realistically address its consequences. However, we also realize that current American politics are unlikely to produce coherent fertility control policies. Indeed, the political debates surrounding birth control and abortion are often far removed from the circumstances of many women's lives.

Much of the political maneuvering that occurs around fertility control has few tangible consequences. For example, our findings in chapter 6 reveal that except for restrictions on abortion funding for Medicaid-eligible women, none of the various state-level restrictions had a statistically significant impact on state abortion rates. At the same time, abortion politics have generated more sound and fury than any other American political issue of the late twentieth century. The end result is a classic case of "symbolic" politics.

We expect symbolic politics to continue and quite likely to become even more divorced from actual problems in the policy area of fertility control. For example, despite the heated debates over partial birth abortion and whether to allow federal Medicaid coverage of pregnancies generated by rape and incest, these issues arise in relatively few cases. Such highly contentious and symbolic issues make good electoral politics but poor public policy.

Creating effective fertility control policies in a legislative context will not be easy. Human reproduction involves sex, and topics surrounding sex are the rubric of morality politics, not policy analysis. However, there are several ways that the dynamics of morality politics might be overcome.

First, our research has shown that advocacy groups can be a positive force. States with more NARAL members are more likely to fund abortions for low-income women. This finding leads us to believe that increased advocacy could lead to more effective fertility control policies, particularly at the state level.

Second, stressing the health benefits of family planning, particularly its capacity to dramatically reduce abortion rates, offers another way out of rigid morality politics. The evidence here is unequivocal, and advocates should reiterate these facts frequently. If the debate can be framed in terms of fewer abortions and healthier babies, politicians may find it difficult not to support family planning.

Finally, we suggest dialogue among those with divergent opinions. While many groups are polarized regarding fertility control issues, there are individuals (even in public life) who are capable of open exchange and even policy learning (Sabatier and Jenkins-Smith 1993). Such discussions will be most beneficial and less emotional if grounded in ethical precepts, which use human reason to assess what is right and wrong (Sheeran 1993). Our hope is that such dialogue will spill over and counteract the dynamics of morality politics.

Notes

CHAPTER 1 FERTILITY CONTROL POLICY: A THEORETICAL APPROACH

1. The figure is 21.5 for whites only.
2. Whether these individuals will also avoid sex is a separate question.
3. We do not consider totalitarian policies of coercion in relation to abortion or family planning. Legge's (1985) study of Romania suggests that the demand for fertility control is so strong that such policies will have major second-order health consequences.
4. This position is held by 88.9 percent of men and 93.5 percent of women.
5. For abortion, payment may well involve transportation costs because the number of abortion providers is decreasing; in many geographic areas, abortion is not available even to those who can pay the cost of the procedure.
6. Fourteen states currently fund abortions for low-income women.
7. Obviously, contraceptive technology and abortion involve some highly technical issues, but these are not the issues that drive the policy adoption process. For the most part, fertility control issues have been framed to focus on results rather than on the technical issues.
8. Emergency contraception refers to postcoital contraception that can be used within seventy-two hours of unprotected sexual intercourse to avert an unintended pregnancy. Emergency contraceptives are not abortifacients; they do not terminate a pregnancy, which is medically defined as the implantation of a fertilized egg (Grimes 1997). Rather, they prevent implantation from occurring. Emergency contraceptives available in the United States are emergency contraceptive pills, minipills, and the copper-T intrauterine device (IUD) (Trussell et al. 1997; Hatcher et al. 1998). Mifepristone, when taken by itself, is an effective abortifacient 65 to 80 percent of the time. When combined with a prostaglandin, such as misoprostol (which has been approved in the United States as an ulcer medication), mifepristone produces a nonsurgical, or "medical," abortion in approximately 95 percent of women when used up to forty-nine days after the last menstrual period (Population Council 1999).
9. Clearly, the Title X program would be better served by looking at the prevalence of unplanned pregnancy within a given population and measuring the impact of a grantee's services. Grantees report that this type of outcome measurement would be particularly important in negotiations with managed care organizations when demonstrating the "value" of their covering contraceptive services.

CHAPTER 2 CONTRACEPTION AND ABORTION: A HISTORICAL OVERVIEW

1. Crocodile dung has no spermicidal properties. The later substitution of elephant dung, which is more acidic, would have improved contraceptive effectiveness (Himes 1970, 62).
2. "Rue is a traditional abortifacient among the Hispanic people in New Mexico and has been used as a tea for abortion purposes throughout Latin America" (Riddle, Estes, and Russell 1994, 32).
3. Albert believed that if a woman would spit thrice in the mouth of a frog or eat bees, she would not become pregnant.
4. Europe's population shrank from 80 million to 60 million between 1320 and 1400; between 1350 and 1450, the English population decreased by 60 percent (Heinsohn and Steiger 1982, 197).

5. The reason for using this population is simply that vital statistics for this group are far more accurate than for women of color or immigrant women (Brodie 1994).
6. Increasing birth intervals among married couples in certain communities suggest the use of this practice (Brodie 1994).
7. *Coitus reservatus* is coitus without ejaculation (Himes 1979, 127).
8. The "social purity" movement included dozens of organizations of men and women interested in promoting temperance and Sunday closing laws, controlling prostitution, ending white slave traffic, and suppressing obscenity (Brodie 1994, 261–62).
9. These states were Colorado, Indiana, Iowa, Massachusetts, Minnesota, Mississippi, Missouri, Montana, Nevada, New Jersey, New York, Pennsylvania, Washington, and Wyoming.
10. These states were Colorado, Indiana, Iowa, Minnesota, Mississippi, New Jersey, New York, North Dakota, Ohio, Pennsylvania, and Wyoming.
11. These states were Colorado, Idaho, Iowa, and Oklahoma.
12. This growth in female participation in the labor force continued a trend from the nineteenth century. Between 1870 and 1900, the number of women working outside the home increased from 1.8 million to 5.3 million (Dienes 1972, 76). Between 1910 and 1920, the proportion of women in nonmanual jobs increased from 17 to 30 percent, "and work outside the home became socially acceptable" (Reed 1978, 59).
13. In 1939, the American Birth Control League and the Birth Control Clinical Research Bureau merged to form the Birth Control Federation of America. In 1942, the Birth Control Federation was renamed Planned Parenthood Federation of America, Inc.
14. *One Package* did not completely end Comstockery. In 1940, the Connecticut Supreme Court of Errors upheld a state law that made the use of contraceptives illegal and denied any exception for physicians (Planned Parenthood 1992).
15. Not very many states took advantage of the opportunity afforded them in 1942; by 1958, only seven states (Alabama, Florida, Georgia, North Carolina, South Carolina, Mississippi, and Virginia) were using maternal and child health monies to provide birth control services and then only in token fashion (Jaffe 1967, 146).
16. In 1985, the risk of death was 0.4 per 100,000 legal abortions compared with 6.6 per 100,000 births (Gold 1990, 28).

CHAPTER 3 FAMILY PLANNING POLICIES: AN INTERGOVERNMENTAL LABYRINTH

1. By 1973, four states (Alaska, Hawaii, New York, and Washington) had already guaranteed a woman the right to choose for herself whether to terminate her pregnancy (Tribe 1992, 49–50).
2. These services include child care, foster care, family planning, employment, and health (AGI 1974, 31).
3. The AFDC welfare program was replaced by Temporary Assistance for Needy Families (TANF) in the mid-1990s.
4. Child Health Act of 1968 (PL 248).
5. DHEW was changed to the Department of Health and Human Services (DHHS) in 1977.
6. The gag rule was a duly promulgated regulation; that is, it went through the entire federal rule-making process. Technically, then, this regulation had to be repealed and replaced through the legally established process of "notice and comment" (AGI 1993f; Kerwin 1999). To date, the process has not been completed. This neglect of the rule-making process by the Clinton administration worries family planning advocates because another president could easily reinstate the gag rule.

7. The health care industry receives payments from Medicaid, so it would not be supportive of converting this entitlement program into a block grant. Moreover, unlike welfare, Medicaid functions as a middle-class subsidy in the financing of nursing home care. The cost of nursing home care is exorbitant and is for the most part not covered by Medicare, but it is covered under state Medicaid programs. However, Medicaid eligibility depends on spending down one's savings. Increasingly, the middle class has viewed Medicaid as an entitlement, a way to protect life savings. "Thus families transfer funds from the elderly person to the other members of the family so that the elderly person can become eligible for Medicaid," which saves the family from having to pay for their relative's long-term care (Patel and Rushefsky 1995, 98; Anton 1997, 707). Support for Medicaid from health care providers and many middle-class persons, along with public opinion that is generally more supportive of health subsidies than of welfare (Schlesinger and Lee 1993), may explain why AFDC was blocked while the larger Medicaid program was not.

Chapter 4 Abortion Policy

1. The Hyde amendment was passed in 1977, but it was enjoined and not enforced until after the Supreme Court's ruling in *Harris* v. *McRae* in 1980.
2. When it issued this requirement in February 1995, ACGME specifically exempted residents who had moral or religious objections to abortion (AGI 1995g).

Chapter 5 State Fertility Control Policies

1. *Categorically needy* individuals are those who would have qualified for welfare cash assistance under AFDC even though it has been replaced by TANF. *Medically needy* recipients are those who meet the nonfinancial standards for Medicaid eligibility but whose income or resources are in excess of AFDC cutoffs (Andrews and Orloff 1995; U.S. DHHS 1996a).
2. Except for a handful of training grants, including grants for nurse practitioners.
3. In 1991, the Medicaid program was administered by the welfare department in thirty-one states, by the health department in six states, by a combined health and welfare department in seven states, and by a specialized agency in six states.
4. DHHS Region I (Boston) administers funds for Connecticut, Maine, Massachusetts, New Hampshire, Rhode Island, and Vermont. Region II (New York City) administers funds for New Jersey, New York, Puerto Rico, and the Virgin Islands. Region III (Philadelphia) administers funds for Delaware, the District of Columbia, Maryland, Pennsylvania, Virginia, and West Virginia. Region IV (Atlanta) administers funds for Alabama, Florida, Georgia, Kentucky, Mississippi, North Carolina, Tennessee, and South Carolina. Region V (Chicago) administers funds for Illinois, Indiana, Michigan, Minnesota, Ohio, and Wisconsin. Region VI (Dallas) administers funds for Arkansas, Louisiana, New Mexico, Oklahoma, and Texas. Region VII (Kansas City) administers funds for Kansas, Iowa, Missouri, and Nebraska. Region VIII (Denver) administers funds for Colorado, Montana, North Dakota, South Dakota, Utah, and Wyoming. Region IX (San Francisco) administers funds for Arizona, California, Hawaii, Nevada, and the Pacific Basin. Region X (Seattle) administers funds for Alaska, Idaho, Oregon, and Washington.
5. In 1999, the federal poverty levels were $8,240 for a nonfarm family of one person; $11,060 for a nonfarm family of two persons; $13,880 for a nonfarm family of three persons; $16,700 for a nonfarm family of four persons; $19,520 for a nonfarm family of five persons; $22,340 for a nonfarm family of six persons; $25,160 for a nonfarm family of seven persons; $27,980 for a for a nonfarm family of eight persons; and $2,820 for each additional family member.

6. A *capitated system* is a payment system in which providers receive a given allocation per person; if the provider can deliver services at lower costs, the difference can be kept as profit.

7. Title X grantees are required to provide client education; counseling, including both contraceptive method and special needs; history, physical assessment, and laboratory testing; fertility regulation; infertility services; pregnancy diagnosis and counseling; adolescent services; treatment and referral for sexually transmitted diseases; and identification of estrogen-exposed offspring. Title X guidelines recommend, but do not require, that grantees provide gonorrhea screening, treatment of minor gynecologic problems, genetic screening and referral, and health promotion and disease prevention. The guidelines also suggest that Title X projects offer some reproduction-related health services— prenatal care, postpartum care, and special gynecologic procedures (e.g., colposcopy and biopsy)—if appropriately skilled personnel and equipment are available (U.S. DHHS 1981, 9–15).

8. The procedures used by HMOs to send statements to heads of households may reveal that a family planning service was provided to a minor (Gold and Richards 1996, 26).

9. These states are Idaho, Illinois, Iowa, Virginia, and Wisconsin.

10. These states are California, Connecticut, Hawaii, Maryland, Massachusetts, Minnesota, Montana, New Jersey, New Mexico, New York, Oregon, Vermont, Washington, and West Virginia.

11. The states that enforce parental consent or notification laws are Alabama, Arkansas, Delaware, Georgia, Idaho, Indiana, Iowa, Kansas, Kentucky, Louisiana, Maine, Maryland, Massachusetts, Michigan, Minnesota, Mississippi, Missouri, Nebraska, North Carolina, North Dakota, Ohio, Pennsylvania, Rhode Island, South Carolina, South Dakota, Utah, Virginia, West Virginia, Wisconsin, and Wyoming. States that have parental involvement laws on the books but do not enforce them are Alaska, Arizona, California, Colorado, Illinois, Montana, Nevada, New Mexico, and Tennessee.

12. These states include Arkansas, Colorado, Illinois, Iowa, Kansas, Minnesota, Nebraska, South Carolina, Virginia, and Wisconsin.

13. These states are Delaware, Illinois, Iowa, Maine, North Carolina, Ohio, South Carolina, and Wisconsin.

14. Title X was then and remains the most evenly distributed funding (McFarlane 1989; McFarlane and Meier 1993b).

15. This has been the case since 1981, when Arizona became the fiftieth state to develop its own Medicaid program, which is known as ACCESS.

16. Some states include rape or incest as reasons for Medicaid funding of abortions, but so few abortions are performed for these reasons that this restriction can be viewed as identical to the mother's life-endangerment restriction. A more elaborate classification of funding policy can be found in Weiner and Bernhardt 1990.

17. Abortion policy data for 1990 are from Gold and Daley 1991; 1987 data are from Gold and Guardado 1988, 231; 1985 data are from Gold and Macias 1986.

18. Data on church membership are from Quinn et al. 1980. The following churches were identified as Protestant fundamentalist: Church of God, Church of Jesus Christ of Latter Day Saints, Church of Christ, Church of the Nazarene, Mennonites, Conservative Baptist Association, Missouri Synod Lutherans, Pentecostal Free Will Baptists, Pentecostal Holiness, the Salvation Army, Seventh Day Adventists, Southern Baptists, and Wisconsin Synod Lutherans.

19. Data on partisanship are from U.S. Bureau of the Census, *Statistical Abstract of the United States,* 1990 and earlier editions.

20. All data are from U.S. Bureau of the Census, *Census of Population,* 1980.
21. In 1996, North Carolina ceased funding abortions.

CHAPTER 6 THE OUTPUTS OF FERTILITY CONTROL POLICIES

1. An exception to this observation is a 1991 study by the Centers for Disease Control and Prevention that collected patient data solely from Title X clinics. This study, of course, missed publicly subsidized patients who were served in non–Title X settings (Smith, Franchino, and Henneberry 1995). For completeness, we also recognize that the Association for State and Territorial Health Officers (ASTHO) collect patient statistics for persons receiving family planning services provided by state and local health agencies only. These data are not complete or comparable. An example of the incomplete nature of these figures is that in 1983, only forty states provided data (California, the state with the largest population, was not among them), and in 1984, only thirty-three states did (California and Texas, another of the most populous states, were among the missing ones).

2. The term *women in need* was used from the late 1960s until 1981, when it was changed to *women at risk.* Notwithstanding the change in terms, only slight modifications over time have been made to the methodology for estimating target populations for publicly subsidized family planning services (Dryfoos 1973, 1975; AGI 1981b; AGI 1988d, vii–xi).

3. Vital statistics bureaus of state health departments report births and deaths to the National Center for Health Statistics, which is not part of CDC.

4. The coefficient of variation is the standard variation divided by the population mean (Ott 1977). This statistic is required because each of the four statutes has a different annual appropriation.

5. In this case, the incrementalism was examined over a two-year period because state family planning expenditures were not available for 1993.

6. Funded abortion data for 1990 are from Gold and Daley 1991; for 1987, they are from Gold and Guardado 1988, 231; and for 1985, they are from Gold and Macias 1986. We calculated the number of women aged fifteen to forty-four by taking the number of women reported in the 1980 *Census of Population,* aging these population figures to get the appropriate year (1985, 1987, 1990), and further adjusting them to account for migration to the state. The data on live births are from U.S. National Center for Health Statistics 1982–88.

7. The rate and ratio measures all had standard deviations twice the size of their respective means. All measures had a large positive skew. To avoid problems with states that funded no abortions, we added a constant of 1 to each rate and ratio before making the log transformation.

8. Wetstein (1995) employs a similar logic in his ARIMA model of national abortion rates, in which he controls for past abortion rates by differencing the dependent variable.

9. The rate of abortions funded in this data set is correlated with public policy in regard to funding at .85. We used the funded rate rather than announced policy because the former captures the nuances of policy, such as the limited amount of funds allocated in states like North Carolina.

10. Abortion funding rates and abortion providers may not be exogenous; that is, the abortion restrictions also might affect these variables directly or indirectly. To determine whether the inclusion of these variables in the model influenced our results, we replicated table 6.12 but omitted abortion funding and abortion providers. The results were identical to those presented here.

11. The decreases found by other researchers in single-state studies may well be balanced out by increases in other age groups. The number of abortions performed on minors is a relatively small proportion of the total.

CHAPTER 7 THE IMPACT OF FERTILITY CONTROL POLICIES

1. During the period of study (1982–88), the Hyde amendment prohibited the use of federal Medicaid funds "unless the life of the pregnant woman is at stake" (AGI 1993q).
2. AGI data on funded abortions and family planning are available for 1982, 1984, 1985 (Gold and Macias 1986), and 1987 (Gold and Guardado 1988).
3. Data are from U.S. Bureau of the Census, *Statistical Abstract of the United States,* various years. For the Hispanic population, individual years had to be extrapolated from the 1980 and 1990 census data.
4. Data are from U.S. Bureau of the Census, *Statistical Abstract of the United States,* various years.
5. Homoscedasticity is "the assumption in linear regression that the size of the errors is not affected by the size of the independent variables" (Meier and Brudney 1997, 45).
6. As expected, the dummy variables improved the fit of the regression line and reduced the autocorrelation. Their inclusion had little impact on the substantive interpretation of either family planning or abortion funding. The apparent impact was to reduce the size of these coefficients; the result was a conservative estimate of impact compared with the ordinary least squares estimates. For low birth weights, we included specific time-point dummies for 1987 and 1988 to correct for time-dependence problems.
7. This finding contradicts Currie, Nixon, and Cole (1993), who found no impact on birth weight. Their model used individual-level data and estimated models using least squares dummy variables. Our inclusion of regional and year dummy variables might have eliminated the impact of state laws, since states that fund abortions do cluster in some regions. We also used a more precise measure of abortion funding.
8. The ecological analysis presented here cannot rule out the possibility that other factors caused these changes, but any such changes would have to be collinear with either funded abortions or family planning expenditures.
9. Teen mothers, especially low-income ones, are less likely than older mothers to receive adequate prenatal care (Singh, Torres, and Forrest 1985). The Institute of Medicine (1995) has noted that "maternal age is an especially important risk factor. . . . Girls under 15 are a particularly high risk group. Except for the very youngest women, however, being a teenager probably does not have an independent impact on the risk of having a baby with a low birth weight. Most of the increased risk probably comes from other factors associated with teenage pregnancy such as low socioeconomic status, poor nutrition, and late or no receipt of prenatal care."
10. Metropolitan areas that provided fewer than fifty abortions per year were counted as not having an abortion provider (Henshaw 1998).
11. We use the total birth rate rather than birth rates by age groups as our dependent variable. Meier and McFarlane (1994) found that family planning expenditures do not affect teen birth rates. If family planning funding affects birth rates in any age group, however, it should also show up in the birth rate for all age groups.
12. The Forrest analysis did not include miscarriages because "the number of pregnancies ending in miscarriage is not well established and because there is no information on the distribution by intention status" (Institute of Medicine 1995, 25). The proportion attributed to each outcome changes, of course, when the incidence of miscarriage is estimated. About 12 percent of pregnancies will end in miscarriage (Gold 1990, 11).

13. Data on total state births are from U.S. National Center for Health Statistics, *Vital Statistics of the United States,* various years. Population data are from U.S. Bureau of the Census, *Census of Population,* annual updates. Except for 1983, 1986, 1989, and 1990, all abortion data are from AGI (Henshaw and Van Vort, 1988, 1990, 1994). To provide estimates for other years, we used an interpolation procedure similar to that of Meier and McFarlane 1994; these estimated data can be obtained from the authors.

14. All data on infant mortality are from U.S. National Center for Health Statistics, *Vital Statistics of the United States,* various years. Additional measures were considered. However, data that measure known risk factors for infant mortality, such as late prenatal care and low birth weight (Institute of Medicine 1985, 1988), were not available for the last three years of the study because of the lag time in the publication of national vital statistics. Similarly, state-level data measuring neonatal mortality, a major component of infant mortality, were not available. These factors are all related to infant mortality, so infant mortality is probably the best overall indicator of child health.

15. Title X data were available for every year (Bickers and Stein 1994). Other family planning data are from the Alan Guttmacher Institute. For specific citations of individual years, see note to table 6.2 (p. 108). We interpolated data for the missing years by averaging data from the year before and the year after.

16. Data are from U.S. Bureau of the Census, *Statistical Abstract of the United States,* various years. For the Hispanic population, individual years had to be interpolated from the 1980 and 1990 census data.

17. Data are from U.S. Bureau of the Census, *Statistical Abstract of the United States,* various years.

18. We ran the Hausman specification test to compare the fixed effects models with random effects models. In each case, the insignificant result suggests that the fixed effects model is the appropriate one. The dummy variables, as expected, have a substantial impact on the fit of the regression line and reduce the degree of autocorrelation. Their inclusion does not have much impact on the coefficients that indicate the impact of family planning. If anything, the introduction of state effects appears to reduce the size of the family planning coefficients; the result is a conservative estimate of the impact compared with the ordinary least squares estimates.

19. Because Medicaid is an insurance program, its impact in a state will depend on the cost and quality of care delivered by the amalgamation of Medicaid providers.

20. In fact, Title X has forbidden the use of its funds for abortion since 1970, when it was first enacted. During the 1980s, the national office of Planned Parenthood Federation of America (PPFA) became a vocal advocate of freedom of choice in the abortion debate. Because of this and because many PPFA affiliates were Title X grantees, the anti-abortion movement tried to link Title X and all Planned Parenthood activities to abortion (McKeegan 1992).

CHAPTER 8 CONCLUSION

1. Indeed, the most encouraging results for abstinence are coming from programs with "more complex messages stressing both abstinence and contraceptive use once sexual activity has begun" (Institute of Medicine 1995, 265).

2. See chapter 1, note 8 (p. 167), for a description of these methods.

3. Other than the condom, vasectomy, and abstinence, current contraceptive methods are women-centered.

4. Although we have demonstrated that family planning funding produces maternal and child health benefits and others have documented savings in terms of welfare expendi-

tures, this research has not been exhaustive in analyzing the benefits of family planning funded by Title X and other programs. While we expect that family planning programs contribute to child welfare, educational attainment, and economic stability, we do not wish to imply that family planning eliminates poverty. That poverty leads to teenage childbearing has been convincingly argued by other researchers (Luker 1996).

Bibliography

Abma, J., A. Chandra, W. Mosher, L. Peterson, and L. Piccinino. 1997. *Fertility, Family Planning and Women's Health: New Data from the 1995 National Survey of Family Growth.* Vital and Health Statistics, series 23, no. 19. Hyattsville, Md.: National Center for Health Statistics.

Adams, G.D. 1997. "Abortion: Evidence of Issue Evolution." *American Journal of Political Science* 41 (July): 718–37.

Advisory Commission on Intergovernmental Relations (ACIR). 1995. *Characteristics of Federal Grant-in-Aid Programs to State and Local Governments: Grants Funded FY 1995.* Washington, D.C.

Alan Guttmacher Institute (AGI). 1973. "One Year Extension of Family Planning Project Grants (Title X) and Other Health Programs Signed by President." *Washington Memo,* 20 June, 1.

———. 1974. *Family Planning, Contraception, Voluntary Sterilization, and Abortion: An Analysis of Laws and Policies in the United States, Each State and Jurisdiction (as of September, 1971).* Washington, D.C.: U.S. Department of Health, Education, and Welfare, publication no. (HSA)74-16001.

———. 1975a. "Ads for Legal Abortions Upheld by Supreme Court." *Family Planning and Population Reporter* 4, no. 4: 75.

———. 1975b. "Antiabortion Policy Found Invalid, Supreme Court Lets Contrary Ruling Stand." *Family Planning and Population Reporter* 4, no. 6: 107.

———. 1976a. "Family Planning Made Universal Service." *Washington Memo,* 16 September, 3–4.

———.1976b. "Supreme Court Says Spouse, Parent Can't Block Abortion." *Family Planning and Population Reporter* 5, no. 4: 1–3.

———. 1977. "States Can Deny Medicaid Benefits, Hospital Services for Elective Abortions." *Family Planning and Population Reporter* 6, no. 4: 41, 45.

———. 1978. *Family Planning, Contraception, Voluntary Sterilization, and Abortion: An Analysis of Laws and Policies in the United States, Each State and Jurisdiction (as of October 1, 1976 with 1978 Addenda).* Washington, D.C.: U.S. Department of Health, Education, and Welfare, publication no. (HSA)79-5623.

———. 1979a. *Data and Analysis for 1978 Revision of DHEW Revision of Five Year Plan for Family Planning Services.* New York: Alan Guttmacher Institute.

———. 1979b. "Relationship between Organized Family Planning Program Budget and Patients Served." Fact sheet.

———. 1979c. "States Spend More on Family Planning in 1977 than FY 1976, Rise Due to Title XX." *Family Planning and Population Reporter* 9, no. 2: 17.

———. 1979d. "Supreme Court Gives Judges Say in Abortion for Minors." *Washington Memo,* 6 July, 1.

———. 1980a. "Family Planning Funds Administered by the States Increased 20 Percent in FY 1978." *Family Planning and Population Reporter* 9, no. 2: 26.

———. 1980b. "1979 Review/1980 Outlook, Part II." *Washington Memo,* 25 January, 2.

———. 1980c. "Supreme Court Upholds Hyde Amendment." *Washington Memo,* 4 July, 1.

———. 1981a. *Data and Analysis for 1979 Revision of DHHS Five-Year Plan for Family Planning Services.* New York: Alan Guttmacher Institute.

———. 1981b. *Data and Analysis for 1980 Revision of DHHS Five-Year Plan for Family Planning Services.* New York: Alan Guttmacher Institute.

————. 1981c. "Family Planning Services Spent by State Health Welfare Agencies Increased 15% in FY 79." *Family Planning and Population Reporter* 10, no. 2: 30–31.

————. 1981d. "States Spent 74.7 Million for 'Family Planning' Services under Medicaid Program in FY 79." *Family Planning and Population Reporter* 10, no.2: 34.

————. 1981e. "Supreme Court Rules on Minors' Cases." *Washington Memo*, 27 March, 2–3.

————. 1981f. "Title X Emerges 'Unblocked.'" *Washington Memo*, 31 July, 1–3.

————. 1981g. "Title X Victory Analyzed." *Washington Memo*, 14 August, 1-3.

————. 1983a. *Current Functioning and Future Priorities in Family Planning Services Delivery.* New York: Alan Guttmacher Institute, 26, table 3.

————. 1983b. "Supreme Court Decisions on Abortion." *Washington Memo*, 22 June, 3.

————. 1983c. "Supreme Court Reaffirms Right to Abortion, Strikes Down Local Restrictions." *Washington Memo*, 22 June, 1–4.

————. 1984. *Organized Family Planning Services in the United States, 1981–1983.* New York: Alan Guttmacher Institute, 52–53, table 9.

————. 1986. "Supreme Court Reaffirms Abortion Right, Strikes 'Baby Doe' Rule." *Washington Memo*, 16 June, 1–3.

————. 1987. "Administration Proposed to Ban Any Abortion Information in Family Planning Clinics." *Washington Memo*, 9 September, 1–2.

————. 1988a. "Abortion Funding Expansions Are Subject of Debate as House Passes Spending Bills." *Washington Memo*, 21 June, 1–2.

————. 1988b. "Fetal Research at Issue Again in NIH Renewal Debate." *Washington Memo*, 12 April, 3.

————. 1988c. "NIH Panel Recommends Lifting Fetal Tissue Research Ban: Decision in Sullivan's Hands." *Washington Memo*, 15 May, 4.

————. 1988d. *Women at Risk: The Need for Family Planning Services, State and County Estimates, 1987.* New York: Alan Guttmacher Institute.

————. 1990. "Further Restrictions on Minors' Right to Abortion Allowed by Supreme Court." *Washington Memo*, 5 July, 1–2.

————. 1991a. "Abortion Issue Tests States, Congress, as High Court Continues to Back Away." *Washington Memo*, 18 January, 1–2.

————. 1991b. "Title X Program Faces Major Upheaval, as High Court Okays Ban on Abortion Speech." *Washington Memo*, 29 May, 1–3.

————. 1992a. "Bare Court Majority Reaffirms Roe, but Standard for Reviewing State Laws Is Relaxed." *Washington Memo*, 2 July, 1–3.

————. 1992b. "Clinton and Appeals Court Signal Death Knell for Title X Gag Rule." *Washington Memo*, 12 November, 1–2.

————. 1992c. "FOCA, Funding on Center Stage to New Dynamic in Abortion Politics." *Washington Memo*, 2 July, 3–4.

————. 1992d. "From beyond the World of Washington." *Washington Memo*, 12 November, 4.

————. 1993a. "Abortion-Related Actions Expected Soon from President Clinton." *Washington Memo*, 12 January, 3.

————. 1993b. "Actions following Bray Decision." *Washington Memo*, 9 February, 1–2.

————. 1993c. "AID to Restore Support to Population Groups Shunned under Reagan and Bush." *Washington Memo*, 24 August, 3.

————. 1993d. "The Clinton Health Care Reform Plan Is Formally Transmitted to Congress." *Washington Memo*, 9 November, 2.

————. 1993e. "Clinton Repeals Antiabortion Policies as Activists Map Out New Strategies." *Washington Memo*, 9 February, 1.

———. 1993f. "FOCA, Funding on Center Stage to Test New Dynamic in Abortion Politics." *Washington Memo*, 12 January, 1–3.

———. 1993g. "From beyond the World of Washington." *Washington Memo*, 25 February, 3–4.

———. 1993h. "Gag Rule Formally Suspended as Title X Renewal Advances." *Washington Memo*, 9 February, 2–3.

———. 1993i. "Hill Attention on FOCA, FACE Increases following Murder of Florida Physician." *Washington Memo*, 25 March, 1–2.

———. 1993j. "House Vote on Hyde Changes Dynamic of Congressional Abortion Debate." *Washington Memo*, 27 July, 1.

———. 1993k. "HHS Bill, with Hyde Language, Gets Final Approval from Congress." *Washington Memo*, 25 October, 3.

———. 1993l. "In the Next Issue." *Washington Memo*, 19 January, 4.

———. 1993m. "Newsbriefs." *Washington Memo*, 25 March, 4.

———. 1993n. "Reform Debate Has Major Implications for Reproductive Health Care." *Washington Memo*, 19 January, 1–3.

———. 1993o. "RU 486: 'It Should Be Available.'" *Washington Memo*, 5 May, 3.

———. 1993p. "Senate Confirms Elders by Wide Margin." *Washington Memo*, 20 September, 3.

———. 1993q. "Senate, 59-40, Defeats Move to Strike Limits on Medicaid Abortion Coverage." *Washington Memo*, 5 October, 1–2.

———. 1994a. "Clinton Bans NIH Research on Human Embryos Created for That Purpose." *Washington Memo*, 9 December, 5.

———. 1994b. "A Compromise Is Floated over Abortion in Health Care Reform." *Washington Memo*, 31 August, 2.

———. 1994c. "Newsbriefs." *Washington Memo*, 29 April, 4.

———. 1994d. "The 104th Congress—It's a Whole New World." *Washington Memo*, 9 December, 1.

———. 1994e. "Paving Way for FDA Review, Roussel Divests Itself of U.S. Patent Rights to RU 486." *Washington Memo*, 23 May, 2–3.

———. 1994f. "President to Sign FACE Bill Aimed at Deterring Abortion Violence." *Washington Memo*, 23 May, 1–2.

———. 1994g. "Some States Resisting Implementation of Federal Abortion Funding Policy." *Washington Memo*, 2 February, 2–3.

———. 1994h. "Supreme Court Allows Judges to Create 'Buffer Zones' at Clinics." *Washington Memo*, 7 July, 3.

———. 1994i. "Supreme Court Unanimously Okays Use of RICO to Combat Anti-Abortion Violence." *Washington Memo*, 2 February, 1.

———. 1995a. "Action Pending in Senate to Criminalize Method of Late-Term Abortion." *Washington Memo*, 21 November, 2–4.

———. 1995b. "Attack on Reproductive Rights Begins with a Flurry of House Antiabortion Votes." *Washington Memo*, 5 July, 1–3.

———. 1995c. "Attacks on Reproductive Rights Takes Place in the House." *Washington Memo*, 30 May, 1–3.

———. 1995d. "Challenge to FACE Rebuked." *Washington Memo*, 5 July, 6.

———. 1995e. "Congress Outlaws Abortion Procedure Despite Vow to Veto; Override Seen Unlikely." *Washington Memo*, 21 December, 1–2.

———. 1995f. "House Hews to Antiabortion Agenda; Medicaid Funds for Abortion Are Narrowed." *Washington Memo*, 29 August, 3–5.

———. 1995g. "Newsbriefs." *Washington Memo*, 6 March, 5.

————. 1995h. "Newsbriefs." *Washington Memo*, 5 July, 6.

————. 1996a. "Clinton's Missive on D & X Ban." *Washington Memo*, 18 March, 4.

————. 1996b. "Clinton to Sign Welfare Reform Bill That Targets Teens, Out-of Wedlock Births." *Washington Memo*, 7 August, 2–3.

————. 1996c. "Fate of Population Aid Funding, Abortion Riders at Stake as FY 1996 Endgame Nears." *Washington Memo*, 18 March, 1–2.

————. 1996d. "Late-Term Abortion Issue Hangs over New Congress; AMA Rejects D & X Ban." *Washington Memo*, 20 December, 1–2.

————. 1997a. *Contraceptive Needs and Services, 1995.* New York: Alan Guttmacher Institute.

————. 1997b. "High Court Okays Fixed Buffer Zone." *Washington Memo*, 12 March, 4.

Althaus, F.A., and S.K. Henshaw. 1994. "The Effects of Mandatory Delay Laws on Abortion Patients and Providers." *Family Planning Perspectives* 26: 228–31, 233.

Anderson, J. 1997. *Public Policymaking.* 3d ed. Boston: Houghton Mifflin.

Anderson, J.E., and L.G. Cope. 1987. "The Impact of Family Planning Program Activity upon Fertility." *Family Planning Perspectives* 19: 152–57.

Andrews, C.Y., and T.M. Orloff. 1995. *State Medicaid Coverage of Family Planning Services.* Prepared by National Governors' Association under contract (no. 500-92-0045) with Health Care Financing Administration (December).

Annas, G.J. 1989. "The Supreme Court, Privacy, and Abortion." *New England Journal of Medicine* 321: 1200–1203.

Anton, T.J. 1997. "New Federalism and Intergovernmental Fiscal Relationships: The Implications for Health Policy." *Journal of Health Politics, Policy and Law* 22: 691–720.

Bardach, E. 1977. *The Implementation Game: What Happens after a Bill Becomes a Law.* Cambridge, Mass.: MIT Press.

Barnes, R.L. 1970. "Birth Control in Popular Twentieth Century Periodicals." *Family Coordinator* 19, no. 2: 159–64.

Barringer, F. 1992. "Court Sets Aside U.S. Restriction on Abortion Counseling at Clinics." *New York Times*, 4 November, p. A1.

Becker, G.S. 1996. *Accounting for Taste.* Cambridge, Mass.: Harvard University Press.

Benda, P.M., and C.H. Levine. 1988. "Reagan and the Bureaucracy: The Bequest, the Promise, and the Legacy." In *The Reagan Legacy: Promise and Performance*, edited by C.O. Jones. Chatham, N.J.: Chatham House.

Berkman, M.B., and R.E. O'Connor. 1993. "Do Women Legislators Matter? Female Legislators and State Abortion Policy." Chap. 15 in *Understanding the New Politics of Abortion*, edited by M.L. Goggin. Newbury Park, Calif.: Sage.

Berman, P. 1978. "The Study of Macro- and Micro-Implementation." *Public Policy* 26: 157–84.

Bibby, J., C. Cotter, J. Gibson, and R. Huckshorn. 1990. "Parties in State Politics." Chap. 3 in *Politics in the American States,* edited by V. Gray, H. Jacobs, and K. Vines. 5th ed. Boston: Little, Brown.

Bickers, K., and R.M. Stein. 1994. *Codebook: U.S. Domestic Assistance Programs Database.* Ann Arbor: University of Michigan Inter-University Center for Political and Social Research.

Blank, R.M., C.C. George, and R.A. London. 1994. "State Abortion Rates: The Impact of Policies, Providers, Politics, Demographics and Economic Environment." Northwestern University, Department of Economics. Mimeographed.

Bogue, D.J. 1970. *Family Planning Improvement through Evaluation: A Manual of Basic Principles.* Family Planning Research and Evaluation, no. 1. University of Chicago, Community and Family Study Center.

Bonavoglia, A. 1997. "Separating Fact from Fiction." *Ms.*, May/June, 54–63.

Brandt, E.N., Jr. 1981. "Block Grants and the Resurgence of Federalism." *Public Health Reports* 96: 495–97.

Brodie, J.F. 1994. *Contraception and Abortion in Nineteenth Century America.* Ithaca, N.Y.: Cornell University Press.

Broun, H., and M. Leech. 1927. *Anthony Comstock: Roundsman of the Lord.* New York: Literacy Guild of America.

Bureau of National Affairs, Inc. 1995. "Summary and Analysis." *United States Law Week* 64, no. 2: 1005.

Carney, E.N. 1995. "Maryland: A Law Codifying *Roe* v. *Wade.*" Chap. 3 in *Abortion Politics in the American States*, edited by M.C. Segers and T.A. Byrnes. Armonk, N.Y.: M.E. Sharpe.

Cartoof, V.G., and L. Klerman. 1986. "Parental Consent for Abortion: Impact of the Massachusetts Law." *American Journal of Public Health* 76: 397–400.

Cates, W., Jr., and E.G. Raymond. 1997. "Annotation: Emergency Contraception—Parsimony and Prevention in the Medicine Cabinet." *American Journal of Public Health* 87: 909–10.

Christian Coalition. 1995. *Contract with the American Family.* Chesapeake, Va.: Christian Coalition.

Cohen, J.E., and C. Barrilleaux. 1993. "Public Opinion, Interest Groups, and Public Policy Making: Abortion Policy in the American States." Chap. 12 in *Understanding the New Politics of Abortion*, edited by M.L. Goggin. Newbury Park, Calif.: Sage.

Colby, D.C., and D.G. Baker. 1988. "State Policy Responses to the AIDS Epidemic." *Publius* 18, no. 3: 113–30.

Congressional Quarterly. 1993a. "Abortion Clinic Blockaders Targeted in New Bill." *Congressional Quarterly,* 6 February, 271.

———. 1993b. "Ruling Favors Blockaders." *Congressional Quarterly,* 16 January, 130.

———. 1995. "Members Pushing to Retain Welfare System Control." *Congressional Quarterly,* 28 January, 280–83.

Corman, H., and M. Grossman. 1985. "Determinants of Neonatal Mortality Rates in the U.S." *Journal of Health Economics* 4: 213–36.

Corsa, L., Jr. 1966. "Introduction." *American Journal of Public Health* 56:2.

Craig, B.H., and D.M. O'Brien. 1993. *Abortion and American Politics.* Rev. ed. Chatham, N.J.: Chatham House.

Currie, J., L. Nixon, and N. Cole. 1993. "Restrictions of Medicaid Funding of Abortion." Working paper 4432, National Bureau of Economic Research, Cambridge, Mass.

Cutright, P., and F.S. Jaffe. 1976. "Family Planning Program Effects on the Fertility of Low-Income Women." *Family Planning Perspectives* 8: 100–110.

Daley, D., and R.B. Gold. 1993. "Public Funding for Contraceptive, Sterilization, and Abortion Services, Fiscal Year 1992." *Family Planning Perspectives* 23: 244–51.

Davis, K., and J. Blake. 1956. "Social Structure and Fertility: An Analytic Framework." *Economic Development and Cultural Change* 4: 211–35.

Dienes, C.T. 1972. *Law, Politics, and Birth Control.* Urbana: University of Illinois Press.

Donovan, P. 1973. "Georgia Governor Jimmy Carter." *Family Planning and Population Reporter* 2, no. 3: 58–59.

———. 1990. "Funding Restrictions on Fetal Research: The Implications for Science and Health." *Family Planning Perspectives* 22: 224–31.

———. 1992. *Our Daughters' Decisions.* New York: Alan Guttmacher Institute, 7–22.

———. 1995. *The Politics of Blame: Family Planning, Abortion, and the Poor.* New York: Alan Guttmacher Institute.

————. 1998. "Falling Teen Pregnancy, Birthrates: What's behind the Declines?" *Guttmacher Report on Public Policy* 1, no. 5: 6–9.

Doring-Bradley, B. 1977. "Financial Resources for Organized Medical Family Planning Services in the United States: An Historical Overview." Working paper, Alan Guttmacher Institute, New York. Mimeographed.

Drucker, D. 1990. *Abortion Decisions of the Supreme Court, 1973 through 1989: A Comprehensive Review with Historical Commentary.* Jefferson, N.C.: McFarland.

Dryfoos, J.G. 1973. "A Formula for the 1970's: Estimating the Need for Subsidized Family Planning Services in the United States." *Family Planning Perspectives* 5: 145–74.

————. 1975. Women Who Need and Receive Family Planning Services: Estimates at Mid-Decade." *Family Planning Perspectives* 7: 172–79.

————. 1976. "The United States National Family Planning Program." *Studies in Family Planning* 7: 80–89.

————. 1980. "The National Reporting System for Family Planning Services—a New Look." *Family Planning Perspectives* 12: 193–201.

————. 1989. "What President Bush Can Do about Family Planning." *American Journal of Public Health* 79: 689–90.

Dryfoos, J.G., and B. Doring-Bradley. 1978. "The Hundred Million Dollar Misunderstanding." *Family Planning Perspectives* 10: 144–47.

Dryfoos, J.G., and W.J. White. 1980. "Organization of Title X Grantees." Paper presented at the annual meeting of the American Public Health Association, Detroit, October.

Eliot, J.W., L. Corsa, Jr., J. McEachern, R. White, and S. Stableford. 1968. "Family Planning Activities of Official Welfare Agencies, United States, 1966." *American Journal of Public Health* 58: 700–712.

Family Planning Perspectives. 1991. "Fetal Tissue Panel Organized." *Family Planning Perspectives* 23: 4.

Federal Register. 1993. "Family Planning Services." *Federal Register* 58, no. 218: 60130.

Finch, B.E., and H. Green. 1963. *Contraception through the Ages.* London: Peter Owen.

Fisher, D., and J.I. Rosoff. 1972. "How States Are Using Title IV-A to Finance Family Planning Services." *Family Planning Perspectives* 4: 31–43.

Forrest, J.D. 1994. "Epidemiology of Unintended Pregnancy and Contraceptive Use." *American Journal of Obstetrics and Gynecology* 170: 1485–89.

Forrest, J.D., and R. Samara. 1996. "Impact of Publicly Funded Contraceptive Services on Unintended Pregnancies and Implications for Medicaid Expenditures." *Family Planning Perspectives* 28: 188–95.

Forrest, J.D., and S. Singh. 1990a. "The Impact of Public-Sector Expenditures for Contraceptive Services in California." *Family Planning Perspectives* 22: 161–68.

————. 1990b. "Public Sector Savings Resulting from Expenditures for Contraceptive Services." *Family Planning Perspectives* 22: 6–15.

Fraley, C. 1995. "States Guard Their Borders as Medicaid Talks Begin." *Congressional Quarterly*, 10 June, 1637–42.

Franklin, C.H., and L.C. Kosaki. 1989. "Republican Schoolmaster: The U.S. Supreme Court, Public Opinion, and Abortion." *American Political Science Review* 83: 751–71.

Frost, J.J. 1996. "Family Planning Clinic Services in the United States, 1994." *Family Planning Perspectives* 28: 92–100.

Frost, J.J., and M. Bolzan. 1997. "The Provision of Public-Sector Services by Family Planning Agencies in 1995." *Family Planning Perspectives* 29: 6–14.

Gamson, W.A. 1968. *Power and Discontent.* Homewood, Ill.: Dorsey Press.

Garand, J.C., P.A. Monroe, and G. Meyer. 1991. "Does the Welfare State Increase Divorce Rates in the American States?" Paper presented at the annual meeting of the Southern Political Science Association, Tampa, Fla., November.

Glasier, A. 1997. "Emergency Postcoital Contraception." *New England Journal of Medicine* 337: 1058–64.

Goggin, M.L. 1993. "Understanding the New Politics of Abortion." *American Politics Quarterly* 21: 7–8.

Goggin, M.L., and C. Wlezien. 1993. "Abortion Opinion and Policy in the United States." Chap. 11 in *Understanding the New Politics of Abortion*, edited by M.L. Goggin. Newbury Park, Calif.: Sage.

Gohmann, S.F., and R.L. Ohsfeldt. 1990. "Predicting State Abortion Legislation from U.S. Senate Votes." *Policy Studies Review* 9: 749–65.

———. 1993. "Effects of Price and Availability on Abortion Demand." *Contemporary Policy Issues* 11: 42–55.

Gold, R.B. 1990. *Abortion and Women's Health: A Turning Point for America?* New York: Alan Guttmacher Institute.

———. 1998. "The Need for and Cost of Mandating Private Insurance Coverage of Contraception." *Guttmacher Report on Public Policy* 1, no. 3: 5–7.

Gold, R.B., and D. Daley. 1991. "Public Funding of Contraceptive, Sterilization, and Abortion Services, Fiscal Year 1990." *Family Planning Perspectives* 23: 201–11.

Gold, R.B., and S. Guardado. 1988. "Public Funding of Contraceptive, Sterilization, and Abortion Services, 1987." *Family Planning Perspectives* 20: 228–33.

Gold, R.B., and D. Lehrman. 1989. "Fetal Research under Fire: The Influence of Abortion Politics." *Family Planning Perspectives* 21: 6–11, 38.

Gold, R.B., and J. Macias. 1986. "Public Funding of Contraceptive, Sterilization, and Abortion Services, 1985." *Family Planning Perspectives* 18: 259–64.

Gold, R.B., and B. Nestor. 1985. "Public Funding of Contraceptive, Sterilization, and Abortion Services, 1983." *Family Planning Perspectives* 17: 25–30.

Gold, R. B., and C.L. Richards. 1996. *Improving the Fit: Reproductive Health Services in Managed Care Settings*. New York: Alan Guttmacher Institute.

———. 1998. "Managed Care and Unintended Pregnancy." *Women's Health Issues* 8: 134–47.

Goldberg, C. 1999. "Insurance for Viagra Spurs Coverage for Birth Control." *New York Times*, 30 June, pp. A1, A15.

Goldscheider, C., and W.D. Mosher. 1991. "Patterns of Contraceptive Use in the United States: Importance of Religious Factors." *Studies in Family Planning* 22: 102–5.

Gonen, J. 1997. "Managed Care and Unintended Pregnancy: Testing the Limits of Prevention." *Insights* 3 (July): 1–8.

Gormley, W.T. 1986. "Regulatory Issues in a Federal System." *Polity* 18: 595–620.

Gorney, C. 1998. *Articles of Faith: A Frontline History of the Abortion Wars*. New York: Simon and Schuster.

Gramlich, E.M. 1977. "Intergovernmental Grants: A Review of the Empirical Literature." Chap. 12 in *The Political Economy of Fiscal Federalism*, edited by W.E. Oates. Lexington, Mass.: Lexington Books.

Greene, W.H. 1993. *Econometric Analysis*. New York: Macmillan.

Greenhouse, L. 1989. "Supreme Court, 5-4, Narrowing Roe v. Wade, Upholds Sharp State Limits on Abortions." *New York Times*, 4 July, p. A11.

———. 1992. "High Court, 5-4, Affirms Right to Abortion but Allows Most of Pennsylvania's Limits." *New York Times*, 30 June, pp. A1, A7, A8.

Grimes, D.A. 1997. "Emergency Contraception—Expanding Opportunities for Primary Prevention." *New England Journal of Medicine* 337: 1078–79.

Grossman, M., and S. Jacobowitz. 1981. "Variations in Infant Mortality Rates among Counties of the U.S.: The Roles of Public Policies and Programs." *Demography* 18: 695–713.

Gusfield, J.R. 1963. *Symbolic Crusade*. Urbana: University of Illinois Press.

Haas-Wilson, D. 1997. "Women's Reproductive Choices: The Impact of Medicaid Funding Restrictions." *Family Planning Perspectives* 29: 228–33.

Halberstam, D. 1993. *The Fifties*. New York: Villard Books.

Halva-Neubauer, G.A. 1990. "Abortion Policy in the Post-Webster Age." *Publius* 20, no. 3: 27–44.

———. 1993. "The States after *Roe:* No Paper Tigers." Chap. 10 in *Understanding the New Politics of Abortion*, edited by M.L. Goggin. Newbury Park, Calif.: Sage.

Hanna, M.T. 1995. "Washington: Abortion Policymaking through Initiative." Chap. 8 in *Abortion Politics in the American States*, edited by M.C. Segers and T.A. Byrnes. Armonk, N.Y.: M.E. Sharpe.

Hansen, S.B. 1980. "State Implementation of Supreme Court Decisions: Abortion Rates since *Roe v. Wade*." *Journal of Politics* 42: 372–95.

———. 1993. "Differences in Public Policies toward Abortion: Electoral and Policy Context." Chap. 13 in *Understanding the New Politics of Abortion*, edited by M.L. Goggin. Newbury Park, Calif.: Sage.

Harkavy, O., F.S. Jaffe, and S.M. Wishik. 1969. "Family Planning and Public Policy: Who Is Misleading Whom?" *Science* 165 (25 July): 367–73.

Hatcher, R.A., J. Trussell, F. Stewart, F. Guest, and D. Kowal. 1998. *Contraceptive Technology*. 17th rev. ed. New York: Ardent Media.

Heinsohn, G., and O. Steiger. 1982. "The Elimination of Medieval Birth Control and the Witch Trials of Modern Times." *International Journal of Women's Studies* 5: 193–214.

Henig, J.R. 1985. *Public Policy and Federalism*. New York: St. Martin's Press.

Henshaw, S.K. 1991. "The Accessibility of Abortion Services in the United States." *Family Planning Perspectives* 23: 247.

———. 1992. "Abortion Trends in 1987 and 1988: Age and Race." *Family Planning Perspectives* 23: 85–86.

———. 1995. "Factors Hindering Access to Abortion Services." *Family Planning Perspectives* 27: 54–59, 87.

———. 1998. "Abortion Incidence and Services in the United States, 1995–1996." *Family Planning Perspectives* 30: 263–70, 287.

Henshaw, S.K., and J.D. Forrest. 1993. *Women at Risk of Unintended Pregnancy, 1990 Estimates*. New York: Alan Guttmacher Institute.

Henshaw, S.K., L.M. Koonin, and J.C. Smith. 1991. "Characteristics of U.S. Women Having Abortions, 1987." *Family Planning Perspectives* 23: 75–79.

Henshaw, S.K., and J. Silverman. 1988. "The Characteristics and Prior Contraceptive Use of U.S. Abortion Patients." *Family Planning Perspectives* 20: 158–68.

Henshaw, S.K., and J. Van Vort. 1988. *Abortion Services in the United States, Each State and Metropolitan Area, 1984–1985*. New York: Alan Guttmacher Institute.

———. 1990. "Abortion Services in the United States, 1987–88." *Family Planning Perspectives* 22: 102–8, 142.

———. 1994. "Abortion Services in the United States, 1991 and 1992." *Family Planning Perspectives* 26: 100–106, 112.

Henshaw, S.K., and L.S. Wallisch. 1984. "The Medicaid Cutoff and Abortion Services for the Poor." *Family Planning Perspectives* 16: 170–80.

Hern, W.M. 1994. "Life on the Front Lines." *Women's Health Issues* 4: 48–54.

Himes, N.E. 1970. *Medical History of Contraception*. 1936. Reprint, New York: Schoken Books.

Hofferbert, R.I., and J.K. Urice. 1985. "Small Scale Policy." *American Journal of Political Science* 29: 308–29.

Holbrook, T.M. 1984. "Economics and Presidential Elections: The View from the States." Ph.D. diss., University of Iowa.

Holbrook-Provow, T.M., and S.C. Poe. 1987. "Measuring State Political Ideology." *American Politics Quarterly* 15: 399–416.

Hsiao, C. 1986. *Analysis of Panel Data.* New York: Cambridge University Press.

Hwang, S., and V. Gray. 1991. "External Limits and Internal Determinants of State Public Policy." *Western Political Quarterly* 44: 277–99.

Institute of Medicine. Committee to Study Outreach for Prenatal Care. 1988. *Prenatal Care: Reaching Mothers, Reaching Infants.* Washington, D.C.: National Academy Press.

———. Committee to Study the Prevention of Low Birthweight. 1985. *Preventing Low Birthweight.* Washington, D.C.: National Academy Press.

———. Committee on Unintended Pregnancy. 1995. *The Best Intentions: Unintended Pregnancy and the Well-Being of Children and Families.* Washington, D.C.: National Academy Press.

Jaenicke, D.W. 1998. "Abortion and Partisanship in the 104th U.S. Congress." *Politics* 18: 1–9.

Jaffe, F.S. 1967. "Family Planning, Public Policy, and Intervention Strategy." *Journal of Social Issues* 23, no. 4: 145–63.

———. 1973. "Public Policy on Fertility Control." *Scientific American* 229, no. 1: 17–23.

———. 1974. "Fertility Control Policy, Social Policy and Population Policy in an Industrialized Country." *Family Planning Perspectives* 6: 164–69.

Jakobovits, I. 1967. "Jewish Views on Abortion." In *Abortion and the Law,* edited by D.T. Smith. Cleveland, Ohio: Case Western Reserve University Press.

Jones, E.F., J.D. Forrest, N. Goldman, S.K. Henshaw, R. Lincoln, J.I. Rosoff, C.F. Westoff, and D. Wulf. 1986. *Teenage Fertility in Industrialized Countries.* New Haven, Conn.: Yale University Press.

Jones, E.F., J.D. Forrest, S.K.Henshaw, J. Silverman, and A. Torres. 1989. *Pregnancy, Contraception, and Family Planning Services in Industrialized Countries.* New Haven, Conn.: Yale University Press.

Jones, E.F., and J.D. Forrest. 1992. "Underreporting of Abortion in Surveys of American Women: 1976 to 1988." *Demography* 29: 113–26.

Joyce, T.J. 1987. "The Impact of Induced Abortion on Black and White Birth Outcomes in the United States." *Demography* 24: 229–44.

Joyce, T.J., and M. Grossman. 1990. "Pregnancy Wantedness and the Early Initiation of Prenatal Care." *Demography* 27: 1–17.

Judge, G.G., W.E. Griffiths, R.C. Hill, H. Lutkepohl, and T. Lee. 1985. *The Theory and Practice of Econometrics.* New York: Wiley.

Kaiser Family Foundation. 1998. *The Medicaid Program at a Glance.* Menlo Park, Calif.: Kaiser Family Foundation. Http://kff.org/archive/health_policy/kcfm/glance/glance. html (October).

Katz, J.L. 1995. "Key Members Seek to Expand State Role in Welfare Plan." *Congressional Quarterly,* 14 January, 159–62.

———. 1996. "After 60 Years, Most Control Is Passing to States." *Congressional Quarterly,* 3 August, 2190–96.

Kennedy, A. 1935. "History of the Development of Contraceptive Materials in the United States. *American Medicine* 30, no. 2: 159–61.

Kerwin, C.M. 1999. *Rulemaking: How Government Agencies Write Law and Make Policy.* 2d ed. Washington, D.C.: Congressional Quarterly Press.

Kirby, D. 1997. *No Easy Answers: Research Findings on Programs to Reduce Teen Pregnancy (Summary).* Washington, D.C.: National Campaign to Reduce Teen Pregnancy.

Klein, R. 1999. *Losing Health Insurance: The Unintended Consequences of Welfare Reform.* Washington, D.C.: Families USA.

Lee, P.R. 1970. "The Roles of Government Agencies." In *Manual of Family Planning and Contraceptive Practice,* edited by M.S. Calderone. Baltimore: Williams and Wilkins, 76–77.

Legge, J.S., Jr. 1985. *Abortion Policy: An Evaluation of the Consequences for Maternal and Infant Health.* Albany: State University of New York Press.

Lindberg, L.D., F. Sonenstein, L. Ku, and G. Martinez. 1997. "Age Differences between Minors Who Give Birth and Their Adult Partners." *Family Planning Perspectives* 29: 61–66.

Littlewood, T.B. 1977. *The Politics of Population Control.* Notre Dame, Ind.: University of Notre Dame Press.

Lowi, T.J. 1964. "American Business, Public Policy, Case-Studies, and Political Theory." *World Politics* 16: 677–715.

Luker, K. 1984. *Abortion and the Politics of Motherhood.* Berkeley: University of California Press.

———. 1996. *Dubious Conceptions: The Politics of Teenage Pregnancy.* Cambridge, Mass.: Harvard University Press.

MacPherson, P. 1995. "Medicare, Medicaid on Table for Possible Cuts." *Congressional Quarterly,* 11 February, 458.

Maddala, G.S. 1992. *Introduction to Econometrics.* New York: Macmillan.

Manhattan Institute. 1985. "Losing Ground: Why the War on Poverty Failed." *Manhattan Report* 5: 1.

Marsiglio, W., and F. L. Mott. 1988. "Does Wanting to Become Pregnant with a First Child Affect Subsequent Maternal Behaviors and Infant Birth Weight?" *Journal of Marriage and the Family* 50: 1023–36.

Maynard-Moody, S. 1995. *The Dilemma of the Fetus.* New York: St. Martin's Press.

Mazmanian, D.A., and P.A. Sabatier. 1981. *Effective Policy Implementation.* Lexington, Mass.: D.C. Heath.

———. 1983. *Implementation and Public Policy.* Glenview, Ill.: Scott, Foresman.

———. 1989. *Implementation and Public Policy: With a New Postscript.* Lanham, Md.: University Press of America.

McFarlane, D.R. 1989. "Testing the Statutory Coherence Hypothesis." *Administration and Society* 20: 395–422.

———. 1992. "Restructuring Federalism: The Effects of Decentralized Federal Policy on States' Responsiveness to Family Planning Needs." *Women and Health* 19: 43–63.

———. 1993. "U.S. Abortion Policy since *Roe* v. *Wade.*" *American Journal of Gynecologic Health* 7: 17–25.

McFarlane, D.R., and K.J. Meier. 1992. "Determinants of Abortion Levels in the American States, 1982–1988." Paper presented at the annual meeting of the American Public Health Association, Washington, D.C., November.

———. 1993a. "The Clinton Administration and the DHHS Office of Population Affairs: The October 1993 Report Card." Paper presented at the annual meeting of the American Public Health Association, San Francisco, October.

———. 1993b. "Restructuring Federalism: The Impact of Reagan Policies on the Family Planning Program." *Journal of Health Politics, Policy and Law* 18: 821–50.

———. 1998. "Do Different Funding Mechanisms Produce Different Results? The Implications of Family Planning for Fiscal Federalism," *Journal of Health Politics, Policy and Law* 23: 423–54.

McKeegan, M. 1992. *Abortion Politics: Mutiny in the Ranks of the Right.* New York: Free Press.

Medoff, M.H. 1988. "An Economic Analysis of the Demand for Abortions." *Economic Inquiry* 26: 353–59.

———. 1989. "Constituencies, Ideology, and the Demand for Abortion Legislation." *Public Choice* 60: 185–91.

Meier, K.J. 1987. *Politics and the Bureaucracy: Policymaking in the Fourth Branch of Government.* 2d ed. Monterey, Calif.: Brooks/Cole.

———. 1988. *The Political Economy of Regulation: The Case of Insurance.* Albany: State University of New York Press.

———. 2000. "Drugs, Sex, Rock and Roll: A Theory of Morality Politics." In *The Public Clash of Private Values*, edited by C. Z. Mooney. New York: Chatham House.

Meier, K.J., and J.L. Brudney. 1997. *Applied Statistics for Public Administration.* 4th ed. Fort Worth, Tex.: Harcourt Brace College Publishers.

Meier, K.J., D.P. Haider-Markel, A. Stanislawski, and D.R. McFarlane. 1996. "The Impact of State-Level Restrictions on Abortion." *Demography* 33: 307–12.

Meier, K.J., and C. Johnson. 1990. "The Politics of Demon Rum." *American Politics Quarterly* 18: 404–29.

Meier, K.J., and M. Licari. 1997. "Public Policy Design: Combining Policy Instruments." Paper presented at the annual meeting of the American Political Science Association, Washington, D.C., September.

Meier, K.J., and D.R. McFarlane. 1993a. "Abortion Politics and Abortion Funding Policy." Chap. 14 in *Understanding the New Politics of Abortion*, edited by M.L. Goggin. Newbury Park, Calif.: Sage.

———. 1993b. "The Politics of Funding Abortion." *American Politics Quarterly* 21: 81–101.

———. 1994. "State Family Planning and Abortion Expenditures: Their Effect on Health." *American Journal of Public Health* 84: 1468–72.

———. 1996. "Statutory Coherence and Policy Implementation: The Case of Family Planning." *Journal of Public Policy* 15: 281–98.

Merz, J.F., C.A. Jackson, and J.A. Klerman. 1995. *A Review of Abortion Policy: Legality, Medicaid Funding, and Parental Involvement, 1967-1994.* Santa Monica, Calif.: Rand (DRU-1096-NICHD).

Michael, R.T., J. Wadsworth, J. Feinleib, A.M. Johnson, E.O. Laumann, and K. Wellings. 1998. "Private Sexual Behavior, Public Opinion, and Public Health Policy Related to Sexually Transmitted Diseases: A U.S.-British Comparison." *American Journal of Public Health* 88: 749–54.

Mishell, D.R. 1975. "Assessing the Intrauterine Device." *Family Planning Perspectives* 7: 103–11.

Mohr, J.C. 1978. *The Origins of and Evolution of National Policy, 1800–1900.* New York: Oxford University Press, vii.

Morgan, D.R., and K.J. Meier. 1980. "Politics and Morality: The Effect of Religion on Referenda Voting." *Social Science Quarterly* 61: 144–48.

National Abortion Federation. 1993. *Incidents of Violence & Disruption against Abortion Providers, 1993.* Washington, D.C.

National Abortion Rights Action League Foundation (NARAL). 1991–93, 1995–99. *Who Decides? A State-by-State Review of Abortion Rights in America.* Washington, D.C.

Nestor, B. 1982. "Public Funding of Contraceptive Services 1980–1982." *Family Planning Perspectives* 14: 198–203.

Noonan, J.T. 1986. *Contraception: A History of Its Treatment by the Catholic Theologians and Canonists.* Cambridge, Mass.: Harvard University Press.

O'Connor, K. 1996. *No Neutral Ground: Abortion Politics in an Age of Absolutes.* Boulder, Colo.: Westview Press.

Ohsfeldt, R.L., and S.F. Gohmann. 1994. "Do Parental Involvement Laws Reduce Adolescent Abortion Rates?" *Contemporary Policy Issues* 12: 65–76.

Orr, M.T. 1983. "The Family Planning Program and Cuts in Federal Spending: Impacts on State Management of Family Planning Funds." *Family Planning Perspectives* 15: 176–84.

Ott, L. 1977. *An Introduction to Statistical Methods and Data Analysis.* North Scituate, Mass.: Duxbury Press.

Pear, R. 1996. "What Welfare Research?" *New York Times,* 15 September, p. E4.

Peterson, G.E. 1984. "Federalism and the States: An Experiment in Decentralization." In *The Reagan Record: An Assessment of America's Changing Domestic Priorities,* edited by J.L. Palmer and I.V. Sawhill. Cambridge, Mass.: Ballinger.

Peterson, G.E., R.R. Bovbjerg, B.A. Davis, W.G. Davis, E.C. Durman, and T.A. Gallo. 1986. *The Reagan Block Grants: What Have We Learned?* Washington, D.C.: Urban Institute Press.

Pindyyck, R.S., and D.L. Rubenfield. 1991. *Econometric Models and Econometric Forecasts.* New York: McGraw-Hill.

Planned Parenthood Federation of America. 1992. "Family Planning in America: Chronology of Major Events." New York: Planned Parenthood of America. Fact sheet.

Population Council. 1996. "FDA Issues Approvable Letter for Mifepristone Medical Abortion." New York: Population Council. Press release, 18 September.

———. 1999. "Medical Abortion with Mifepristone and Misoprostol: Frequently Asked Questions." New York: Population Council. Http://www.popcouncil.org/faqs/emergency-contraception.html.

Posner, R.A. 1992. *Sex and Reason.* Cambridge, Mass.: Harvard University Press.

Powell-Grinder, E., and K. Trent. 1987. "Sociodemographic Determinants of Abortion in the United States." *Demography* 24: 553–61.

Public Law (PL) 248. 90th Cong., 1st sess., 2 January 1968. *Social Security Amendments of 1967.*

Public Law 572. 91st Cong., 2d sess., 24 December 1970. *Family Planning Services and Population Research of 1970.*

Public Law 45. 93d Cong., 1st sess., 18 June 1973. *Health Programs Extension Act of 1973.*

Public Law 626. 95th Cong., 2d sess., 10 November 1978. *Health Services and Centers Amendments of 1978, Title VI, Grant Program.*

Public Law 35. 97th Cong., 1st sess., 13 August 1981. *Omnibus Budget and Reconciliation Act of 1981, Title IX, Subtitle D, Family Planning, and Subtitle G, Adolescent Family Life Act.*

Public Law 193. 104th Cong., 2d sess., 22 August 1996. *Personal Responsibility and Work Opportunity Reconciliation Act of 1996.*

Public Law 78. 105th Cong., 1st sess., 13 November 1997. *Departments of Labor, Health and Human Services, and Education and Related Agencies Appropriations Act, 1998.*

Purdum, T.S. 1996. "President Vetoes Measure Banning Type of Abortion." *New York Times,* 11 April, pp. A1, B10.

Quinn, B.H., H. Anderson, M. Bradley, P. Goetting, and P. Shriver. 1982. *Churches and Church Membership 1980.* Atlanta: Glenmary Research Center.

Radecki, S.E., and G.S. Bernstein. 1989. "Use of Clinic versus Private Family Planning Care by Low-Income Women: Access, Cost, and Patient Satisfaction." *American Journal of Public Health* 79: 692.

Reagan, L.J. 1997. *When Abortion Was a Crime.* Berkeley: University of California Press.

Reed, J. 1978. *From Public Vice to Private Virtue.* New York: Basic Books.

Richard, P. 1989. "Alternative Abortion Polices: What Are the Health Consequences?" *Social Science Quarterly* 70: 941–51.

Riddle, J.M., J.W. Estes, and J.C. Russell. 1994. "Ever Since Eve . . . Birth Control in the Ancient World." *Archaeology* 47: 29–35.

Rogers, E.M. 1973. *Communication Strategies for Family Planning.* New York: Free Press.

Rogers, J.L., R.F. Boruch, G.B. Stoms, and D. Demoya. 1991. "Impact of the Minnesota Parental Notification Law on Abortion and Births." *American Journal of Public Health* 81: 294–98.

Rosenbaum, S., P.W. Shin, A. Mauskopf, K. Fund, G. Stern, and A. Zuvekas. 1994. *Beyond the Freedom to Choose: Medicaid Managed Care and Family Planning.* Washington, D.C.: George Washington University, Center for Health Policy Research.

———. 1997. "Medicaid Managed Care and the Family Planning Free-Choice Exemption: Beyond the Freedom to Choose." *Journal of Health Politics, Policy and Law* 22: 1191–1214.

Rosenblatt, R. 1992. *Life Itself: Abortion in the American Mind.* New York: Random House.

Rosenfield, A. 1994. "The Difficult Issue of Second-Trimester Abortion." *New England Journal of Medicine* 331: 324–25.

Rosenstone, S.J. 1983. *Forecasting Presidential Elections.* New Haven, Conn.: Yale University Press.

Rosoff, J.I. 1972. "Medicaid, Past and Future." *Family Planning Perspectives* 4: 26–33.

———. 1981. "Blocking Family Planning." *Family Planning Perspectives* 13: 125–31.

———. 1990. Afterword to *Abortion and Women's Health: A Turning Point?* by R.B. Gold. New York: Alan Guttmacher Institute.

Rubin, A.J. 1993a. "Freedom of Choice Bill Returns; Too Early to Predict Outcome." *Congressional Quarterly,* 20 March, 675.

———. 1993b. "High Hopes Turn to Uncertainty for FOCA." *Congressional Quarterly,* 8 May, 1154–55.

———. 1993c. "Reno Supports Protection for Women and Doctors." *Congressional Quarterly,* 15 May, 1235.

Ryder, N.B., and C.F. Westoff. 1971. *Reproduction in the United States, 1965.* Princeton, N.J.: Princeton University Press.

Sabatier, P.A. 1988. "An Advocacy Coalition Framework of Policy Change and the Role of Policy-Oriented Learning Therein." *Policy Sciences* 21: 129–68.

Sabatier, P.A., and H.C. Jenkins-Smith. 1993. *Policy Change and Learning: An Advocacy Coalition Approach.* Boulder, Colo.: Westview Press.

Sabatier, P.A., and D.A. Mazmanian. 1981. "The Implementation of Public Policy: A Framework of Analysis." In *Effective Policy Implementation,* edited by D.A. Mazmanian and P.A. Sabatier. Lexington, Mass.: D.C. Heath, 10–15.

Sable, M.R., J.W. Stockbauer, W.F. Schramm, and G.H. Land. 1990. "Differentiating the Barriers to Adequate Prenatal Care in Missouri, 1987–88." *Public Health Reports* 105: 549–54.

Salganicoff, A., and S.F. Delbanco. 1998. "Medicaid and Managed Care: Meeting the Reproductive Health Needs of Low Income Women." *Journal of Health Management and Practice* 4, no. 6: 13–22.

Saul, R. 1999. "Teen Pregnancy: Progress Meets Politics." *Guttmacher Report on Public Policy* 2, no. 3: 6–9.

Schlesinger, M., and T. Lee. 1993. "Is Health Care Different? Popular Support of Federal Health and Social Policies." *Journal of Health Politics, Policy and Law* 18: 551–628.

Schneider, A.L., and H. Ingram. 1993. "Social Construction and Target Populations: Implications for Politics and Policy." *American Political Science Review* 87: 334–47.

Schnucker, R.V. 1975. "Elizabethan Birth Control and Puritan Attitudes." *Journal of Interdisciplinary History* 4: 655–67.

Segers, M.C., and T.A. Byrnes, eds. 1995. *Abortion Politics in the American States.* Armonk, N.Y.: M.E. Sharpe.

Sheeran, P.J. 1987. *Women, Society, the State, and Abortion: A Structuralist Analysis.* New York: Praeger.

———. 1993. *Ethics in Public Administration: A Philosophical Approach.* Westport, Conn.: Praeger.

Shelton, J., E.A. Brann, and K.F. Shultz. 1976. "Abortion Utilization: Does Travel Distance Matter?" *Family Planning Perspectives* 8: 260–62.

Shiano, P.H., and R.E. Behrman. 1995. "Low Birthweight: Analysis and Recommendations." *Future of Children* 5, no. 1: 4–18.

Shroeder, L.D., D.L. Sjoquist, and P.E. Stephan. 1986. *Understanding Regression Analysis: An Introductory Guide.* Newbury Park, Calif.: Sage.

Singh, G.K., and S.M. Yu. 1995. "Infant Mortality in the United States: Trends, Differentials, and Projections." *American Journal of Public Health* 85: 957–64.

Singh, S., A. Torres, and J.D. Forrest. 1985. "The Need for Prenatal Care in the United States: Evidence from the 1980 National Natality Study." *Family Planning Perspectives* 17: 118–24.

Smith, J.C., B. Franchino, and J.F. Henneberry. 1995. "Surveillance of Family Planning Services at Title X Clinics and Characteristics of Women Receiving These Services, 1991." *Morbidity and Mortality Weekly Report* (5 May): 1–21.

Smith, K.B. 1994. "Abortion Attitudes and Vote Choice in the 1984 and 1988 Presidential Elections." *American Politics Quarterly* 22: 354–69.

Smith, P.J. 1991. Letter to D.R. McFarlane, 2 October.

Smolowe, J. 1993. "New, Improved, and Ready for Battle." *Time,* 14 June, 48–51.

Sollom, T., R.B. Gold, and R. Saul. 1996. "Public Funding for Contraceptive, Sterilization, and Abortion Services, 1994." *Family Planning Perspectives* 28: 167–73.

Stein, R.M. 1984. "Policy Implementation in a Federal System." In *Policy Formulation and Implementation,* edited by R. Eyestone and G. Edwards III. New York: J.A.I. Press.

Stimson, J.S. 1985. "Regression in Space and Time." *American Journal of Political Science* 29: 914–47.

Suitters, B. 1968. "Contraception in Ancient and Modern Society." *Royal Society of Health Journal* 88, no. 1: 9–11.

Tatalovich, R., and B.W. Daynes. 1988. *Social Regulatory Policy: Moral Controversies in American Politics.* Boulder, Colo.: Westview Press.

Thomlinson, R. 1965. *Population Dynamics: Causes and Consequences of World Demographic Change.* New York: Random House.

Tietze, C. 1965. "History of Contraceptive Methods." *Journal of Sex Research* 1, no. 2: 69–85.

Torres, A. 1983. "The Family Planning Program and Cuts in Federal Spending: Initial Effects on the Provision of Services." *Family Planning Perspectives* 15: 184–91.

Torres, A., P. Donovan, N. Dittes, and J.D. Forrest. 1986. "Public Benefits and Costs of Government Funding for Abortion." *Family Planning Perspectives* 18: 111–18.

Torres, A., and J.D. Forrest. 1988. "Why Do Women Have Abortions?" *Family Planning Perspectives* 20: 169.

Torres, A., J.D. Forrest, and S. Eisman. 1981. "Family Planning Services in the United States, 1978–1979." *Family Planning Perspectives* 13, 132–41.

Tribe, L.H. 1992. *Abortion: The Clash of Absolutes.* New York: Norton.

Trussell, J., J. Koenig, C. Ellertson, and F. Stewart. 1997. "Preventing Unintended Pregnancy: The Cost-Effectiveness of Three Methods of Emergency Contraception." *American Journal of Public Health* 87: 932–37.

Trussell, J., F. Stewart, F. Guest, and R.A. Hatcher. 1992. "Emergency Contraceptive Pills: A Simple Proposal to Reduce Unintended Pregnancies." *Family Planning Perspectives* 24: 269–73.

Upchurch, D., L. Levy-Storms, C.A. Sucoff, and C.S. Aneshensel. 1998. "Gender and Ethnic Differences in the Timing of First Sexual Intercourse." *Family Planning Perspectives* 30: 121–27.

U.S. Bureau of the Census. Annual updates. *Census of Population.* Washington, D.C.

———. Various years. *Statistical Abstract of the United States.* Washington, D.C.

U.S. Commission on Population Growth and the American Future. 1972. *Population and the American Future: The Report of the Commission on Population Growth and the American Future.* Washington, D.C.: GPO.

U.S. Department of Health and Human Services (DHHS). 1978. "Briefing Manual for Deputy Assistant Secretary for Population Affairs." Washington, D.C.: Office of Population Affairs. Mimeographed.

———. 1980. *Five Year Plan for Family Planning Services and Population Research.* Washington, D.C.: Office of Population Affairs.

———. 1981. *Program Guidelines for Project Grants for Family Planning Services.* Washington, D.C.: U.S. Public Health Service, Health Services Administration, Bureau of Community Health Services.

———. 1988. *State Medicaid Manual, Part 4—Services.* Washington, D.C.: Health Care Financing Administration, transmittal no. 36 (September).

———. 1991. Office of Population Affairs. *Family Planning Grantees, Delegates, and Clinics: 1991/1992 Directory.* Washington, D.C.: Family Life Exchange.

———. 1992. *Medicaid: spDATA System: Characteristics of State Medicaid Programs.* Vol. 11, *State by State Profiles.* Washington, D.C.: Health Care Financing Administration, publications no. 10959 (December).

———. 1994. "Family Planning History Table." Washington, D.C.: Office of Population Affairs. Mimeographed.

———. 1995. *Review Guide for Section 1115 Research and Demonstration Proposals for State Health Care Reform.* Washington, D.C.: Health Care Financing Administration. Draft (30 January).

———. 1996a. "Link between Medicaid and Temporary Assistance for Needy Families (TANF)." Washington, D.C.: Health Care Financing Administration. Fact sheet no. 1. Http://www.hcfa.gov/MEDICAID/wrfs1.htm.

———. 1996b. *State Health Care Reform Demonstrations Fact Sheet.* Baltimore: Health Care Financing Administration, Office of State Health Care Reform Demonstrations.

U.S. General Accounting Office (GAO). 1984. *Maternal and Child Health Block Grant: Program Changes Emerging under State Administration. Report to the Congress by the Comptroller General of the United States.* Washington, D.C.

———. 1998. *Medicaid: Early Implications of Welfare Reform for Beneficiaries and States.* Washington, D.C.: Superintendent of Documents.

U.S. National Center for Health Statistics. 1982–88. *Vital Statistics of the United States.* Washington, D.C.

———. 1993. "Advance Report of Final Natality Statistics, 1991." *Monthly Vital Statistics Report* 42, no. 3, supplement (9 September), tables 30 and 31.

Van Meter, D., and C. Van Horn. 1975. "The Policy Implementation Process: A Conceptual Framework." *Administration and Society* 6: 445–88.

Weinberg, D. 1974. "Family Planning in the American States." In *Population Policymaking in the American States,* edited by E. Bergman, D.N. Carter, R.J. Cook, R.D. Tabors, D.R. Weir, and M.E. Urann. Lexington, Mass.: D.C. Heath, 75–99.

Weiner, J., and B.A. Bernhardt. 1990. "A Survey of State Medicaid Policies for Coverage of Abortion and Prenatal Diagnostic Procedures." *American Journal of Public Health* 80: 717–20.

Weller, R.B., I.W. Eberstein, and M. Bailey. 1987. "Pregnancy Wantedness and Maternal Behavior during Pregnancy." *Demography* 24: 407–12.

Wetstein, M.E. 1995. "The Abortion Paradox: The Impact of National Policy Change on Abortion Rates." *Social Science Quarterly* 76: 607–18.

———. 1996. *Abortion Rates in the United States: The Influence of Opinion and Policy.* Albany: State University of New York Press.

Williamson, R.S. 1990. *Reagan's Federalism: His Efforts to Decentralize Government.* Lanham, Md.: University Press of America.

Index

About the Authors

DEBORAH R. MCFARLANE is a professor in the Department of Political Science at the University of New Mexico. She holds master's degrees in Public Health/Population Planning (University of Michigan) and in Public Administration (Harvard University) and a doctorate in Public Health from the University of Texas. She has published many articles in the fields of public health, reproductive health, and public policy; worked as a family planning program administrator; and consulted for numerous organizations involved in reproductive health. In 1998–99, she was chair of the Population, Family Planning, and Reproductive Health Section of the American Public Health Association in Washington, D.C.

KENNETH J. MEIER is the Charles Puryear Professor of Liberal Arts, Professor of Political Science, and coordinator of the Program in American Politics at Texas A&M University. He earned his M.A. and Ph.D. in Political Science at the Maxwell School of Citizenship and Public Affairs at Syracuse University. He is the author of *Politics and the Bureaucracy: Policymaking in the Fourth Branch of Government* and *The Politics of Sin: Drugs, Alcohol, and Public Policy*. He has published numerous articles on a variety of subjects in American politics and public policy, and he serves on the editorial boards of several scholarly journals.